Low Risk, High Reward

Starting and Growing Your Business
with Minimal Risk

BOB REISS

WITH JEFFREY L. CRUIKSHANK

THE FREE PRESS

New York   London   Toronto   Sydney   Singapore

THE FREE PRESS
A Division of Simon & Schuster, Inc.
1230 Avenue of the Americas
New York, NY 10020

The authors gratefully acknowledge permission from the following sources to reprint material in their control:

Daniel Ebenstein for the three-page letter of July 18, 1994, from Daniel Ebenstein to David Pfau, Executive Vice President of Afterthoughts Boutiques, a Division of F. W. Woolworth Company.

Harvard Business School Publishing for permission to use the Harvard Business School Case R&R 386-019. Copyright © 1985 by the President and Fellows of Harvard College.

United Feature Syndicate, Inc. for the North American English reprint rights to Dilbert 2/7/91, 6/6/96, 2/24/94, and 2/18/93.

This publication contains the opinions and ideas of its authors and is designed to provide useful advice in regard to the subject matter covered. It is sold with the understanding that the authors and publisher are not engaged in rendering legal, accounting, investment, or other professional services. Laws vary from state to state, federal laws may apply, and if the reader requires expert assistance from a registered investment adviser or legal advice, a competent professional should be consulted.

The authors and publisher specifically disclaim any responsibility for any liability, loss, or risk, personal or otherwise, which is incurred as a consequence, directly or indirectly, of the use and application of any of the contents of this book.

Designed by Susan Hood
Manufactured in the United States of America

10   9   8   7   6   5   4   3   2   1

Library of Congress Cataloging-in-Publication Data

Reiss, Bob, 1930–
  Low risk, high reward : starting and growing your business with minimal risk / Bob Reiss, with Jeffrey L. Cruikshank.
      p.   cm.
    Includes index.
    1. New business enterprises.   2. Entrepreneurship.   I. Cruikshank, Jeffrey L. II. Title.
HD62.5.R43   2000   00-021786
658.1'141—dc21

ISBN 0-684-84962-3

CONTENTS

CONTENTS

To the women of my life:
Grace, Valerie, Nicole, Melody, Jereann, and Georgie

FOREWORD

by Howard H. Stevenson

Serafim-Rock Professor of Business Administration
Harvard Business School

I remember very well the first time I talked to Bob Reiss. It was in 1983, shortly after I had returned to the Harvard Business School to help build a new faculty group focused on entrepreneurship. Somehow, Bob heard about the effort, and called me up.

"I'm glad the School is finally doing something about entrepreneurship," Bob said in so many words. "Come see me next time you're in New York."

So I did, and I wasn't disappointed. He greeted me warmly in the spartan offices of R&R, and within a few minutes was regaling me with a fascinating story about a recent adventure he and his company had gone through. Quickly, that story turned into a case, and that case is included as an appendix to this book. I've written lots of cases, but none was easier than "the R&R Case."

For many years thereafter, I used "R&R" as the subject of the first class session in my entrepreneurship courses. It was almost always a lively class. "Risky business, this fad-game business, right?" I'd ask my class. Yes, most people agreed; very risky. "So, if it's so risky," I'd continue, "who took all the risks?" Suddenly, my class had trouble finding the risks. "Hey," I'd ask next, "where did all those risks go?"

Bob's special genius, my students gradually came to realize, was in getting a whole basket of contingent commitments lined up. When the last one fell into place, there literally *was* no risk.

I would usually go on to describe a managerial spectrum, which had what I called *entrepreneurs* at one end, and *managers* at the other. Entrepreneurs, I suggested, were opportunity-driven. They used few resources—and when they did, they tended to be other people's resources. They committed quickly, and in small increments. They rewarded people for the value they created.

Bob embodied all of those traits. In fact, he practically anchored the entrepreneurial end of the spectrum, and his example helped me think through what distinguished entrepreneurial management from other kinds of management. If Bob was doing it, it was almost certainly entrepreneurial.

Those traits shine through the pages of this book. So do many of the other characteristics that make Bob a fun person to know, and distinguish him from the run-of-the-mill business person. For example: Many people in business tend to divide things into either cooperation *or* competition. But in business, as in most things in life, you're *both* competing and cooperating. In *Low Risk, High Reward,* Bob shows how to do both. He emphasizes the satisfaction of "getting your share of the pie"—but also the importance of making the pie bigger.

And by the way, Bob extends that prescription all the way to the end customer. He reminds us that success lies in delivering value to the customer. At the same time, Bob's book is an antidote to all the business books on the market today that argue for a *passionate, single-minded dedication* to one thing or another. The customer is very important, says Bob. So is the product. So is the order. So is the reorder.

That's one of the things I noticed first about this book, in an early draft. Most authors of business books (who tend to be either professors or consultants) try very hard to boil things down to "seven key points" or "six good habits" or some other small collection of precepts. Bob is a business person, who operates in the real world. His lists never have fewer than a dozen or two key ideas—and sometimes many more. The real world, Bob reminds us, is very complicated.

Another thing that Bob reminds us of—and it's one reason why I gave the manuscript to my daughter to read—is that entrepreneurship is not about having the great idea. It's about having at least a pretty good idea, and executing it with skill and passion. It's about the million details you have to get right if you want to have the right people work with you, successfully. I noted with interest the emphasis that Bob places on relationship building. As noted, he makes the pie bigger for everybody. He doesn't burn bridges. He can call again (and people will be glad to hear from him).

I believe we should teach Bob's approach to financial analysis at the Harvard Business School. What are the numbers that you have to watch, and how often do you have to watch them? For the founder and grower of a business, Bob's chapter on numeracy alone is worth the price of the book.

In fact, there's a great deal in Bob's experience—colorful and unusual as it has been—that turns out to have universal appeal and importance. Maybe you won't have your wristwatches "knocked off," as Bob did. But the minute you have a good idea, someone out there is going to figure out how to make it cheaper, better, and faster. Are you prepared to respond? Bob tells you how.

And maybe you won't use a manufacturer's representative (as Bob often did, and which he sometimes was himself). But if you make a product, you will almost certainly be distributing through channels that you don't control yourself. Do you know how to create incentives for all the people in that supply chain? Bob has lots of good ideas for you.

I couldn't be happier that *Low Risk, High Reward* makes Bob's ideas and example accessible to a new and broader audience. I hope that the many people who've always wanted to start a business will buy this book, read it, and—if they decide entrepreneurship is for them—take the plunge with Bob's help. And I hope that those entrepreneurs who are already in business will dip into this book for help, new ideas, encouragement, and a timely pat on the back.

Entrepreneurship is a strange and exciting road, and Bob Reiss is one of my favorite tour guides.

INTRODUCTION

This is a book for people interested in entrepreneurship.

But that's not specific enough. If you look at the magazine stands, or tune in to CNBC, or visit either your local neighborhood bookstore or your favorite business-related Web site, *everybody* is interested in entrepreneurship.

So, let me be more specific. This is a book for people who want to start or buy a business and who want to run that business in a way that generates relatively high rewards with relatively low risks. It's a book for people who already own a small business, and want to push that business up to the next level of success. To some extent, it's for those people in the ranks of corporate America who have the entrepreneurial bug, and want to break out and go their own way. And finally, it's a book for people who think they might want to go into business for themselves, and want to know more about the day-to-day reality of working for yourself. Who does it? Is it better than the alternatives?

Although I'll necessarily be presenting some of the basics, my emphasis will tend to be on the things they don't teach in school. My emphasis, too, will be on things with which I've had a lot of personal experience. As a result, certain kinds of topics (e.g., marketing) get more attention than other kinds of topics (e.g., manufacturing). Again, this reflects both my experiences and my biases.

Where did this book come from? An interesting thing happened to me when (in 1985) I became the subject of a Harvard Business School case study. (That case is reprinted as Appendix 3 in this book.) I started thinking about how I was living life, and doing business. Not that I hadn't been aware of what I was doing in the previous thirty years or so. Yes, I had plans, but they were mostly in my head. (I never had a written business plan. I think they're highly overrated—except that you usually need one to raise money.) But now, as I talked with smart people about the particular way that I had tried to do business, I found myself forced to be a little more articulate on that subject.

This was reinforced when the *Wall Street Journal* wrote an article about some of my exploits, which the *Journal* writer seemed to think were interesting. It was reinforced again each time I saw the Harvard Business School case on my company taught to a group of undergraduate or graduate students.

Pretty soon I found myself wanting to find out more about how other people looked at their business careers. I read books and articles by people who had done interesting things. I sought out certain people at trade shows and conventions. I found good pretexts to call people on the phone and pick their brains about their particular approach to entrepreneurship.

When the Free Press asked me in 1997 to put my ideas into book form, I realized that this was a perfect opportunity to go public with all this snooping. I bought a tape recorder, made a new list of "targets," and asked for the opportunity to talk to a group of entrepreneurs in all kinds of industries. To my surprise, almost every one of them agreed to be interviewed. Most of them were extremely generous with their time, and amazingly candid about their businesses. I also did a formal survey of salespeople, many with years of experience in their respective fields. With their permission, I have used their stories to illustrate themes throughout this book.

Finally, about a year ago, I started getting systematic about my approach to my "guest shots" at colleges and graduate schools. Rather than simply asking for feedback on my teaching, I started asking students to fill out a questionnaire. This survey was designed to help me understand more about how young people look at business in general, and entrepreneurship in particular. The results have been revealing; and they, too, are built into the chapters that follow.

In setting out to write this book, I resolved to make it as *practical* as possible. I have nothing against theoretical approaches to business problems. Good theories eventually lead to good business practices. But most of the time, entrepreneurs have to act, quickly, taking advantage of opportunities that may be short-lived. I believe in the power of intuitive thinking. If you understand a problem intuitively, you usually can get to the right answer without ever solving that problem intellectually.

Let me emphasize the "low risk" part of this book's title. I'm nothing less than a missionary on this subject. I believe that in most business situations, risk can be managed. Not *eliminated*—nothing in life is certain—but managed in ways that will definitely increase your odds for success.

Contrary to popular belief, entrepreneurs don't like risk. They don't get up in the morning and go looking for it. In fact, they do what they can to anticipate it, minimize it, offset it, circumscribe it—pick your favorite appropriate verb. This doesn't mean that you don't take risks, or that you don't make mistakes. You'd better! (The fear of mistakes is one virus that is deadly to creativity.) But it means that you take risks that you've built some firewalls around.

Low risk with high reward: Does this sound like a pipe dream? Well, I think I can persuade you it's not. As a forty-year veteran of the entrepreneurial trenches, I think I have a set of skills, ideas, and experiences that add up to low-risk, high-reward (LRHR) entrepreneurship. They're neither hard to learn, nor hard to use once you've learned them. The best evidence for that is me.

But let's figure out first who *you* are. There are several key audiences I'm writing for in this book. If you're in one of these audiences, then keep reading. If you're not, then wrap this book up as handsomely as you can, write a nice card, and give it to that friend of yours who's always making noises about how he or she is definitely going to get into business someday.

WHO AM I WRITING FOR?

The first audience is people who are already decision makers in their own businesses, and are looking for ways to make those businesses work smarter. That's a key message in this book: Working smart can be even more important than working hard.

A second audience is those people who currently work for large companies, but would like to find a way to get out off the 9-to-5, forty-years-and-a-pension treadmill. Have you always felt a little bit out of place in that big, slow-moving, intensely political company? Do you suspect you may be laid off, despite the fact that you've done a great job for your company? Are you reaching the nasty conclusion that there are no more promotions coming your way because you're not political enough, or won't go along with questionable practices, or don't have the right color skin, or are of the "wrong" gender, or didn't go to the right school?

Are you underappreciated? Underpaid? Have you ever wondered if you could have more *fun* while making a living?

A third audience is closely related to the second. I call these people the "closet entrepreneurs." They can be found in many places—law firms, medical offices, and other professional settings, as well as business settings. These people aren't necessarily unhappy where they are, but for one reason or another, they yearn to be their own boss. In some cases, they want to prove something to themselves. In other cases, they are convinced they could make more money. By and large, they lack the know-how or the self-confidence to proceed—or even openly acknowledge their dream.

A fourth audience is young people who are currently in school— high school, college, or graduate school. Some of you may have had little or no exposure to business and can only wonder what it's all about. Others of you may have several years of work experience behind you, may have studied at a leading business school, and may even have investigated what it takes to start your own company.

Maybe you're even farther down this road. Maybe you've already got an absolutely great idea for a business, you've got access to some start-up capital, and you're ready to work your tail off. Be advised, however, that most successful businesses don't grow out of a "great idea." Most grow out of a more or less mundane idea—but one that is made or marketed a little bit better than all the competing ideas out there. Don't wait for lightning to strike!

Also be advised that the act of creating a business doesn't make you an entrepreneur. We'll return to this idea in the next section, when I define entrepreneurship.

Every year, I meet and speak with hundreds of students, ranging from undergraduates to MBAs-in-training to participants in executive education programs. My perspective is not an academic one, though. In fact, I think some of my professor hosts see me as some sort of exotic species, brought in to illustrate the fact that entrepreneurship can come in many packages. I'm glad to help make that point, since I think it's true.

A final audience for this book are the future leaders of entrepreneurial businesses. Maybe you're formally or informally in a line of succession at a good and growing company. Or maybe you're a prospective heir to a family business. In either case, you're in a special situation. You may well be slotted to take over someday, but take it from me: You'll still have to earn your stripes. You'll have to demonstrate to those around you that you're the right person for the job. The best way to do this is to chart an effective path for the company, and then implement that plan effectively. Many of the ideas in this book should serve you well in those difficult tasks.

WHAT'S "ENTREPRENEURSHIP"?

This is the easiest section of the book for me to write, because I can borrow it almost entirely from Howard Stevenson, who largely invented the Entrepreneurship faculty group at the Harvard Business School (and was kind enough to write a foreword for this book).

Professor Stevenson, himself a very successful entrepreneur, has spent almost two decades trying to make a respectable academic field out of a subject that academicians used to avoid like the plague. Before Howard and a few colleagues at other schools tackled the subject, entrepreneurship was not something that a self-respecting scholar would take on. It was barely "teachable," let alone "researchable." Yes, there were certainly lots of people out there who were starting and growing a wide variety of businesses; and yes, colleges showed a lot of interest in those guys (and more recently, gals) when it came time for fundraising. But no one could define entrepreneurship in a way that was useful for knowledge building.

It was not so long ago that entrepreneurs were described in such unflattering terms as: shiftless, unfocused, shady, money-hungry, misfits, sharks, quick-buck artists, unreliable, shoot-from-the-hip operators, and so on. The focus was all on the personality and character of the individual—and in my opinion, badly misinformed.

What Howard did was to define *a way of thinking,* rather than a personality type. He said that entrepreneurship is a set of behaviors. He distinguished entrepreneurs (who are opportunity-driven) from managers (who are resource-driven). The entrepreneur tends to use other people's resources to pursue opportunities that would otherwise stay out of reach. The manager, starting from a corporate resource base, focuses on trying to find ways to protect corporate assets, and to meet profit, sales, return on investment, or other goals imposed from above, or by the stock market.

Howard didn't say one was good and one was bad—just that they were different in fundamental ways. I agree.

A key feature of Howard's definition is that it is a pretty wide open, even welcoming idea. In other words, you don't have to be born with certain personality traits to succeed as an entrepreneur. You just have to *act* in certain ways. Or, if you can't act that way yourself—for example, if you're not likely to be a great salesperson—you have to be good at understanding and supporting that function. If you had to possess a certain gene sequence to be an entrepreneur, there'd be no reason to go to business school or to read this book. You'd either have it or you wouldn't.

But it doesn't work that way. So, let me adopt Howard's definition of entrepreneurship, with a few little amendments of my own. I think that *entrepreneurship is the recognition and pursuit of opportunity without regard to the resources you currently control, with confidence that you can succeed, with the flexibility to change course as necessary, and with the will to rebound from setbacks.*

Throughout this book, I'll argue that entrepreneurship is all about flexibility. Flexibility is one asset that a small company almost always has more of than a large company. So *flexibility* and *opportunism* are key. And flexibility is important on the individual, as well as the corporate, level. Entrepreneurship is about competitive people who can withstand adversity, and recover from—and learn from—failure, on their way to success.

WHAT'S IN THIS BOOK?

So, what's in this book? I've divided my ideas into ten chapters and four appendices. All of them consider various aspects of starting and growing a business. All of them also sound the general theme of managing and minimizing risk, while maximizing profit.

Chapter 1 contains a summary of the skills and attributes that I think are important for the individual entrepreneur to develop. These include creativity, flexibility, salesmanship, passion, a hunger for knowledge, the ability to build trust, integrity, and so on.

So far in this introduction, I've stressed flexibility, even including it in my definition of entrepreneurship. Now I'm going to make the point that there are some things—like integrity—where flexibility works *against* the entrepreneur. Don't give people out there the idea that you'll give up your personal integrity just to close a deal. Don't compromise core values!

This is as good a place as any to make a point that maybe I should have made earlier. My goal in all of this is to give you new things to think about, or maybe new ways of thinking about things you're already involved in. I certainly don't think that my way is the only way of doing things. (Indeed, "my way" of doing things has changed over the years, and I hope it will keep changing.) That's one reason why I've tried to pick the brains of so many smart people out there, ranging from students to experienced entrepreneurs and salespeople.

Chapter 2 puts a spotlight on one more skill set that's absolutely vital to the LRHR entrepreneur: the ability to understand and use numbers. I call this *numeracy:* the numbers equivalent of literacy. Chapter 3 focuses specifically on *risk:* how to spot it, manage it, and—in as many cases as possible—reduce it. Chapter 4 is a short chapter focused on a big topic: *the idea.* If businesses are founded on ideas, where do ideas come from?

The next chapter, chapter 5, is about getting the company started, a task that seems to frustrate many would-be entrepreneurs. How do you start? Where does the money come from? How do you find and grow the right people? How do you keep track of the numbers? Above all, how do you manage risk—avoiding it, reducing it, sharing it, staging it, eliminating it, accepting it, and evaluating it against potential rewards?

Chapter 6 is about building your business. How big? That depends in part on what you want. I'll confess in advance that I'm not the world's best authority on growing a large company. I never wanted to grow one of those. But I *have* included lots of good ideas from people who have created successful enterprises, and I hope this will give you at least an introductory road map to growing that Really Big Company.

Products are the focus of chapter 7. I may not love huge companies, but I *do* love products. I love developing them, introducing them, defending them against other people's knockoffs, knocking off my products before somebody else does, pulling the plug on them, and so on. Believe me: There are few, if any, processes in business that will give you more of a kick than getting an idea for a product, making that product come to life, and then seeing it on retail counters across the country—or in some cases, around the world.

My own experience has been in consumer goods, games, and novelties, beginning with personalized pencils and continuing through games that require either mental or physical dexterity, or both. But I've tried hard to complement my own experiences with those of people in other sectors, so—in addition to ideas based on selling magic kits and Rubik's Cubes—you'll learn lessons derived from more typical products.

Chapter 8 is about *getting the order.* You're not in business until you get an order. This is the process of "selling in" to businesses, or to some sort of distribution chain. For most of my own business career, this has meant selling into a retailer network, but these same ideas apply when you're selling, either to businesses or direct to the consumer.

But selling, as we'll see in later chapters, is getting harder. With the continuing and accelerating consolidation of the retail sector—companies going out of business or gobbling each other up—the power of the remaining retailers has increased to such an extent that there is a real imbalance of power in the market today. (The retailer—the buyer—holds a lot more cards than the seller.) They often use this leverage mercilessly.

Some people say that the Internet will be the death of retail as traditionally practiced. If and when this happens, my guess is that not everyone will be sad. Meanwhile, we entrepreneurs have to know how to mitigate the power of the retailers. We need to get orders at a profit, and minimize the risks that dealing with retailers pose. We need to know how to get in to see these characters, how to sell to them, how to use manufacturers' reps, how to license products, how to use advertising and public relations and other marketing gambits, and so on, and so on.

Or even smarter: Let's figure out some way to do an end run around the traditional retailer. Can we go direct to the consumer? Can we sell to the direct response industry, which in turn will sell to the consumer without all the baggage that comes with a store?

I don't mean to imply that all retailers are dangerous, of course. There are many niche retailers, with whom it pays off to build long-term relationships. I *am* raising the caution flag, however, when it comes to dealing with the largest and most powerful retailers. They've got the leverage; you probably don't.

Next comes a chapter (chapter 9) about the *reorder*. I'm making an explicit distinction between your first wave of orders and your second. You can't get into business without your initial order; you can't stay in business without that all-important reorder. This is "selling through," which is the necessary complement to selling in. Again, I look at advertising, PR, and marketing. I also look at building an appropriate infrastructure, building relationships, building trust across a spectrum of institutions, dealing with the problems (and opportunities) of knock-offs, and so on.

Finally, in chapter 10, you'll find lots of ideas about you and your company, and about success and failure. (Most important: *you* get to define them both.) I provide a kind of running counterpoint between individual and corporate lessons. What happens to your company when it succeeds? (What happens to *you*?) What happens to your company when it fails? (What happens to *you*?) Should you go public? If so, when and how? If you build a corporate juggernaut, will you be happy catering to analysts and stockholders?

If not, will you resign? Then what will you do? My personal vision of purgatory is endless cocktails on the beautiful patio alongside the tenth fairway under an eternally blue sky, with tanned folks in pastel shorts playing through, complaining about the dog-leg on Nine. Let me keep working, and *learning,* please!

WHAT'S IMPORTANT?

To me, money and the trappings of power are only moderately important. Having enough money means that my car will start on cold mornings, that my shoes won't hurt my feet, that I don't have to check any particular bottom line on any given day of the week (stock listings, the price of gold, or whatever). Having enough money means that I'm able—within reason—to respond to my kids' *pleeezes* for the cash to buy tickets for some upcoming *totally awesome* event.

Having power is basically an extension of having money. When the last flight out gets canceled, I don't have to sleep in the airport lounge. When I call somebody powerful, they (may) call me back.

To me, what *is* important in life are things like trust, balance, satisfaction, family, love, happiness, self-esteem, and helping others. What's great about entrepreneurship is that, done right, it's been an effective way for me to get to some of those things that are important. And getting to some of those things—for example, trust—has in turn made being a good entrepreneur easier.

I think I've been lucky in life, and lots of people have been very generous to me. I want to repay those debts. This inclination—and probably the strange process of getting older—has led me into teaching. Increasingly, being a good teacher is important to me. I enjoy my sessions as a diamond in the rough at business schools. I've enjoyed sharing what I've learned with my interview subjects, almost as much as I've enjoyed learning from them. I've enjoyed writing this book, although it's a hell of a lot easier to start a company than to write a book.

When I read a book, I try to take away at least one actionable idea from it. Now I'm the author, and of course, I want to excel at being an author. So I hope that those of you who are already in business can take away at least *two* actionable ideas that will help make your business stronger. Or maybe even more than two.

And if I can persuade even a few young people to engage in low-risk, high-reward entrepreneurship—bright young people who might otherwise have gone into some less happy calling—I will have done something worthwhile.

I

ATTRIBUTES AND SKILLS FOR LOW-RISK, HIGH-REWARD ENTREPRENEURSHIP

The formal academic studies I've read indicate that there is no one, definitive profile of the "successful entrepreneur." My own experiences and observations confirm this conclusion. Entrepreneurs come in all kinds of packages. Gender, age, income, educational background, race, geography, personality, experience: nothing seems to rule people out, or rule people in.

So, we can't program or genetically engineer the perfect entrepreneur. But based on my experience, observations, and interviews, I'd like to propose a collection of attributes and skills that I think most successful entrepreneurs tend to have, in greater or lesser amounts. This list may be helpful to you as you decide whether you should take the plunge and go into your own business. Or it may be helpful to you as you decide whether to partner with a particular individual, or invest in a new enterprise that seems to have certain skills. Finally, if you're already in business, it may help you think about yourself in a slightly different way.

As you read through these attributes and skills, don't be too hard on yourself or your associates. If you (or they) lack something, there's plenty of room for hope. Attributes are sometimes inherited, but they can also be cultivated. Skills are the result of determination, hard work, and continuous learning. If you lack a skill today, you can probably pick it up quickly enough—if you decide that you really need it for success in your business.

Two more cautions: First, attributes and skills alone don't make a business. There are many, many other factors that come into play, including the right idea, good timing, great implementation, adequate resources, and, yes—sometimes a little luck. (We'll review all of these other building blocks in subsequent sections of the book.) And second, these are my own opinions, which are derived from a particular set of experiences. If you think you've got a different set of skills and attributes that will set you up for entrepreneurial success, hey—prove me wrong!

Meanwhile, I'll focus on the attributes and skills that have proved themselves in *my* eyes.

TEN ATTRIBUTES

Attributes are personal qualities. They may be innate, or they may lend themselves to being cultivated, and this may vary from individual to individual. I'll let you decide which is which, in your case.

You may decide you lack one or more of these attributes, or you may decide you've got way too much of one of them. Having just the right amount of one of these qualities may be your personal "strong suit." But lacking one isn't necessarily a killer. If you think you come up short in one or more, figure out whether there's some way to compensate for that shortfall.

1. Passion

If you, as the person heading the venture, don't have a strong passion for the idea, the company, or the great things that this company makes possible for you and other people, you're dragging a huge anchor. Why should anyone else believe in you, and invest in you, if you don't believe in yourself?

Passion is the best way to get investors, employees, customers, and suppliers to buy into your vision. It's the ultimate sales tool. The enthusiasm generated by your passion is contagious. People who are exposed to your passion are far more likely to want you to succeed than if they read your prospectus—no matter how good the numbers look on that prospectus.

Passion can make up for many shortcomings. For example: Young people with plenty of passion can overcome their almost unavoidable lack of experience. Senior people with relevant experience are far more likely to want to mentor you if they detect a lot of passion in you.

Passion is a highly personal thing. It can have both positive and negative elements. "For me," admits Dennis Boyer, the former head of Brothers Gourmet Coffee, "it was more than being inspired by an idea. The idea of being free to create my own workplace, to invent my own products and services, to satisfy more fully every customer, and to help other people live fresh careers—these ideas were no doubt inspirational. But just as forceful was the reality that, damn it, I'm *hungry*. I don't want to ever be poor again. I don't want to live my life working for others, or in fear of arbitrary supervisors and managers."

I recently met a wonderful young woman, Amy Love, in one of the Harvard Business School classes I sat in on. She was about to launch a new, women-oriented sports magazine. If you know anything about the magazine business, you know that new launches have a spectacularly high failure rate. Between January and June 1998, according to *USA Today,* almost 600 new magazines were launched. There's only so much room on the shelves. New magazines need to push old magazines off the shelves to have a chance—no easy task in itself. Then they have to succeed quickly, or be pushed off the shelves themselves. This is a tough business!

Amy's business plan was very solid and thorough, but so were the plans for all those magazines that have failed over the years. But it was Amy's belief in herself that ultimately convinced me and a few other individuals to invest in her proposal. She was confident enough about her plan, by the way, to offer to personally guarantee any "seed" investments she got.

Not everybody gets won over by passion, of course; I later learned that some hard-nosed venture capitalists, skeptical about yet another magazine venture, chose not to invest at that time. But I also heard that they were impressed by Amy's heartfelt salesmanship, and intend to listen hard when she comes up for her next round of financing.

Passion gets you off the ground, and it helps sustain you when you hit the rocky periods that are sure to come. In later chapters, we'll talk about the critical importance of orders and reorders, all of which are at least in part dependent on good salesmanship—which in turn is dependent on your passionate belief in your product and your company. And guess what? Success creates the need for *more* passion, not less passion, because your success is surely going to engender competition. If you get complacent as new, hungry, *passionate* competitors enter your market, watch out!

What do you do if you're not passionate about your idea? I'd say, *Get a new idea.* You're going to be living with this thing around the clock for more months and years than you'd care to admit. If you can't love it, for goodness' sake, don't live with it! You won't fool anybody, starting with yourself. Your lack of passion will come ringing through in the ears of all your crucial constituencies, and may short-circuit your enterprise before it starts.

What do you do if your passion starts to flag a little bit? Go find an inspirational well and drink deeply from it. I recently read a story in *Tennis* magazine about Mark Philippoussis, one of the great young Australian tennis players who burst on the tennis scene in the 1990s. At one point, Philippoussis got down on himself, and seemed to lose interest in competing at the highest levels of the tennis world. His coach contacted Monica Seles's coach, and asked if Philippoussis could spend some time training with Seles. Philippoussis's coach thought that if his demotivated star could spend a little time with the fire-eating Seles—who's nothing if not passionate about her game—he might snap out of his slump. Philippoussis did go a few rounds with Seles, and apparently the treatment worked. (He made it to the finals of his next Grand Slam event: the U.S. Open.)

What's the business equivalent? Seek out some successful peer in an industry that's far removed from your own. Attend a convention or a business school seminar. Get a pep talk from a trusted adviser outside the company who knows you and your business well. Figure out why you've stopped having fun. Do less of the irritating stuff and more of the fun stuff. Get passionate again!

Dennis Boyer makes a good point when he says that there are some business settings that *don't* begin and end with passion. The gas station on the corner or the Burger King franchise down the street—these are businesses that to their owners may be a way of making a living, pure and simple. Inherited companies, too, sometimes lack a fueling passion. All I can say is, (1) I've never seen a business that passion hurt; and (2) I'd rather get my oil changed at a gas station with a passion for giving good service.

Passion has many faces. Sid Young founded and runs a very successful maintenance and painting contracting company, focused mainly on commercial properties. His customers are mostly repeat customers. He has no sales force, doing all the selling himself. (It doesn't take a lot of his time.) He has no thought of retiring, or selling, or going public.

Sid is the first to admit that he has no great passion for his business. So why do I include him here? Because he *does* have a passion for what the business has done for him. It has allowed him a lot of free time to indulge in the good things of life, and it has provided security for him and his family. I'd note, too, that a major key to Sid's success is his fanatical dedication to customer service. This is another kind of passion, and it pays off. Sid has one customer who has built more than 700 strip shopping centers during the last 15 years. Sid has painted each of those centers at least twice, and in many cases three times. His passion—focused as it is—creates highly satisfied customers.

2. Curiosity

I've conducted a lot of job interviews over the years. Now—like the major league umpire who confessed in his autobiography that he never really understood what a "balk" was—I'd like to confess that the job interview process always baffled and frustrated me. I could never figure out what questions to ask. I was pretty sure I didn't have the skills that would allow me to predict job performance based on an interview. I'm not sure *anybody* has those skills.

In retrospect, I was doing it all wrong. If I were interviewing a job applicant today, my questions would be geared toward determining if that applicant had a healthy curiosity.

Curiosity is the beginning of creativity (see the section on skill sets below). A strong dose of curiosity *makes* you ask the questions you need to ask about your products, people, company, industry, and environment. The answers to these questions open the door for opportunities and solutions.

Curious people read constantly. (Good interview question: "Tell me something you've read recently that really surprised you.") They read strange, all-over-the-map kind of stuff. They don't worry about connecting the dots; they figure the dots will connect themselves.

A roomful of curious people isn't necessarily a prescription for peace and quiet and predictability within your company. But in most cases, peace and quiet aren't what your entrepreneurial business needs to succeed. Some companies go so far as to hire a "vice president of knowledge" or a "chief knowledge officer." (Now when you see "CKO" in a magazine article, you'll know what it stands for.)

Other companies focus on the "intake" function. John Altman, founder of six start-ups and a professor of entrepreneurship at Babson College, once told me that his biggest mistake over the years was that he "didn't hire enough flute players." I took that to mean that he valued people who challenged the status quo, thought "outside the box," applied unique skills to business problems, and kept themselves happy and motivated by taking on new challenges. These people aren't easy to find, according to Altman: "Kids come out of the womb extremely inquisitive. But as parents we put limits on kids, and start to destroy their curiosity and inquisitiveness. Then we put them in school for sixteen years, and insist that they walk between two railroad tracks. Then I get them at the end of their college careers—second semester, senior year—and I want them to be creative and innovative. Well, I have to spend the first several weeks empowering them to be risk takers."

Curiosity is where learning starts, and it's the fuel source for continuous learning. Many of the entrepreneurs I talked with—including Jim McCann, Ed Hajim, and Bill Doyle—say that *learning for one's lifetime* was an absolutely indispensable trait. I couldn't agree more.

3. Work ethic

A strong work ethic is so much a given among the entrepreneurs I've worked with that I almost forgot to mention this attribute. Starting and growing a business takes hard work, dedication, and long work days (and nights!). This may sound onerous, but in fact, if you're passionate about your work, you won't notice the long hours, and even an extraordinary time commitment won't seem like too high a price to pay.

Some entrepreneurs succeed simply because they're the last ones standing—they outwork and outlast the competition. I can't argue with that kind of dedication, especially in this particular section. But I want to stress again that working smart and good planning are crucial contributors to success. And having said that, I want to make the main point of this section again: that smarts and great planning won't cut it, unless they are accompanied by hard work.

4. Energy

One thing I've noticed, in my conversations with dozens of entrepreneurs in recent months, is the incredibly high energy levels most of them possess. It would be interesting to find out whether they've always been that way, or whether they started working at higher energy levels as the amount of fun and reward in their lives began to increase. I suspect it's some of the one and some of the other. "I didn't have a lot of energy when I worked for someone else," Earl Peek of Intellectual Technologies, Inc., told me; "but when it's your baby, you have much more drive."

What I *am* sure of is that we make our own energy, to some extent. I'm convinced that, within reason, physical activity generates more energy than it consumes. All the years when I was on the road, I made a point of working out almost every day. (This was back in the days before running became popular, and I used to attract some interesting looks from hotel guests as they encountered this character running around the periphery of the parking lot in the dark.) Physical exertion makes you sleep better and think better, and may permit you to sleep fewer hours with no ill effects. And the more stress you're under, the more you will benefit from exercise.

I recently heard a Goldman Sachs partner, Connie Duckworth, give an informal talk at my kids' school. (The talk was sponsored by Dare to Dream, a foundation headed by my wife, Grace, that tries to inspire girls and young women to aspire to high professional achievement.) Duckworth was telling her young audience about her schedule, which might best be described as murderous. She has three children (ages one, two, and five), works a million hours a week, and has no free time. But she treasures her exercise. Her solution? To work out at 4:00 a.m. three or four times a week. Duckworth is performing at a high energy level!

You will have to do the same. Think about it: The engine that makes your small business go is you. So take care of your engine. Give it a proper physical regimen and diet. Read a book on fitness, get a video, put an exercise machine in your home office, hire a trainer—whatever it takes to get into the habit. But above all, use common sense (don't red-line the engine). And don't let yourself say that you don't have enough time. Make exercise a priority, and you'll be paid back with increased efficiency, and a good shot at a longer and more satisfying life.

And believe it or not, your habits can be passed on to the people you work with—and this, too, will benefit you. John Korff, a terrific events impresario, told me, "I have to teach my staff, and convey energy. If I don't convey the energy, it will get flat. That's the only thing that sets me apart from everybody else: the energy."

5. Flexibility

Maybe this one is self-evident. Business is a slice of life, and life is all about change. Yes, entrepreneurs sometimes fit the stereotype of stubborn, single-minded types who don't know when to quit. Tenacity is a good thing. Folding your cards at the first sign of trouble is a *bad* thing.

But staying open to new options is critically important to successful entrepreneurship. Very few businesses I've ever heard of carried out their business plans—if, indeed, they ever had any. Instead, most stepped sideways in the face of opportunity (or huge obstacles). They trimmed, adjusted, regrouped, and moved forward. Staples, the office superstore, began as a low-service, concrete-floored, no-delivery, no-frills enterprise. Gradually, its management broke all these rules to pursue new opportunities.

There was a Dilbert T-shirt that featured Dilbert's handsome face. Above his face, in big letters, was the phrase: "Change is good!" And below his face, in smaller type, was: "You go first." Dilbert works for a large company, where protecting the status quo is critical and change is threatening. Rigidity is the rule. Flexibility (the tool for dealing with change) is irrelevant.

Think of it this way: Flexibility is one of the few advantages that a new and small company has over an old and big one. *Use* that advantage!

6. Balance

Entrepreneurs (and lots of other people) sometimes think in terms of dichotomies: on/off, good/bad, friend/foe, etc. In many cases, I think, this is a kind of mental shortcut. It can speed up decision making: *Don't bother me with all these shades of gray; I've got to act.* To that extent, thinking in black and white can sometimes be helpful.

But this same trait can be harmful when it sets up false dichotomies. If you say, "It's either my company or my family," you may be heading for trouble. If you say, "It's either work or play, but not both," you may be hurting yourself and your company in the long run. Yes, there are very successful entrepreneurs who will tell you that they had to make a choice—company or family—and that putting the company first was the only way they could succeed. I don't doubt that's true, in some situations, but I'm sure glad I never put myself in one of them.

I suggest you don't put yourself in such a terrible situation. Look to build balance into your life. Take breaks; spend time with your young children; be a Big Brother or Big Sister; take up white-water rafting or cave diving. Balance supports curiosity and energy, which I've already persuaded you are important. Admit that you have batteries, and recharge them.

This task can be a simple one. "It's more of a zen approach to what's important and how to spend my time," Bill Doyle, Johnson & Johnson's VP of licensing and acquisitions, told me. "I try to spend at least an hour a day alone. The phones and meetings really catch you. I look for some absolutely alone time. It's okay if I'm in the office, but I'll close the door and take my shoes off, put my feet up, look out the window."

I am not a religious person, but I find that a surprisingly large number of the entrepreneurs I talk to also stress the importance of religion in their lives. It's where some combination of their passion, energy, and balance comes from. (Bud Paxson, the creative genius behind the Home Shopping Network and more recently the "Pax-Net" TV network, leans heavily on his religious beliefs.) If you're one of those people, protect and nurture your beliefs as a resource, and as a way to keep your eye on what's really important.

7. Mental toughness

Having argued on behalf of flexibility and balance, now I'll make a pitch for what I call *mental toughness*. Business is about change, which means it's about turbulence, aggravations, and obstacles. Growing a business sometimes feels like pushing a slippery boulder up a mountain in the dark. You get tired; you seem to lose your footing at just the wrong moment; you feel like nobody else understands what you're going through; you can't even see how high this mountain is.

Well, just how competitive *are* you, anyway? Are you determined to succeed? Can you dig down a little deeper when you have to, and summon up the will to carry on?

The sports arena makes for good analogies to business. I'll use a couple here. I remember when Pete Sampras played Alex Corretja in the semifinals of the U.S. Open in 1995. It was a marathon five-hour match. In the later stages of this slugfest, Sampras was physically sick—cramping, vomiting on the court—but he hung on to win. (He was practically carried off the court.) It was an astonishing display of mental toughness.

I'm convinced that above a certain level of competence, what separates winners from losers is not their relative ability but their relative *will to win*. Is Michael Jordan a superlative athlete? Of course. What makes him a superstar? His will to win, and his mental toughness.

Entrepreneur Jim McCann, the CEO of 1-800-FLOWERS.COM, told me, "I see entrepreneurs take a blow all the time. A key person leaves. You lose a big account. You have the financing yanked, due to a bad market. They take it in the labonza. Then, a half-hour later, their shoulders are starting to come up a little bit. Then their heads start to come back up. In their minds, they're spinning their own version of 'Okay, here's what I've gotta do to recover.' The people who don't have that skill are talking two years later about how the bank screwed them and that's why they're out of business."

Part of mental toughness, it seems, is dealing with *fear*. Bill Russell, the former Celtics center and Hall of Famer, threw up before big games. But when he stepped out on that parquet floor, he was ready to play. Coming to grips with what you're afraid of, and putting your fear to work for you, is a trick that many entrepreneurs have mastered.

Mental toughness has many faces in business. It shows itself when a salesperson, rebuffed dozens of times by a key prospect, makes yet another phone call. It shows itself when an entrepreneur makes the umpteenth pitch for that last $150,000 of financing he or she needs to get the business off the ground. It shows itself when a young person personally guarantees a note. In my mind, it's an indispensable quality for an entrepreneur.

8. Egotism

And speaking of indispensable qualities, a healthy dose of ego is a great thing. You've got to believe in yourself. You've got to believe that you can succeed, and that you *deserve* to succeed.

When I talk to college and business school students who think they might be interested in entrepreneurship, they tend to tell me two things that might scare them off from the world of small business. The first I'd describe as a healthy respect for their own ignorance: They don't know enough to start and grow a business. But the second I'd summarize as a fear of failure.

Think back to when you were a kid. Back then—I bet—you were reluctant to try new things, because you hated to fail at things and look bad in front of your family and friends. It probably got worse when you were a teenager, and you thought of yourself as too fat or too skinny, or your complexion went to hell, or you blushed and stammered at all the wrong moments. Some people carry this baggage throughout their lives. They derive their self-esteem from other people's opinions of them. They think that failing at something will make other people think less of them. They don't think that failure can be the first step toward success; instead, they get stuck in the negative.

Egotism is what lets you sidestep all that. I don't like to fail at *anything,* ever. Failing bugs me (even though I know, intellectually, that it can be very good for me). But I don't spend a lot of time worrying about whether Susie thinks I should stop embarrassing myself on the golf course or John thinks my last business venture was supremely dumb. When it comes to the important stuff, who cares what Susie or John thinks, anyway?

Egotism has to be kept under control, of course. At the far end of the spectrum are egomaniacs. Egomaniacs are obnoxious. People try to avoid them, or—if they're stuck with them—they try to sabotage them. *Anything* to get rid of this jerk!

More dangerous, in my eyes, are the people I'll call "stealth egomaniacs." These are the quiet egomaniacs who make business decisions that are driven mainly by ego. I couldn't begin to count the number of entrepreneurs I've met who, in their first year of making good profits, plowed those profits into a fancy office, expensive cars, extravagant gifts, junkets to exotic places, and so on. Yes, you should reward yourself and your colleagues for succeeding. No, you shouldn't build the Taj Mahal to gratify your ego. You'll hurt the company, and you probably won't enjoy the Taj Mahal as much as you thought you would.

9. Greed (in small doses)

Here's another helpful attribute that has to be kept under control. Let's define greed in a neutral way: *the state of wanting more money than you currently have, or have a good chance of making in the future.* Defined that way, greed can be a good thing. It can be a strong motivator to work hard. It can help generate the income needed to provide good things to good people: security, education, fun, a satisfying retirement, and so on. It may be inseparable from the passion that I advocated earlier. If greed gets you out of bed in the morning, and reinforces your mental toughness, great. Be greedy.

Now for the sermon: Greed, like ego, can cause great mischief when it slips its leash. When you start coveting money that's not rightfully yours, that's a bad sign. When you start cutting corners to make that extra buck—even though you know you'll be hurting good people in the process—that's a *very* bad sign. When your greed starts feeding on itself, you'll be in major trouble.

10. Integrity

I've included integrity at this point in my list mainly to offset egotism and greed. Otherwise, I would have put it up front, ahead of passion.

When I look at the business world today, I see a general deterioration of what I would call business ethics. Heightened competition, large-scale mergers and sales, downsizing, "right-sizing," and so on— these trends have all helped tear up the social contract that held businesses (and particularly large businesses) together. I've had lots of people tell me in recent years that they don't believe in loyalty any more.

I hope I never get to that advanced state of disillusionment, because it sounds like the beginning of the end of integrity. Business is all about relationships. I've worked with you for years, and it's been mutually beneficial. Turning on you would be a betrayal not only of you but also of me.

Why have integrity? I can think of four great reasons: First, and maybe most important, it's a very comfortable way to live your life. You'll sleep better. Your family and friends will take pride in being associated with somebody whom they trust and admire. When the phone rings, you won't get that bad feeling in your stomach. As entrepreneur Don Bakehorn of the American Stationery Company once told me, "Most people you deal with are good people, because they either fear ostracism or have an innate goodness. In my industry, there are lots of people you do business with on a handshake, and there are others I wouldn't trust. I don't see much change over the years. There have always been some shits out there. My boss once told me, a long time ago, 'You don't have to be a shit to be in business.' And I liked that. We're working here, having fun, making a living, and not screwing anybody. That's the way I like it. Sleep with a clear conscience."

Second, your employees will work harder for you, and look out for you. They'll be much more fun to be with. They'll feel that it's safe to take chances and be creative on your behalf. Third, your customers and suppliers will want to do business with you. (Take it from me: you will *definitely* stand out in the crowd.) They will bring you new ideas and opportunities. They will alert you to problems and help you out of problems. They will forgive your mistakes, and help you out of cash

BUILDING TRUST

Sometimes when people hear me talking about "building trust," they tune out. I can almost see it on their faces: "Wake me up when the sermon's over, Bob."

But building trust is critical in business. In that spirit, I offer Reiss's Rules—35 ways to let people around you know that you want them to trust you, and you want to trust them. I know that this is a lengthy list, but I think it warrants the space, because it may help you think up practical ways to build what I call a "mosaic of trust." Think of these as concrete, action-oriented ideas, rather than platitudes. How would you add to the list?

- Listen to the people you're dealing with
- Be honest at all times
- Set an example by your behavior. (Give it a lot of thought)
- Admit mistakes right away. (This is never easy)
- After admitting a mistake, immediately move to correct it and pay for any necessary remedies
- Pay your bills on time. (If you can't, call and explain why, and say when you will pay)
- Give credit where credit is due
- Acknowledge what you don't know (don't B.S. people). Then go get the answer

Continued on next page

- Push quality. Demand quality
- Don't knock others
- Keep your promises
- Undercommit and overperform
- *Try* to be fair. (In many cases, it's the effort that counts.)
- Don't betray confidential information. (Buyers will press you for information about their competition. Don't get trapped!)
- Treat the "little people" well; they deserve it—and by the way, they get promoted. In fact, be respectful to everybody you deal with
- Don't duck problems. Don't procrastinate. Take that call you're dreading—or better yet, call them first
- Be knowledgeable about your product, and share this knowledge
- Inform customers of problems as soon as you know about them. Offer solutions to the problems as soon as you have them
- Don't sell a product that you know is bad
- Look people in the eye when you talk to them
- Don't be embarrassed to make a profit
- When people break their promises to you, call them on it
- Set down explicit and specific rules of behavior for your company, communicate them, and review them regularly
- Keep people informed
- When starting a relationship, be as specific as you can about what you expect from that relationship
- Attack problems
- Return overpayments
- Say "please" and "thank you" at every possible juncture. ("You're welcome" is also good.)
- Pay attention to detail
- Be on time
- Go the extra mile
- Speak candidly to customers and employees, even when you know you're delivering bad news
- Present solutions, rather than problems
- Don't take on assignments you're unqualified for, or for which you don't have the time
- Do unto others as you would have them do unto you. (The Golden Rule, often reiterated by my mom. Thanks, Mom.)

crunches. Fourth, your integrity is portable. When you leave this current business, you may or may not take a pile of money away—but you'll definitely carry your reputation along with you.

And what other people say or hear about you can be crucial. Bill Doyle of Johnson & Johnson confirms this: "In buying an entrepreneurial company, we look for honesty and integrity. That's the very first thing. If we suspect someone of playing it too close or over the line, if it doesn't feel right, then I don't care if he's got the cure for cancer, we probably won't deal with him."

I talked earlier about the virtues of flexibility. Now I'm going to argue that there are some things you *can't* be flexible about. Core values should not be compromised. Honesty, like pregnancy, is not a halfway kind of commodity: you're either honest or you're not. Either you treat people with respect or you don't. Either you and your company stand for something or you don't. Either you're someone who can be trusted or you're not. In my opinion, you need a moral compass, and you need to be prepared for the day when that compass gets tested.

Ask yourself today—before the test comes—whether you want to be remembered for your integrity or your greed. If you're a religious person, ask yourself what standard you're ultimately going to be judged against.

FOUR SKILL SETS

So much for attributes. Now I want to focus on certain skills that I'm convinced can absolutely be acquired and sharpened. You can probably compensate for coming up a little short on the ego scale, or for a tendency to let your life get a little out of balance. But there's no way around the following skills. If you don't have them, acquire them. The good news is that you *can* acquire them! Once you've acquired them, use them.

The skills I am referring to are: (1) creativity; (2) communications; (3) salesmanship; and (4) decision making. (A fifth skill, which has to deal with understanding and using numbers on behalf of your business, is covered in the following chapter.)

Creativity

I'm sure that most entrepreneurs would agree that creativity is a key contributor to the success and continuity of a business. That's certainly *my* belief. I therefore list creativity as one of the key skills of low-risk, high-reward entrepreneurship. Creativity is where your new products, new methods, and new markets begin.

That's the easy part: endorsing creativity. The hard part is figuring out exactly how to bottle this genie. "Creativity" means something different for every business, and every individual. For my part, I depend a great deal on *intuition* to guide me in my creative decision making. (Intuition that is derived from experience allows you to think and act without necessarily employing a conscious reasoning process.) In this section, I'll begin by offering some personal observations on creativity—guided in part by intuition—and then I'll add some interesting perspectives from academics who think and write on this subject.

What is "creativity"? In a business context, it's the spark that drives the development and implementation of new products or ideas that are actionable. These innovations can apply to any aspect of the business; they are not limited to "artistic" sides of the business. In my experience, many people mistakenly equate creativity with "being artistic."

From my perspective, that's a cop-out. Creativity has to infuse all corners of your business. You need better ways to move goods through your warehouse; you need innovative ways to enhance your cash flow; you need new sales techniques; you need new motivational programs for employees; you need new accounting methods—fill in the blank. These are all functions that call for creativity. I honestly believe that if your business is structured well, everybody can find ways to put their creativity to work on behalf of the company.

How?

I've already implied the first prerequisite: You have to create an environment that welcomes new ideas. Would *you* suggest a new way of doing something if you thought the most likely response would be, "We don't do things that way," or—worse—"Boy, *that's* dumb!"? I wouldn't!

This is not to say that every new idea is good. Most of them aren't good, and many won't even be new. People who are relatively new to an organization lack the historical knowledge to avoid reinventing the wheel. People who are deeply immersed in a particular function—say, accounting—are unlikely to understand the complexities of another function. These two factors are always in play, limiting someone's ability to make a creative contribution.

On the other hand, it sometimes takes fresh eyes to ask the right question. It may take someone who's not burdened with the baggage of the past, or isn't bogged down with deep functional expertise, to put the right idea on the table at the right moment. To make this possible, you have to demonstrate your commitment to idea generation, and your patience when (for whatever reason) the new idea doesn't work out.

I've found that the greatest catalyst for creativity is *knowledge*. You can't ever have too much knowledge about your industry, company, customers, market trends, product, employees, supervisors, peers, and so on. Having this knowledge of how things work and what people are thinking will alert you to opportunities and solutions that others with less knowledge won't see. Logically, this applies across your organization. No, you shouldn't bury people in information they couldn't possibly use. But you do have to give people enough information so they can make their best possible contribution.

Here are some of the tactics that I employ to enhance my own knowledge base (and, I hope, my creativity):

CREATIVITY IN CONTEXT: THE RUBIK'S CUBE BOOK

Most creative business moves are context-dependent. That is, your knowledge of a particular context (or several contexts) enables you to do something inventive and profitable. Let's look at a specific episode (from my own experience) to underscore this point.

When the Rubik's Cube puzzle took America by storm in the early 1980s, it created an opportunity to produce a solution book for this most difficult puzzle. For some reason, Ideal—the company marketing the Rubik's Cube—didn't offer such a book. Quickly, two book companies created solution books that eventually reached the top of the *New York Times* best-seller list.

By this time, I had already had experience as a partner in a toy/game company. I was shopping the game department in Macy's one day and noticed a big display of Rubik's Cube solution books adjacent to the

Continued on next page

cubes. Back then, and to some extent even today, the idea of selling a book outside the book department was a radical idea.

But in those days, the Macy's book department was adjacent to the adult game department, and the same buyer—whom I knew, and who was a very creative and entrepreneurial type—bought for both departments. As I surveyed the game department, I spotted the buyer and asked her how the solution books were selling. She told me the books were doing great. In fact, she said, her impression was that for every three cubes that were sold, two books were sold.

I immediately bought the book, which retailed for $2.00. I then called the book publisher to inquire about buying the books in quantity to resell them into the toy field, so that toy retailers could sell them adjacent to their cubes, à la Macy's.

Book publishers sell books on a "guaranteed sale" basis, which means the retailer can return all unsold books for credit. To minimize their exposure in this potentially risky relationship, publishers work on high margins, and give retailers lower-than-average profit margins as compared to non-guaranteed sale products. Knowing this, I asked them to sell me the book for 50 cents, with the idea of reselling them to toy buyers at $1.00—but on a non-guaranteed sale basis, which was the standard in the toy business at that time.

The publisher's best price for this $2.00 retail book, up to that point, was about $1.10, and that price had been offered only to the largest book chains. You can imagine the publisher's reaction when an unknown person from an unknown company (R&R) proposed to buy their products at less than half the price they extended to their best customers. They were prepared to reject my proposal out of hand—until I told them I would purchase all my books from them on a non-guaranteed basis.

These were the magic words. After a brief back and forth, they agreed to my offer, which I had designed to offer them a series of goodies. These included:

- **A healthy profit** at a 50-cent sales price, because they had no marketing costs or commissions to pay.
- Access to **new channels of distribution.**
- **Economies of scale.** The cost of printing paper products, like books, decreases dramatically with volume. My volume, when added

to their planned print runs, would reduce their cost per book and give them additional profits on all of their regular sales.

The book that they agreed to supply to me was identical in every way to the standard product, except that they printed our name (R&R) on the back cover instead of theirs. This was good for them, because it clearly identified which books could not be returned. At the same time, it was good for us, because it got our company name out there. Working with quality retailers like Toys "R" Us, J. C. Penney, and Sears, we sold more than 600,000 copies of the book in a short period of time, and our name was on every copy.

We also kept looking for ways to reduce our risk. For example, we asked the publisher to ship large orders direct from their factory under our label. ("Large orders" were defined as anything over 1,000 books.) In those cases, we never touched the books. We also entered into a relationship with a distributor who shipped small orders, many of which we turned over to them. Everybody involved—publisher, distributor, retailer—was paid well for their efforts, and it was a win-win solution all around.

What are the lessons for risk management and creativity?

- The creativity in the deal grew directly out of our knowledge of how the book industry works. We offered non-guaranteed sales, economies of scale, and incremental distribution that was otherwise unavailable.
- Key risks normally associated with publishing disappeared, because we needed no warehouse or inventory. (We didn't buy any books unless we already had a purchase order for them.)
- There was no development cost. We latched onto an existing product, and put that product into a new market that the owner couldn't penetrate on his own.
- Relationships were crucial. My relationship with the Macy's buyer persuaded her to share her experience with me. Our relationships with the toy retailers and toy reps allowed us to move quickly, and get sales in what was likely to be a short window of opportunity. (Toy items like Rubik's Cubes tend to have short lives.) We enjoyed doing business with these people, and they enjoyed doing business with us.

Reading. Trade periodicals, newspapers (especially the *Wall Street Journal*), general interest and entrepreneurial magazines, and so on—all give me an endless supply of data points, some of which eventually come together in unexpected ways. I also review best-seller lists regularly to keep an eye on what people are reading out there. (Spotting an increase in titles on magic once gave us the idea to produce a line of magic products.)

Here's an unlikely source of valuable reading material: the so-called junk mail that comes to your offices. In too many companies, this is reviewed by nobody. What I've found is that if you're selective, you can pick up a lot of valuable information in these letters and solicitations. How are companies selling themselves? What are they pointing to as new and exciting? Are they bad-mouthing products or practices that are at the heart of *your* business?

Roaming. I haunt mall stores and other retail outlets to see what other industries and companies are doing with their packaging, presentation, display, and so on. As often as possible, I talk with people who sell or use my products.

Studying. At least twice a year, I try to go to some type of educational seminar or business conference. These can be one-day affairs, or can last several days. Inevitably, I wind up doing some schmoozing and networking at events like these, but my real goal is to bear down on a topic of interest and *learn* about it. You can't just hope this will happen—you have to make it happen.

Interacting. I regularly interact with other entrepreneurs, both inside and outside my industry. I attend lunches, dinners, conferences, and chat on the phone with smart people. I attend business breakfasts organized around guest speakers. I visit trade shows both in and outside of my industry. I meet with suppliers. I have meetings off-premises with my customers (off *their* premises, that is).

When I'm a licensee, I always attend the two-day retreats that most licensors put together (usually every other year). This is the best way to stay on top of the product—and also to get to know your fellow licensors.

Questioning. I ask questions of my employees, particularly those who deal with customers and/or consumers. What's going on out there? I extend this questioning process to include the people who are producing, packaging, and shipping my products.

So that's a quick primer on knowledge building. Here are a few more tips, in no particular order, for fostering creativity, both specifically and in general:

- When you find yourself stuck on a problem, **try to list as many potential solutions as possible.** These can come from your employees, customers, suppliers, even yourself. Think about these solutions from various perspectives. Does one start to stand out from the crowd as increasingly appealing?

- **Walk away from seemingly intractable problems.** Work them for a while, and then give them a break. If you're like me, you'll probably find that "marinating" tough problems softens them up.

- **Recast problems as opportunities.** Maybe it's old hat to tell people that every cloud has a silver lining, but this kind of perspective can really turn your day around. The obstacle blocking your path might vanish—or it might transform itself into the obstacle blocking your *competitor's* path. Event-owner extraordinaire John Korff puts it this way: "If you're creative, you can make adversity your friend. So what if it's harder and harder to get corporate sponsorship for one of my events? That just makes it harder for my competition. And makes me look even more competent when I get the sponsorship."

- **Get yourself out of your normal routine.** I'm a great believer in three-day vacations. There's no better way to look at a problem with fresh eyes. If that's too great a luxury, go for a long run, or block out time for reflection on your next long plane trip. As long as your seatmate doesn't need a lot of attention, a plane trip can be very conducive to a creative connecting-of-the-dots.

- **Get other people out of *their* normal routine.** For example, off-site meetings of all your employees can be very productive. The trick here is to combine freedom with structure, so that good ideas can bubble up without too much random noodling. In my experience, a detailed agenda helps strike this balance.

Such meetings need not be expensive. A full-day session on a Saturday, with lunch served in the middle, has worked out well for me. You might want to invite key suppliers or customers for parts of the meeting, for lunch, or for both. Make it clear that one key goal is to come up with good ideas for the company. You should be prepared to share relevant information, either in advance or on site. In return, you should expect to hear a range of perspectives on that information.

- **Be prepared for that flash of insight.** If you're like me, great ideas can come to you in the middle of the night—sometimes even in your sleep. Take the time to turn on the light and *jot that idea down*. Your sleepy brain is great at putting things together, but it's not great at remembering them.

- **Talk to people who aren't just like you.** This is good for specific problem solving: Maybe that oddball next door, who seems pretty accomplished in his own specialized field, could bring a whole new perspective to this problem.

  This is also good policy for your company in general. Resist the temptation to hire people with the same skills and outlook as you. (What will you learn?) Assume that artistic people—designers, artists, inventors—will welcome the kind of structure that you can provide to them. This may seem counterintuitive, but in my experience, it's true: artistic people work better with constraints, and they actually welcome such constraints—as long as they come in the problem-definition stage. When I took over a struggling needlecraft company, for example, we had seventeen designers on staff, who were floundering in part because there were no clear directives from the company about what was important, and what was not. They welcomed clarification of this critical point, and subsequently did great creative work.

  As Teresa Amabile, a Harvard Business School professor with a specialty in creativity, writes, "Creativity thrives when managers let people decide how to climb a mountain. They needn't, however, let employees choose which one."

- **Create incentives for creativity.** I believe strongly in recognizing the contributions of individuals. This can take the form of financial incentives, or public recognition, or both. The 3M Company, famous for its creative output, has an elaborate employee-recognition system. But an effective system need not be elaborate. Bob Savage, at one time the president of Compton Advertising, told me that Compton used to give an "Excitement Award" every month to a leading innovator in every department. Savage personally presented the awards, and always pointed out that to "excite" means to "move to action."

- **Do things that excite you.** This is an addition suggested by Professor Amabile, and I agree wholeheartedly. When you're *excited* about going to work in the morning, your creativity levels are likely to soar. "You must like what you're doing," mail-order maven Don Seta once told me, "because then your mind becomes very creative. If you are with a beautiful woman, the soul comes up with beautiful words you want to tell her. But if she's not very attractive and you don't like her, nothing comes out. It's the same with a business. It's a love affair. If your business is something you love, you'll be surprised at how quickly you can learn and how creative you become."

In other words, do less of the things you don't like and more of the things you do like. This is bound to get your creative juices flowing.

Communications skills

There must be a million books (and videos, and CDs, and software packages) on the market today that aim to teach you one or more of the Big Three communication skills: writing, making presentations, and listening. Some of these are very useful tools, as are some of the coaches, seminars, and other resources out there. In this context, I'll only touch briefly on the Big Three.

1. Business writing. Writing is not a dying art. (E-mail, for one, is breathing new life into the written word.) A piece of writing is *you,* in the eyes of the world. Your letters, memos, business plans, prospectuses—all of them make you naked in front of the world. Among other things, they tell the world either that you are or are not able to express yourself. Good writing arises out of good thinking. If you're not thinking straight about something, you can only write badly about it. And your readers may work backwards from your bad writing. They may ask, "Can't our friend Bob think straight?"

In my opinion, good business writing is concise. It fits on a page (maybe two). It assumes that business readers have to get to the point quickly—and it helps them do that. Good business writing uses simple language, short sentences and paragraphs, and as many "road signs" as possible: Here's where you've been, where you are, where you're going.

AMABILE ON CREATIVITY

Thousands of articles and books have been written on the subject of creativity. But almost all of them have focused on the concerns of large, Fortune 500–type firms, and this is a peer group that in most cases doesn't have a lot to teach small businesses. When it comes to creativity, though, I think the circumstances are different. If *big* businesses can build creativity into their relatively inflexible, slow-moving systems, then surely small businesses can steal a page from their books.

To do so, I recommend that readers study the work of Teresa Amabile of the Harvard Business School faculty. Her article in the September–October 1998 issue of the *Harvard Business Review*— entitled "How to Kill Creativity"—is a fascinating analysis of the challenge of fostering creativity.

Amabile writes that in each individual, creativity is a function of three components:

- **expertise** (technical, procedural, or intellectual knowledge)
- **creative thinking skills** (the ways in which people approach problems)
- **motivation** (passion for the work)

The first two categories are the individual's "raw materials" for creativity. The motivational structure created in the work environment either brings that creativity to the surface, or stifles it. For a full catalogue of the kinds of mistakes that managers can make to kill creativity, read Amabile's article—or for that matter, look at a collection of Dilbert cartoons. They include, for example:

- Granting autonomy in name only
- Creating vague goals, and changing them frequently
- Setting fake (or impossibly tight) deadlines
- Condemning failure
- Allowing corporate politics to inhibit information sharing and collaboration

This is not to say that good business writing needs to be sparse and boring. A well-chosen anecdote, or a bit of humor or a flash of passion, can make all the difference. Writing is communication between people, and in many cases, injecting some of yourself into your writing is extremely helpful.

The most useful course I took in business school was the notorious WAC course: the Written Analysis of Cases. We were given a case in the morning. We were told to read it, assess it, and write no more than one page about it—all before 11:00 p.m. If your analysis went over a page, it was rejected. If your analysis was a minute late, it was rejected. I *hated* that course. And yet it drummed into me some crucial lessons about thinking and writing that I had never encountered before. For example: Shorter is harder, but better. Your reader almost *always* wants to read less, not more.

2. Making presentations. Business presentations are another critical basket of skills. One piece of this is public speaking, the prospect of which drives some people screaming out of the room. (In most polls, it shows up as the thing most people are most terrified of.) Believe me, with good coaching, and a willingness to figure out and work within your own limitations, *anybody* can learn to be an effective public speaker.

Practice is the best (and only) way to get better. Force yourself to do more public speaking and your nervousness will gradually dissipate. I'm reminded of a friend of mine who has a terrible stammer. Despite this affliction, he makes the rounds as an inspirational speaker on the subject of product quality. I saw him perform one night. He began his speech by saying, "Ladies and gentlemen, I have a slight stammer, so I'll ask you to bear with me. On to tonight's topic. There are three things you have to understand about quality. The first is—" And here he got absolutely stuck. He couldn't get the word out, whatever it was. He got red in the face. The audience started to squirm uncomfortably. He took a deep breath. "Ladies and gentlemen," he began again, "there are only *two* things you have to understand about quality." The audience ate it up.

New York Life used to have annual get-togethers to celebrate their top-producing salesmen. A friend of mine attended these confabs, at which the members of the Million Dollar Roundtable were toasted and held up as inspirational examples. Every year for about five years running, when it came time for the *highest-producing salesperson* to address the crowd, he did so from behind a screen. According to my friend, this guy—the top salesman for New York Life for several years running—was so shy that he could only speak to crowds through a screen.

My point in telling these two stories is that if these two guys can get up in front of a crowd, one way or another, so can you. Practice! Learn to make the microphone your friend.

When you do get up in front of that crowd, try to keep the focus on *you,* and your ideas. Try to build a relationship between yourself and the individuals in that audience. (One old trick is to pick out one person in the crowd and speak directly to him or her.) Try *not* to be dependent on visual aids: flip charts, PowerPoint presentations, and so on. Yes, some situations call for an endless succession of charts. And some things really are best conveyed through a great chart, or a powerful video clip. But in my experience, people don't buy from projectors; they buy from people. Especially after a nice meal with some wine, they tend to fall asleep in the dark. And by the way: sooner or later, that projector is going to break down, and you'll be on your own. Be ready!

It's more than likely that most of your oral presentations will be to small groups (between, say, two and twenty people). If you're going to address a prospective customer or some other group in which you don't know all the parties, try to determine early on who the decision makers in the room are. Take the time to get everyone's name, title, and function. In most cases, this will help you deliver a more effective presentation.

As much as possible, make your talk interactive. Ask questions at key moments—while still controlling the meeting. One of your key tasks is to get any objections or doubts that they have about your company or product on the table while you are there, so you can alleviate those concerns. Encourage questions, and if there's a time limit, make sure to leave time for questions at the end of your presentation. In most cases, it's a mistake to hand out literature or written highlights of your presentation before you speak. (People will read while you're talking.) One exception is a case where you want to take your audience step by step through complicated material, in which case a written summary, handed out to your audience at the beginning of your talk, can be a useful tool.

3. Listening. Is listening a communications skill? Yes. In my opinion, listening is a major, major contributor to entrepreneurial success. Is listening a skill that is all too often neglected and undervalued? Yes, again.

Listening is different from hearing. Hearing is one of the five senses that God gave to most of us—something that, assuming you're awake and sober, is going to happen whether or not you want it to. Listening, by contrast, doesn't happen unless you make it happen. Most of us are blessed with two ears and only one mouth, and yet our mouth is employed far more often than our ears.

How many times have you been introduced to someone and then immediately forgotten his or her name? How often have you sat in on a lecture, a sermon, or a dinner conversation, and suddenly realized that you have almost no idea what's being said? You're *hearing,* in most of these cases, but you're not listening.

I learned this lesson early, working as a waiter during the summers of my college years. These were resort hotels, which meant we usually had the same three dozen people sitting at our tables three meals a day for an entire week. At the end of the week, they'd tip us for the twenty-one meals that we'd served to them—and this was how you really made your money, given our dollar-a-day salaries. We soon learned that our tips soared if we learned the names of those three dozen people quickly. Based on one introduction, you had to be able to say—four hours later, when you saw them walking around the grounds—"Oh, hi, Mr. and Mrs. Jones. How do you like it here, Sally? Are you and Billy going swimming this afternoon? I hope you're working up an appetite for tonight!"

I think we're bad listeners in part because humans process ideas faster than they can be delivered verbally. How often have you known where a particular sentence was headed, and wished you could fast-forward to the next one? The trouble is, (1) you may be wrong in your guess, and (2) you're being disrespectful to the speaker.

Being a good listener in many cases means being an active listener. When someone is talking to you, look them in the eye. When he or she says something you don't understand, ask an intelligent question to clarify things. (This may involve summarizing what was said just before you started getting confused.) Keep the focus on the speaker's ideas rather than your own ideas. Don't interrupt someone's train of thought gratuitously. Don't spend a lot of time planning what you're going to say. Don't start sifting through your arsenal of war stories, looking for the most relevant one. (This is a sure sign that you've stopped listening.)

Bear down on the speaker, mentally. While you're focusing on the words they're saying, also focus on their inflection, and on their body language. Without losing your grip on what they're saying, try to figure out what's behind what they're saying. Sometimes, if you listen hard and move carefully, you can help the other guy figure out exactly what they're trying to say.

So, how does all this pay off in business? Let me count the ways. Take selling, for example. Many buyers I've run into will more or less instruct you in how to sell them if you ask a few good questions—and then sit back and listen, actively.

"Listening is the most important skill for an entrepreneur," says John Altman, who has started up six companies so far. "We talked to everybody who came in our front door. Every one of those guys brought a fresh idea, and all we had to do was listen for it. But listening is a learned skill. It's something we have to struggle with."

The questions you ask buyers will vary from setting to setting. I like to ask buyers in large corporations, for example, how the company measures their performance and how bonuses (if any) are determined. Since this tends to change from year to year, it's good to be current, and most people are happy to talk about it. I remember a Sears buyer, many years ago, who told me that in that particular year, Sears was paying bonuses based on the cash discounts that buyers were able to obtain from vendors. Well, I was a small company, and I was nothing if not flexible. I offered a 4 percent cash discount on new items—and at the same time, with the buyer's knowledge, raised the list price 4 percent.

Good negotiations depend on good listening. One key challenge in negotiations is to find out what the other team really wants, as opposed to what they *say* they want. The best path to this critical knowledge is good and active listening.

Bring your good listening skills home, too. Being in business can put you into conflict with family members, who feel that they have to compete with the business for your time. Imagine that you're one of these family members, and you need to have a heart-to-heart with Dad. But when you try to initiate that discussion, Dad riffles through papers in his briefcase, or takes a phone call from the office, or starts looking over your shoulder with that distracted look on his face. That's frustrating, right?

So listen hard at home, too. Just the act of listening to your family will lessen the sense of competition with the office. And there's no better way to learn what's important to the most important people in your life.

Salesmanship

The act of selling—securing orders for your company's products or services—is one of the most critical skills for the success of your enterprise. *Getting that order* starts everything! In real estate, they say it's "location, location, location." In entrepreneurship, I say it's "sales, sales, sales!"

Maybe you're already shuddering at this one. Maybe you're already saying to yourself, "Hey, I'm no salesperson. When I need to get those orders, I'll just go find myself a super salesperson."

Let me make the case that you probably *are* a salesperson already, in one or more corners of your life. Selling is the act of persuading other people to see things from your point of view, and then *acting* on that new perspective. Think back to your childhood. Did you ever try to persuade your parents to buy you something, or let you do something new? If so, you were selling. If they agreed, you were selling effectively. Now move on to your time in school. Did you ever get some tough professor to see things your way, as a result of a paper you wrote or a class presentation you made? If so, you *sold* that professor. And how about your social life? Ever try to persuade somebody that you were actually an interesting and attractive human being, and one who was worth spending time with?

Have you ever worked for somebody? If so, you've surely tried to sell that person on the idea of giving you more money or more responsibility. Have you ever had somebody work for you? If so, you've probably tried to sell that person on the idea of working harder, or more effectively.

Selling, selling, selling. We do it all the time. And yet so many people today seem to shy away from it, and even look down upon the people who do it for a living. It's a misunderstood and thankless calling. I'm constantly amazed at how many college students tell me they would *never* get involved in sales. I always wonder where they're going to go to get *away* from sales. The legal profession? Better be prepared to sell in court—and also in those out-of-court settlements. Academia? Better be prepared to sell your dissertation, and to sell yourself at every step along the tenure track. The arts? Get ready for those guest spots on the talk shows, or those long dinners with your patrons. Advertising? Enough said!

So everybody sells, and—generally speaking—successful people sell more and better than unsuccessful people. Why this disdain for salesmanship? I think there are four reasons. First, and probably most important, lots of people are intimidated by the prospect of selling. They think that, on some basic level, they don't have what it takes. They have a mental image of a salesperson as someone who is extroverted, thinks on his or her feet, comes up with the right joke at exactly the right moment, and orders the right wine at the overpriced restaurant. They don't see those traits in themselves, and they doubt that they can acquire them.

In my mind, this is nonsense. I've already mentioned the example of the New York Life salesman—the top producer for several years running—who literally couldn't get up in front of a crowd. There are a million ways to sell effectively, and you probably already own several of them. If you can't, you can acquire one. (More on this below.)

Second, I think some people equate "selling" with "bribing." They think that sales equals payola, and that you can't sell without getting your hands dirty.

I can't be quite so categorical about dismissing this objection. Yes, bad stuff still goes on, especially in certain industries, and especially overseas. But in my personal experience, both the buying and the selling professions have been substantially cleaned up in the past quarter century. Companies that might have winked at abuses on the part of their buyers a decade or two ago now go out of their way to make examples of rotten eggs. Several years back, a national retailer with whom I've done a lot of business over the years caught one of their buyers taking money. They turned him over to be prosecuted, and gained a lot of national attention in the process.

Third, I think some of us think of salespeople as lonely, bored, and underchallenged. This is what I call the Willie Loman phenomenon—in which a character in a play comes to represent an entire profession, unfairly and inaccurately. (It's like saying *Citizen Kane* represents all journalists.) Yes, the life of the stereotypical "traveling salesman" can at times be isolating and tedious. But that kind of selling is only one tiny slice of a much larger pie. Most professional salespeople I know think that their work is exciting and challenging, and puts them in a complex web of human relationships. Most will tell you that there's no thrill in life quite like *making that big sale*.

And finally, I suspect that some people think of the sales function as unimportant. This is easy to counter. Salespeople literally make the wheels of the economy go round, collectively accounting for billions of dollars in sales volume annually. In many cases, the best of them are making more money than the CEOs of their respective companies. And many CEOs are themselves former star salespeople. When a board of directors goes looking for someone to help their company succeed, they most often settle on somebody who has a proven ability to *sell that product*.

"Salespeople are our eagles," says Barbara Todd, founder of Orchids Only and the Good Catalog Company. "We feed and take care of them *very* well. We make sure they are well motivated. We spend a lot of time and money training them. We recognize that they have a very important job, and that—in many cases—they are people who need a lot of recognition. We make sure they get that recognition."

I've already argued that selling is a "learnable" skill. I have to confess that some of the people I've talked with in recent months disagree with that assessment. Some say it's something you're born with. I like the distinction made by Barbara Todd. "You *do* have to have an innate ability," she says, "and that ability is empathy—the ability to put yourself in someone else's shoes. That's really important, and some people just don't have it. But you also have to have the skill sets, which is something that you can learn."

Where can you go to learn these skill sets? Unfortunately, you can't learn them in business school. I have yet to find a graduate business school that has a course called "Sales." (I hope someone will prove me wrong!) Schools like to teach sales management, but that's a different kettle of fish. You have to *make* a sale before you can manage it.

Fortunately, there are companies (like Barbara Todd's) that take this responsibility very seriously. There are also zillions of books, videotapes, and seminars out there to help you sharpen your sales skills. Dale Carnegie is probably the granddaddy of them all, and it's amazing to me how many successful entrepreneurs in their sixties and seventies will eventually confess to having been trained in "how to win friends and influence people." I'm sure you can find a modern-day equivalent, including the modern-day Dale Carnegie. Ask someone who's made a successful transition from a non-salesperson to a salesperson how they did it. Don't be surprised if they tell you that they simply watched somebody else sell—somebody whom they admired, and felt comfortable emulating. And don't be surprised if they tell you that good selling comes from inside yourself.

Maybe you're wondering, at this point, why I'm spending so much time on *salesmanship* in a book that is supposed to be about *entrepreneurship.* I'm not arguing that you have to spend years on the road, going door to door, as a prerequisite for starting your own company. I am arguing that *if you can't sell, your company won't make it.* As the founder, visionary, conscience, and sparkplug of your business, you will constantly be selling. You will be selling to investors, customers, suppliers, and employees.

You will be persuading everybody else in your company to sell, too—selling them on selling. Peter Benassi, head of the MRI barter company in New York, puts it this way: "Sales is critical. We try to instill the idea that *everybody sells.* I sell. Our media people sell. My inventory guy sells. In fact, he's a great example. He's in contact with guys in warehouses. If there's a return of 50,000 cases of something, it's that guy in that warehouse who is likely to say to my inventory guy, 'Hey, by the way, we just got another 50,000 cases of so-and-so.' So our guy contacts the salesperson on the account and says, 'Did you hear there's another 50,000 cases of so-and-so hanging around?'

"Even the people who are cutting our checks can be involved. They talk to Accounts Receivable people, who are well aware of receivable issues at the other end of the line. So most jobs are full of selling potential—endless!—if your people are properly trained and motivated."

A closing thought: Strong sales can make up for a lot of mistakes in other parts of the business. This is a book about reducing your risks, and increasing your chances for success in business. Having those orders pouring in is a great way to tip the odds in your favor. So be an "eagle," as Barbara Todd puts it—and get the people around you to be eagles, too.

Decision making

Small and large companies alike are continuously making decisions. Generally, small companies make their decisions more quickly than large ones, and this is one of their advantages. An entrepreneur who is indecisive, or who procrastinates, squanders this edge. I'd rather make quick decisions and make more mistakes and not miss out on opportunities than move slowly and give up those opportunities.

Another aspect of decision making is the risk/reward calculation. In large companies—as explained to me by the manager of catalogue operations for a Fortune 500 company—employees tend to avoid making any decisions that involve innovation. If they take chances and are successful, the best thing that can happen is that they'll keep their jobs—which they probably would have done anyway. But if they take chances and *fail,* they may actually lose their jobs.

One of the big questions about decision making is the intuition-vs.-science balance: how much should you go with your gut, and how much should you depend on information that has been gathered systematically? My answer is that intuition should be used as often as possible. I'm well aware that there are many people who feel that "your gut" is the same thing as "your emotions," and therefore not to be trusted. But it seems to me that if you're working in a realm you're very familiar with, your gut is based on the sum total of your past experience in this realm. If you're driving down a road in a city where you've never been before, you haven't looked at the map in the glove compartment, and there are no landmarks with which to orient yourself, then your intuition about which direction to head in is probably worth very little.

If you're on your own turf, by contrast, your intuition is worth a lot. It may not be something you can articulate as a rational process, but it's definitely a tool you should use. So: if you've got a lot of experience, trust your gut more. And if you've got a lot of time—and some resources—try to adopt a systematic approach to the decision at hand.

Maybe some real-life approaches to decision making would be helpful. Ed Hajim, chairman and CEO of Ing Furman Selz Asset Management LLC, points out that the size of a company has a large bearing on that company's decision-making process. When one is working for oneself, he says, decisions are largely based on gut. (There's no money for more systematic approaches, and the stakes are too small to warrant such approaches.) As a company gets bigger, the stakes get bigger, there's more in the way of discretionary resources. And my own experience tells me that a lot of the "research" conducted by large companies is not designed to generate useful knowledge; instead, it's CYA-driven (cover your backside). To me, this verges on the sinful. There's got to be some more productive way to spend that money!

Don Bakehorn, who runs a fairly sizable company, confesses that he and his colleagues do a lot of research, and then pretty much make their decisions on instinct. Dan Blau, who works in children's books, says that he makes his business decisions based primarily on testing and research rather than instinct. When it comes to "human" issues—such as dealing with customers, vendors, and employees—Blau admits that intuition plays a much larger role.

Jerry Shafir, who has built a very solid growth business, Kettle Cuisine, over a decade, tells me that he uses something he calls "informed gut." Where things are quantifiable, he says, research should be used to get at the vital information. For example, when choosing where to locate a new factory, a company should thoroughly research the available labor supply, the local tax and incentive structure, local regulations, and so on before making a decision. But other decisions, such as those having to do with future trends in consumer tastes, have to have some degree of intuition built into them.

Time and experience are major factors in decision making. The more time you have, the more research you can afford to do. A high experience factor, as noted above, will hone your instincts. As in most business situations, there's no one success formula. My bottom-line advice, though, is, *Don't understimate the validity of your instincts.*

———

So there you have it: my vision of a set of attributes and skills that collectively can help you on the road to entrepreneurial success. If it seems like a long list, don't be discouraged. Pick and choose; find your own combination; add your own ideas to the ones I've laid out. And conversely, if you think you've already got all these attributes and skills in spades, then I encourage you to go for it!

There's one more critical skill set that I've pulled out and stuck in the following chapter. *Numeracy*—the ability to understand and use numbers to help your business—deserves the special attention that a separate chapter gives it.

2

NUMERACY

Do you want to do everything you possibly can to ensure the survival and growth of your company? Of course you do. Well, one of the most essential skills that you, *personally,* can bring to your company is understanding, tracking, and using certain numbers.

This section started out in a later chapter of the book. But as I thought about it, I decided that a section on *numeracy*—the numbers equivalent of *literacy*—was so important that it belonged up front. Numeracy is a way of thinking. I don't speak a second language, but when people describe the process to me, I recognize it. "Thinking in numbers" is a vital, vital skill.

Let me explain. In my experience, far too many people feel that they aren't good at math, or didn't take accounting, or whatever. Using this as an excuse, they hire someone else to watch the numbers for them. This is two mistakes in one. First, they're selling themselves short. *Anybody* can work with numbers, and the kind of number-tracking I'm talking about requires no advanced mathematical training or professional degree. Second, there's no substitute for *you* in this process. Nobody else out there is as motivated as you are to get the numbers working on behalf of your business.

Yes, your accountant can prepare your P&L statements, tax returns, and balance sheet, and offer certain kinds of advice based on rules-of-thumb and industry norms. (An accountant with lots of experience working with companies like yours can be a gold mine of comparative information.) But you simply can't count on quarterly meetings with your accountant to do what you need to do with the numbers. In order to run your company properly, and dramatically reduce your risk of failure, you need to get access to certain numbers *quickly,* and use those numbers effectively.

Follow the example set by business innovator Raymond Lo. "I hire people to watch the numbers," he once told me, "but I also look at them myself, every day. I'm not sure how other entrepreneurs in Hong Kong do this. I know I have friends who don't watch the numbers. As long as they have money in the bank, they're okay, and that's all they keep track of. Some of them are successful, but not all of them. If you're not looking at the numbers, you can easily get lost."

In a nutshell, here are the numbers you should have at your fingertips:

- a snapshot of the company
- cash flow statements that are regularly updated
- cost analysis of your product(s)
- break-even analyses, both for the company overall and for each new product

In the following pages, we'll look at each of the above. My goal is to get you comfortable with all of them—by which I don't simply mean that you'll be able to generate them, but that you'll understand them and be able to adapt and use them effectively. In general, my prescription is, Know and love these numbers! I'm not saying you have to prepare them yourself. When you're small, you can have your accountant or bookkeeper prepare them for you; and if your company grows to the point that you can afford a chief financial officer, then he or she will take responsibility for preparing the numbers.

But again, none of these people can be an effective substitute for you. In order to guide their activities, you have to be able to "think in numbers." Take it from me: once you get into this method of thinking, it will come easily to you, it won't take much of your time, and it will be an invaluable tool. It can be particularly helpful to you in negotiating with suppliers and customers.

THE COMPANY SNAPSHOT

Exhibit X is an example of what I refer to as a *snapshot*. I sometimes call it a *weekly snapshot,* because that's been the interval that's proved most helpful to me in my businesses. One huge manufacturing company I've worked with does a similar report daily. (They call it the *flash report*.) Depending on the nature of your business, you might find a

EXHIBIT X: COMPANY SNAPSHOT

Current assets
    Cash . . . reg.   _____
    Cash . . . MMA   _____
    Receivables   _____
    Other   _____

       TOTAL   _____

Inventory
    Finished   _____
    Component   _____

       TOTAL   _____

Current liabilities
    Payables   _____
    Misc.   _____
    Accrued commissions   _____
    Accrued royalties   _____

       TOTAL   _____

Fixed monthly expenses   _____

Loans outstanding   _____
Monthly sales to date   _____
Yearly sales to date   _____
Future orders to ship   _____
Open purchase orders   _____

bi-weekly report adequate, particularly during slow seasons. In certain situations—for example, where your company is temporarily flush with cash—you may decide that a monthly snapshot is adequate.

But you can't make that decision until you understand the snapshot, and how your company performs against that snapshot. So my advice is: start weekly, and adjust as necessary.

The snapshot is meant to be *simple*. It's meant to be easy to prepare—your secretary or bookkeeper should be able to do it—and able to be digested by you in no more than five minutes. Depending on the specifics of your business, you may want to add or subtract categories from the following exhibit. You might also want to use comparatives from a prior period. Just remember: *Keep it simple.*

The point of this report is to get the quickest possible handle on key aspects of your company's operation, such as:

- Do I have enough cash to pay my bills?
- Are my receivables running too high? (If so, is it because payments are running late? Or is it because my credit-checking system has fallen apart, and we're selling more non-credit-worthy customers?)
- Do I have enough inventory to handle future demand? (A caveat: This report can't tell you if you have the inventory in the right categories; only a detailed inventory report can tell you that.)
- Have we overcommitted ourselves in terms of inventory? (Most companies hit this stumbling block sooner or later. If your inventory figure is too high, it's a signal that you need to get the kind of detailed report that would let you take the right immediate action—such as canceling existing product orders, heading off the placement of future orders, putting certain items on sale, or closing out certain items.)

Now take a look at Exhibit Y, which is the same report, this time dated "September 30, 1999," and filled in with some sample numbers.

When I look at this report, I reach some quick (but tentative) conclusions:

- Receivables look like they're too high, if terms are net 30 days. Average monthly sales are about $60,000 ($540,000 divided by 9), so one-third of receivables are 30 days late, and one-third are 60 days late. These numbers should encourage you to ask the person responsible for collections to give you an "aging report," which states the dates all your receivables are due. (Aging reports should be done monthly, in any case.)

Pay close attention to the reaction to your request. Is the report slow in coming? Does that suggest that your collections person is too busy on other projects to pay enough attention to your re-

EXHIBIT Y: COMPANY SNAPSHOT

September 30, 1999

Current assets

	Cash . . . reg.	50,000
	Cash . . . MMA	79,000
	Receivables	180,000
	Other	
	TOTAL	$309,000

Inventory

Finished	91,000
Component	12,000
TOTAL	$103,000

Current liabilities

Payables	110,000
Misc.	22,000
Accrued commissions	15,000
Accrued royalties	21,000
TOTAL	$168,000

Fixed monthly expenses	14,000
Loans outstanding	$600,000
Monthly sales to date	51,000
Yearly sales to date	540,000
Future orders to ship	110,000
Open purchase orders	119,000

quest—and to receivables in general? When the report hits your desk, ask yourself if it's accurate and up-to-date. (If it's not, what does that say about your collections person?) In any case, a large percentage of overdue receivables probably requires action by both the sales force and someone in management, or the owner.

- Inventory (which includes open purchase orders) may also be too high. The combined figure is $210,000, not counting components ($91,000 + $119,000). If average monthly sales are $60,000 and your initial markup is 50%, then you have seven months' supply of inventory, with future orders of only two months. (Where did seven months come from? 210,000 × 2 = 420,000 ÷ $60,000 = 7.)

  This may be okay if you have a large order pending which doesn't yet have official confirmation. Or perhaps your $91,000 in finished inventory includes $50,000 of "dead" inventory; or perhaps the future orders are for shipment three months from now. It's perfectly okay for this line to depart from the norm, if you know why that's happening. If you don't know why it's happening, the bells will go off, and you can investigate and take corrective action as necessary.

- "Accrued commissions" looks out of line on this report. Is your bookkeeper late in paying commissions to the sales force? If so, this is a cardinal sin. (Yes, I'm a former salesman.) If sales are $60,000 a month and 80% are commissionable and your average commission is 10%, then your average monthly commissions total is $4,800, which means that your report shows more than three months' worth of commissions as being unpaid. This is a big red flag. Go ask some questions.

- I've put in a line, "Fixed monthly expenses," after current liabilities, so you'll always have a reminder of how big this number is—the number, in other words, for which you have to write checks every month. This figure should change only rarely, since it includes costs that you incur every month regardless of your sales volume: rent, wages, phone, withholding taxes, and lease payments (for photocopiers, computers, phone systems, etc.). You might find it helpful to compare things in terms of percentages, as well as actual numbers. For instance, inventory as a percentage of sales each week, expenses as a percentage of sales, a particular expense (such as travel) as a percentage of all expenses, etc. The idea is to be able to spot changes that may need your attention. Remember, though—*keep it simple.*

THE CASH FLOW STATEMENT

Projecting cash flow is one of the most important ways you can use numbers to manage and grow your business. The cash flow statement also can have important outside-world significance, since you'll probably have to submit a cash flow statement in almost all cases where you're looking for outside money.

Let me try to walk you through a typical cash flow exercise. I'll begin by summarizing the six steps you'll have to take before generating the cash flow statement. Than I'll go back and explain each of these six in depth:

1. List all the assumptions you will make in creating this statement.
2. Project monthly sales for the entire year.
3. Add up all cash revenues for the month.
4. Add up all cash expenditures for the month.
5. Subtract your expenditures (#4) from your revenues (#3) to determine your monthly balance, which can be a plus or a minus.
6. Do a monthly cumulative cash position (in other words, a summary of your #5's). This can be a positive or a negative number. This is the critical step in determining when in the year you will need more cash (the minuses), and when you will have the cash needed to pay back loans or pay bonuses (the pluses).

1. Assumptions

Before you start laying out your numbers, you should list the assumptions that you will use in determining some of those numbers. Here is a sample list of some general ones you'll need to make. Your specific type of business will probably require others:

- Determine your average receivables. (How many days will it take for you to receive your check after the invoice is made and the receivable is created?) You might also build in the number of days it takes for the bank to clear your deposited checks.
- What is your average rate of commission and what percentage of sales are commissionable? In this vein, when do you pay these commissions—e.g., 15 days after the close of the month for the previous month's shipments? Or—as at some companies—do you pay commissions when the bill is paid?

- What is your average cost of goods, which will determine your average gross margin? For instance: every $1,000 of sales will yield you $450 of profit. Therefore, your average cost of goods is 55% (550 divided by 1,000). You will need this percentage when determining your cash outlay for purchases, which will vary by your sales projections.
- How far in advance must you purchase products or components, before you ship goods and payment to the vendors of same? Must you pay vendors upon receipt, or—if not—how many days afterward? If your product is made overseas, do you pay before receipt, and if so, how much before?
- Do the different components of your cost-of-goods-sold have different cash requirements? This is usually true in a manufacturing business. Purchases, for example, may have a 30-day turnaround, whereas labor may need to be paid every week.
- If any of your products need to have royalties paid, when are these royalties due? Monthly? Quarterly? How soon after the close of the period?
- If you have a debt, how much interest is paid, and when is it paid? When is the principal due?
- When are taxes due, and when are they paid?
- When are insurance payments due?
- What new hires will you make, and when? What wage increases will be given (if any)?
- How much inventory will you need to maintain in anticipation of orders, and what rate of turn do you anticipate on it?
- If you give cash discounts, how many dollars of receivables will be affected by those discounts, and how much sooner will the receivable become cash?
- How many of your vendors offer cash discounts for early payment, and how many dollars of your payables will be affected, and for how much in terms of dollar savings?

2. Projecting monthly sales

To do this, you can look at last year's sales (assuming this is at least your second year in business) as a guide. As you record each month's sales, indicate any large orders you received, so that when you look at the figures next year, you can think about whether that large order is likely to be repeated. Be sure to recognize the seasonal nature of your business—if any—in your projections. Don't just do averages!

Remember that last year's numbers are history, and that projections are looking into the future. The more mature your business is, the more likely that the past has a correlation to the future. Newer companies or those with fad products should rely less on the past to project the future.

Your sales management and sales force should give key inputs into developing cash projections. The entrepreneur/manager needs to know the salespeople well, in order to figure out whether they are giving him or her inflated sales projections (to ensure adequate inventory to maximize sales and commissions). Large customers should also be consulted in this forecasting. The good ones should cooperate with you on this, as it is in their best interest to do so. They want you to have enough inventory to maximize their sales, as well. Again, someone in your company needs to know the buyer in question to determine his or her reliability in putting forth purchase expectations.

One thing is for sure: your accountant, bookkeeper, or chief financial officer should not be the only person involved in creating your sales projections. Triangulate—use one person's information to verify or contradict another's.

Another element of this monthly projection is a number for average returns, whether due to quality problems or plain old customer dissatisfaction. If this number historically runs at 5 percent, then this figure should be deducted from your projected sales figure. If you don't, your planned revenues are likely to experience a mysterious 5 percent shortfall.

3. Monthly cash revenues

These revenues will consist of the following components:

- payment of receivables
- cash sales (if any)
- royalty, commission, or fees income
- sale of assets
- miscellaneous income (such as rebates)
- loans or sale of stock

4. Monthly cash expenditures

I like to divide my cash costs into *fixed* and *variable*. The fixed costs are usually the same every month, regardless of volume; while the variable costs can change with volume (or cost in a certain percentage). Some fixed costs (e.g., rent) are paid every month, and others (e.g., insurance, taxes) fall only in certain months.

Examples of fixed costs:

- rent
- wages and payroll taxes
- telephone
- office supplies
- utilities
- postage
- travel and entertainment
- leases (computers, faxes, cars, etc.)
- accounting/legal
- insurance
- interest expense
- subscriptions

Examples of variable costs:

- commissions
- royalties (can sometimes be fixed, or a combination of fixed and variable)
- warehouse expenses
- advertising (can also be fixed)
- purchases (can also be fixed)

Some expenses can be a combination of fixed and variable, such as a warehouse expense that is based on a percentage of dollar shipments, but has a guaranteed monthly minimum. Insurance of goods shipped can be variable, while health insurance is fixed only if the number of employees remains constant. Liability insurance can be either fixed or variable.

There are also onetime expenses that draw on your cash, such as equipment purchases or project-based consulting fees.

Whatever cash payments are made during the year should be accounted for in this cash flow statement under "monthly cash expenditures." Some expenditures, like the phone bill, are fixed (in that they occur every month), but can vary. In these cases, take your best guess, which can be based on last year's bills, or on your estimate of increased or decreased activity in certain months. And don't forget to add a "miscellaneous" expense line, because you can be sure that there will be expenses you haven't thought of.

5. Determine the monthly balance

This is the bottom line for each month: whether you plan to take in more revenue than expenditures going out, or vice versa. It is a simple calculation: subtract the sum of all your monthly expenditures (#4) from the sum of all your revenues (#3).

6. Monthly cumulative cash position

This is simply a running total of all your pluses and minuses each month (#5), added to or subtracted from the cash on hand you started with each month.

For example: let's say you started January 1 with a cash balance of $135,000. For the month of January, you spend $60,000, and have revenues of $52,000. Therefore, you have a negative monthly balance of $8,000. This is subtracted from the opening cash balance of $135,000, leaving you with an end-of-month cash balance of $127,000. This $127,000 then becomes the opening cash balance for February.

These ending cumulative figures are critical in determining future cash needs, or when you can pay back existing loans. As soon as they become negative, then you know that in that month, you will need additional funds to cover that negative figure. You may conclude that you'll have negative cumulative figures in only three months a year. With that knowledge, you can go to your bank for a short-term loan, and show them your statement, which will indicate the month you will have enough of a surplus of cash to repay the loan.

Build in a mid-month cash cushion, or at least be very aware of the need for it. Your receipts may come in at the end of the month—and in the meantime, you may incur expenses (such as payroll or contract labor) that can't wait until the end of the month.

In another scenario, a monthly cumulative negative number may persuade you to go see some key suppliers to get an additional amount of time to pay your bills. An extension from 30 days to 60 days on your payable terms can have a big positive impact on your cash flow statement.

This cash flow statement is a document that needs to be revisited regularly. If you are flush with cash, you might only want to revise it quarterly. If you're in a tight cash position, however, you'll need to revisit it monthly (or even more often). A change in sales from your forecast can dramatically alter your needs. A sudden large increase in sales is not necessarily good news, as it will require more cash to support it than you have budgeted for that purpose. (Of course, I'd rather have that problem than a sales shortfall!)

The message is: *Pay extremely close attention to this statement, or you can find yourself in serious trouble!*

For more detail on cash flow statements, see Appendix 1, in which I provide examples with commentaries. Once again, I strongly recommend that you take the time to get comfortable with all this stuff. Why? Because cash is the lifeblood of your company. Businesses fail for lots of reasons, ranging from bad ideas to bad execution. But the immediate reason for most failures—the "proximate cause," as the lawyers put it—is running out of cash. Yes, many entrepreneurs run a good show without any formal cash flow statements. I've never met a good one yet, though, who didn't have all the critical information (cash positions, cash needs) in their heads. The ones who worried least about cash flow, at least temporarily, were those who were flush with cash.

Most of us aren't so lucky. The best way to inoculate yourself against running out of cash is to have solid knowledge in advance about your cash needs. Your accountant or financial adviser may have ideas about how to generate numbers that represent your particular business most effectively. (There are computer programs on the market that help you generate cash flow statements in a generic kind of way, but these may not give proper weight to the most important variables of your particular business.) However you generate your statement, it's absolutely imperative that you understand how this statement works, and what all of its component parts are. I can't state this too forcefully. You can't make the daily decisions you need to make to run your company if you aren't the master of your cash needs.

Your statement shows your peak cash needs and when they will occur. By understanding your impending cash peaks and valleys, you can start planning exactly how you're going to handle any cash crunches that hit the company. And *planning* is the key idea, here. It takes time to borrow or otherwise raise money. You will be able to make better deals if you're not under a cash-crunch gun. And as noted above, if you're jumping off the equity cliff—selling stock to raise money—your investment bankers and venture capitalists will need clear proof that you have a firm handle on your business.

I probably don't have to tell you that the only constant in business is *change*. Sales forecasts—a key component in building the cash flow statement—change constantly. Each of these changes means changes (big or little) in your cash flow. Changes in product costs, seasonal costs, advertising costs, capital needs, and market opportunities all necessitate changes in your cash flow statement. Computers are extremely helpful here, because you can change one or more assumptions and watch the impact of those changes flow through without having to do endless number-crunching. But once again: *You've got to be in charge of these exercises.* An assumption is only useful if you understand it, and why you're tinkering with it. When the assumptions start getting built into the program and you stop understanding them, you're probably heading for trouble.

THE PRODUCT COST ANALYSIS

Should understanding the cost of your product on an evolving basis be a big challenge? I don't think so. But I'm constantly surprised at how many people forget certain component costs when they do this kind of analysis. This leads to big problems: If your cost assumptions are wrong, then your profit margin projections have to be wrong as well, which will affect both your cash flow statement and your profit and loss statement. Without accurate product costs, your pricing will be wrong.

A cost sheet should be developed for every new product and reviewed by all the appropriate parties before the product is introduced. Any disagreements about the assumptions behind this analysis should be worked out ahead of time, or they may come back to haunt you later.

There are differences of opinion as to what should be included in the costing of a product. Many people don't include royalties or commissions in these costs (including them in overhead instead). I include these costs in my product cost accounting, mostly because they are (1) real, and (2) attributable to each product. It's fine to go either way, as long as you adjust your markup to cover all your costs.

Once you settle on the key building blocks in your product cost analysis, you have to be consistent in your costing—in other words, the same elements must be included each time, so that apples get compared to apples and oranges to oranges.

PROFITS

I'll present some ideas about profits, and their importance to sustaining your company, in Chapter 7. In this chapter, I'll simply suggest that you get your accountant to set up a communication system for you to monitor the profits of your company. If yours is a multi-product company, you should monitor and analyze the profitability of each product. This will help you allocate dollars as effectively as possible—for example, how many advertising or product-development dollars should be expended in each product category, or in each channel of distribution.

THE BREAK-EVEN ANALYSIS

This is a tool that is sometimes overlooked, even though it is easy to use and gives you valuable information in a number of different contexts. The breakeven tells you in dollars or units what amount of sales you need to achieve in order to recoup all your fixed costs or investment. I am always amazed, when I visit MBA classrooms, at how few students take the time to make these relatively simple calculations. Are you trying to decide whether to proceed with a new product introduction? Are you trying to understand exactly where costs stop and profits start for your company? Are you trying to decide whether to buy a company? In all of these cases, the break-even analysis should be your tool of choice.

To do a break-even calculation on a *product:*

1. Determine the cost of the product (let's say it's $9)
2. Determine the average selling cost ($20)
3. Subtract #1 from #2, which gives you your profit per unit ($11)
4. Determine the total investment required for that product ($80,000)
5. Divide #3 into #4. The result is the breakeven (in this case, 7,273 units)

Once you know the break-even figure for a given product, you can ask the critical questions. Is it reasonable to attain the break-even sales figure based on (1) the offering, and (2) our knowledge of the current market? In light of the resources that will be required to bring this product to market, how risky is this bet? (See Appendix 3—the Harvard Business School case on my *TV Guide*–based trivia game—for a step-by-step run-through of a product breakeven.)

OTHER KINDS OF ANALYSES

Are there really only four kinds of reports and analyses that are useful for low-risk, high-reward entrepreneurship? Of course not. Every company and every industry presents opportunities for specialized kinds of analysis, and you should figure out what's potentially useful to you. I suggest, though, that you first get a handle on the four analyses described above. Once you start "thinking in numbers," you'll be better equipped to pick and choose the kinds of reports and ratios that make sense for you.

Additional reports include, for example:

- *Sales reports.* These are used to record sales bookings and shipments for a given period, and to compare them against the same period for previous years. The periods can be weekly or monthly (or even daily, in high-volume periods). Bookings are an important indicator of potential problems or opportunities.
- *Sales by style number or by channel of distribution.* Again, these can be compared to previous years' totals. They can help you pick up important sales trends, and help Purchasing make the right choices in terms of style numbers.
- *Accounts receivable agings.* I'm sticking this in here again just to underscore an important point. Unfortunately, there are more and more companies out there that don't pay their bills unless you follow up on your first invoice(s) and demand a payment. You need an identified person who's responsible for collections, for whom this report will serve as the bible. As your company grows, keep an eye on this person and this function. Eventually, you'll have to make sure that other tasks aren't pulling this individual away from the all-important collections function.

- *Sales and bookings by salesperson compared to previous years.* This is an important tool for the sales manager to monitor individual salespeople's performance, and to act accordingly.
- *Profitability.* Aside from knowing your product profits and your over all profits as a company (monthly, quarterly, or yearly), you might want to track profitability by channel of distribution, sales territory, or some other measure that is meaningful to your business. These analyses can be useful tools in determining where resources should be applied, and where changes need to be made.

Ratios are another way to monitor the progress (or lack of progress) of the business. The ones that you personally find most useful can be incorporated into the company snapshot described earlier in this chapter. One way that you may find ratios useful is to help you compare your company's performance with that of your competitors and your industry averages (when these numbers are available).

Keep in mind that the outside world tends to have opinions about ratios, too. When you go out to borrow money, for example, your prospective lender is likely to ask you for some or all of these ratios. You can't afford to draw a blank at that moment. You need to be able to say, "No problem, I can get them for you by the end of the day." Or better: "No problem. Have them right here."

Here are some of the *common ratios,* and how they are obtained:

Current ratio: $\dfrac{\text{current assets}}{\text{current liabilities}}$

As you will recall from late grade school days, this format means that you divide your current assets (the nominator) by your current liabilities (the denominator) to get the current ratio. This number gives an indication of a company's relative liquidity. A low current ratio might indicate that a company may have trouble meeting its maturing obligations. Put another way, it's a measure of the company's working capital. (Is there enough?)

Incidentally: Inventories, which are part of current assets, should be valued at *your cost,* rather than your wholesale price. Your cost figure should include any freight cost incurred in bringing raw materials or finished product to your factory or distribution center, and any duties incurred if it's an imported item.

Quick ratio: $\dfrac{\text{cash} + \text{cash equivalents} + \text{accounts receivable}}{\text{current liabilities}}$

This ratio is the same as the current ratio, except that inventory and non-cash assets (such as prepaid expenses) are excluded from current assets. It's a better measure of your ability to meet your obligations (particularly your short-term obligations) than is the current ratio. This is true because your inventory—which may be substantial—may take a long time to sell off, or it may not be salable at the price at which you're carrying it.

Debt to equity ratio: $\dfrac{\text{total liabilities}}{\text{total shareholders' equity}}$

This ratio is used to measure the extent to which the company is *leveraged* (i.e., in debt). A certain level of debt is acceptable, but too much will inhibit your ability to obtain more money. This is one ratio that your bank is sure to look at carefully.

Receivables turnover: $\dfrac{\text{net sales}}{\text{receivables}}$

Here you are dividing yearly net sales by one month's worth of receivables. For instance: yearly sales of 3 million divided by receivables at end of year of 500,000 gives you a sales/receivables ratio of 6, which means that receivables turn over six times a year. In terms of days, divide 365 days by this 6, which tells you the average receivable is collected in 61 days.

This is an important figure for developing your cash flow statement. The weakness in this ratio, done this way, is that it doesn't reflect seasonality. You might want to average out your monthly receivables to minimize this problem. You may also have a few large accounts to whom you give special terms. If so, pull them out of this calculation and add them back with their own specific terms.

Inventory turnover: $\dfrac{\text{cost of goods sold}}{\text{inventory}}$

Here you're dividing yearly cost of goods sold by one day's inventory (again, inventory is at cost, rather than selling price). This ratio measures the number of times your inventory turns over (i.e., is gotten rid of and replaced) during the year. (As in receivables turnover, this ratio does not account for seasonality.) A high turnover can indicate good liquidity or excellent merchandising. It also means that the company is likely to require less cash.

A low inventory turnover ratio may mean too much stock, too many style numbers, obsolete inventory, or poor sales execution. A high number mostly means good things, but if it's *too* high, it may suggest that you're missing out on potential sales.

Payables turnover: $\dfrac{\text{cost of sales}}{\text{trade payables}}$

Here you are dividing yearly cost of sales by one day's "trade payables" (in other words, money you owe as a result of having made purchases). This, again, does not take seasonality into account. You can reduce this distortion by using an average trade payable taken for 12 months. A high turnover of payables indicates a shorter time between purchase and payment by the company for goods and services, which could indicate poor negotiation of buying terms, early payment to gain cash discounts, paying bills sooner than you need to, etc. A low turnover number can be an indicator of cash shortages, invoice disputes with suppliers, or good buying terms. Increasing this ratio will ease your cash needs. This payables turnover number should be compared to your buying terms.

Gross profit margin: $\dfrac{\text{gross profit}}{\text{sales}}$

Your gross margin is your excess of sales over the cost of sales. This gross margin percentage must be higher than your operating expenses (overhead) in order to yield a profit. This is a useful monthly measurement, as well as a good yearly benchmark. It will help you detect and track increases in costs, and figure out if you're selling too many of your products at sale prices. The latter could be necessitated by competitors, retailer pressure, or poor buying decisions.

Return on sales (or net profit ratio): $\dfrac{\text{net after-tax profit}}{\text{net sales}}$

This is the best general measure of the overall profitability of the company. Comparing this ratio year to year, and across your industry, gives you a solid measure of your progress.

Once again, there is an almost infinite variety of reports that can be generated, and ratios that can be tracked, especially as a business grows and gets more complicated. My advice is, *Don't scrimp on the analysis, but don't overdo the reporting.* Only generate reports that are read and used. (If they don't get read and used, they're literally useless.) Keep reports simple. Figure out exactly who needs to see which report, and don't send reports to people who can't use them.

After a certain amount of time has passed, start looking for what I call "vestigial reports." These are reports that somebody once wanted, but nobody can remember who or why. When you find a vestigial report, either change it to make it useful, or eliminate it.

I'll end this chapter where I began it: Numeracy is critical to the successful operation of your company. You (and other key people) must understand the numbers, if you're serious about your business.

———

In the next chapter, we'll look at some more specific ways of thinking about, and dealing with, risk. If you take the right ingredients out of these two chapters, and apply them to your idea—the subject of chapter 4—you'll be well on your way.

3

MANAGING RISK

"Risk" is a topic that I address throughout this book. Managing risk is an essential piece of the low-risk, high-reward approach to entrepreneurship that I'm advocating. Because risk rears its head at every stage of the entrepreneurial process, I'll be suggesting ways to deal with it chapter by chapter.

But I'd like to get the subject of risk on the table now in a general way. In this chapter, I'll try to give you some general perspectives on risk, and also some specific ideas for managing risks, particularly in the early days of your company's existence. These specific ideas—for example, the use of incubators—are included here as illustrations of useful ways to think about risk. In later chapters, I'll be more specific phase by phase.

Here, I'm talking about risks to the *business,* or to the money that sits behind the business. I'm not talking about the risk of rejection, for example—getting turned down for an order, a loan, a license, or whatever. These are risks that you'll have to take every day, and they are basically risks to your ego. If you keep your self-confidence well fed and your ego under control, you can stop thinking about rejection (and similar disappointments) as a "risk." They're learning experiences.

THINKING ABOUT RISK

Up to a point, risk—like beauty—is in the eye of the beholder.

What do I mean by that? I mean that if you, as an outsider, were to review almost any of my various business ventures in a cursory sort of way, you might say, "Boy, that Bob Reiss loves to get up on that high wire and hop around."

My response would be, "I've *never* knowingly gotten up on a high wire, and I don't intend to start now."

In a lot of cases, entrepreneurs like me forge ahead because they don't perceive risk. Looking at a good opportunity from the inside out, the entrepreneur sees mostly potential with some boundaries around it. The more work the entrepreneur puts into understanding a given situation, the less risky that situation is likely to appear. It's a little bit like throwing more wood on the campfire: more and more space around the periphery gets illuminated, and it's clear that—at least as far as you can see—there really aren't any wolves lurking out there.

That's not to say that there aren't any wolves *anywhere*. This is where the analogy to beauty begins to break down. Objectively, there *are risks* out there in the world. Stepping off the curb into fast-moving traffic is risky business. So you can find risk if you want it. But as I noted in the introduction, the good entrepreneur doesn't go out looking for risk. Instead, he or she seeks to identify and understand the risks inherent in a given situation. If the risks are too big and can't be managed, the good entrepreneur will most often walk away.

If the risks look manageable, the good entrepreneur plunges in. He or she tries to make as many of those risks as possible disappear. And risks that refuse to get "disappeared" get minimized, mitigated, circumscribed, shared, or phased in.

And when the good entrepreneur finds himself in the thick of it, wrestling with risks that turn out to be bigger than anticipated, he or she keeps trying to find new ways to manage them—and also keeps recalculating the odds. How can I make this work? Or how will I know when I can't make it work, and that it's time to bail out?

Sometimes the recalculations will give you a new perspective. Gourmet coffee marketer Dennis Boyer has this to say: "I think entrepreneurs have a talent for capitalizing on opportunities that have a lot of *perceived* risk, but because an entrepreneur's math is a little more insightful, those risks aren't quite the same as for those who see the situation from the outside."

Think of the best skier or gymnast you've ever watched in action. These are two sports that can't be undertaken without the assumption of some risks. But I'm at far greater risk on the top of a mountain than that skier you imagined, and I'd sure rather see a young Olympic gymnast on a balance beam than me. The difference, of course, is preparation and ability. *Risk is variable,* depending on who's taking it.

Consider two people trying to start a gift mail-order catalogue business from scratch. Would-Be Entrepreneur number one has worked for fifteen years for a mail-order catalogue and he has held a succession of jobs: picker, buyer, list manager, and vice president of operations. Would-Be Entrepreneur number two has just graduated from a prestigious business school. His prior work experience consisted of three years as an analyst at a Wall Street investment banking firm.

Who's your money on? Mine's on number one, even though I'm a firm believer in the value of an MBA. So *experience* (sometimes including education, but sometimes not) can be critical.

So can *confidence,* which in many cases is intimately bound up in background. Unlike me, skier Picabou Street doesn't stand on the top of that mountain thinking about the likelihood of failure. She knows the risks she faces, and—on her way down the slope—she is able to make the necessary decisions on a timely basis. She can act, with skill and wisdom.

Knowledge, experience, confidence: what other factors can help you mitigate risk in the business setting? Among other things, I'd list:

- **Relationships.** Who do you know who can help you succeed? What exactly will those relationships mean to you? "I prefer to share risk or lay it off," says Raymond Lo. "In Chinese, we have an expression about risk, that it is a big piece of meat and we can't eat it all on our own. If we did, we'd have a stomachache. Also, that is not the kind of working environment that exists in Hong Kong. It is nearly impossible to work entirely on your own, to start from scratch and produce an end product, without relying on others."
- **Planning.** This is a theme that runs throughout this book: good planning lowers your risks and greatly increases your chances of success. You have to learn absolutely everything you can about your product, your industry, your competition, your niche, your

goals, and so on, and you have to bring all this information to-gether in a coherent plan. The goal here is not necessarily a written document—although you'll definitely need one of these if you're raising money from a bank, a venture capitalist, or the public—but rather, clear thinking aimed at a goal.

- **Creativity.** We've talked about this one in the first chapter, but it's worth bringing up again here. It's not just the power of a great idea; it's also the power of an organization that brings out the best in its people. Are people less creative when they walk in your door or more creative?

- **Effective partnering.** Look for key customers to whom you can give special incentives, in return for something you need (large orders, early orders, quick payment, etc.). Can you give someone an exclusive on manufacturing your product? Are there opportunities for special pricing, private labels, in-store demonstrations, special servicing, or the right to "break" first with your product in a given city? If so, what do you need in return? Can you pay a key supplier more money in return for advantageous payment terms?

- **Licensing.** Licensing (which we'll talk about further in chapter 6) is an effective way to buy into someone else's proven formula. There are lots of ways to take the risks out of licensing: for example, paying a higher percentage royalty in return for a lower guarantee.

- **Leadership.** Goes without saying, right? A great leader is one who (among other things) manages down the risks. How many such leaders are there in your organization?

- **Adequate cash.** If you're not a billionaire yourself, take on partners with deep pockets. (This will help you avoid the sometimes deadly personal guarantee.) Yes, in return you'll have to give up some stock, which presents its own risks. But if you pick your partners well and if you don't lose control of the company, these risks should be manageable.

Note that I'm not suggesting that you must take on partners to solve your cash problem. Most new businesses "bootstrap," using savings and borrowings from family and friends. But most business failures stem from a lack of cash. Find a way to stay ahead of the cash curve, and your chances of survival will be greatly enhanced.

Business entrepreneur Len Levey can back me up on this. "Most of the time," he told me, "you underestimate the capital needs—

which means you're underestimating the risk. As the capital needs increase, so does the risk. The water is rising, you're in up to your shoulders, but you always think you have a way of swimming to safety. Then before you know it, the risk has become much larger and deeper than you'd anticipated it would be."

- **Sales power.** What did I say in the last chapter? Booming sales can cover up a multitude of organizational sins (unless one of those sins is bad pricing!). Make your product better. Treat your sales force like eagles. Assume that *everybody* in the organization can contribute, directly or indirectly, to the all-important sales activity.

Having said that, I should also emphasize that there's a flip side to this sales coin. As important as sales are to the continued health of your company, there may be occasions when too many sales, too fast, can put you at risk. You need to be prepared to grow. Rapid growth that causes you to ship sloppily, or too slowly, can jeopardize the good name you've worked so hard to build.

- **The caliber of your employees.** This is another no-brainer, but it probably deserves to be called out. Hiring people is a little bit like buying your first home: Set an absolute ceiling, and then go right through it when the right person shows up. Hire the best. Then invest in *training* and *retaining* them.

Try to understand who and what will serve your interests best. For some, like catalogue expert Barb Todd, this doesn't necessarily mean finding people who will always agree with you. "We're really focused on finding people who can communicate well, say what their ideas are. We look for *lively* people. Which makes for lively meetings, sometimes. Contrarians, too; contrarians are good to have around."

And remember to keep an eye on the people you've hired, even when the hiring process is behind you. You will learn whether they can cut the mustard by watching them in action. And don't assume that calm means competent. As John Korff explains, "The key is, how far in advance do they wake up crying in the middle of the night? The further out they wake up crying, the better organized they are. The person who walks in ten days ahead of time and says, 'No problem!'—that's who scares me to death! The girl who's crying five months in advance will have her act together."

- **The motivation level of your employees.** This is in part driven by compensation (of all kinds), but it's also driven by whether your workplace is stimulating, rewarding in non-monetary senses, and fun. People who are having fun will kill themselves for you.

I had an interesting conversation with Jim McCann, the very flexible and energetic head of 1-800-FLOWERS.COM. He told me about his "new employer/employee covenant for the next century." As he sees it, the day of the thirty-five-year employee is over, for better or worse. There will be fewer and fewer gold-watch-into-retirement ceremonies. The result, says McCann, is a need for a new and explicitly defined relationship between employer and employee. Here's how he summarizes that "covenant":

> First, I'll do my best to keep our brand very high in the sky, so you're proud to put us on your resume, and you're proud to tell your friends at the high school reunion that you work at 1-800-FLOWERS.COM.
> Second, I'll try to keep your job interesting and engaging. I'll challenge you all the time.
> Third, I'll try to make sure we're well run, so we don't go out of business just because we've done something really stupid.
> Fourth, I'll invest in you—and not by putting together the greatest pension plan, because most of you are not going to be here to benefit from it. So I'll do things for you that are portable. I'll invest in a 401k that you can take with you. I'll also make every day that you're here a learning experience for you. I'll formalize it, and call it "Floraversity," and you can go to a future employer and say, "Here's my resume, including my transcript from Floraversity, including the courses I took internally and externally."
> And finally, I'll try and do all this in a fun environment, in a context that's a pleasant place to work, where you're often caught off-guard in a positive way. I'll make it so that the people at your backyard barbecue will say, "That must be a great place to work!"

I invite you to run down that list and think about it from a motivational point of view. Isn't everything McCann's proposing to do for his employees at least partially about motivation? For example: why is 1-800-FLOWERS.COM investing substantial sums every year in Floraversity—a "virtual" university? In part because it will help McCann and his colleagues recruit better people, and motivate them more fully. He's betting that people will work smarter (and happier), and stay with the company longer. These seem like good bets to me.

- **Flexibility (yours and the company's).** I'm ending this list with two more criteria we encountered in the last chapter—but this time, from the standpoint of risk management. Big companies are more at risk from change than small companies, because big companies (by and large) are rigid. Make sure your company can step sideways, as necessary. Think of that business plan as the crudest sketch of where you're going—and rewrite it as often as necessary. As for yourself, keep an eye on your spine. Why is it stiffening, at this particular moment? Are you digging in your heels to protect a vital interest of the company (good), or are you protecting your own ego (bad!)?
- **Energy.** Get there first. Do it harder and better and more often. Impress the *hell* out of the people you deal with. Overwhelm the opposition (wherever it is).

STAGING RISK

Here's another way to manage risk: *stage it.*

Even if you're committed to a product or an enterprise, you don't have to incur all your costs at once. For example, the direct response industry (those people that advertise kitchen gadgets on late-night TV and collectible plates in *Parade* magazine) uses extensive testing to figure out how to stage risk. I think other businesses should learn from them.

It's not unusual for a direct response company to have a mailing list of 5 million names. I've never heard of such a company offering a new product to 5 million people. Instead, they offer to 50,000 or 100,000 names first—holding off the production run until they have an initial reading on the response. Even if the response is overwhelmingly positive, a good direct response company will still take those 5 million names in bites.

Do you have to go national with your new product right away? Can't you take it into a small city first? (Even the big guys do this.)

Can you make a prototype of your product—maybe with some extra care on the packaging—and show it to prospective major buyers? Maybe they'll tell you they won't take this thing under *any* circumstances. Or maybe they'll suggest some changes that you can incorporate before the next stage of investment.

CONVERTING FIXED COSTS
TO VARIABLE COSTS

This strategy will come as no surprise to anyone who's had responsibility for starting and running a small business, but it's worth stating clearly in the context of risk management.

First, definitions: a *fixed cost* is one that your business incurs whether or not it makes any sales. An example is rent: it has to be paid every month whether or not you're generating any income, and, it's the same every month.

A *variable cost,* by contrast, is incurred only when you make that sale. A variable cost usually varies directly with the amount of the sale. A commissioned salesperson, for example, is a variable cost. If the person is getting paid 10 percent of sales and the sales for a given month are $25,000, then that person gets $2,500 in commissions. If sales drop to $1,000, then the commission drops to $100.

A variable cost can also turn up on the purchasing side, especially where your cost changes with the size of your order, or you can earn rebates based on certain purchase volumes or combinations of purchases over specified time periods.

Key lesson for new and small businesses: variable expenses are highly, highly desirable. Maximizing variable expenses reduces the amount of capital you'll need to handle overheads and operating expenses in slow selling periods. A low monthly "nut" ensures that you'll get to breakeven (and even profits) faster. As a general rule, investments in overhead should be made only when you have a degree of certainty about the product, and when customer demand is (1) strong, and (2) well understood.

There are downsides to this strategy, of course. When sales are booming, your variable costs will be high. In some cases, too, you have less control than you would if you were dealing with a fixed expense. For example: Your sales rep working on commission is an independent contractor, who doesn't take orders very well from people in the company. Persuasion and incentives tend to work; command-and-control doesn't work.

Here are some examples of fixed costs that can be converted to variable:

• **Sales.** This is implied above. Instead of hiring full-time salespeople and getting burdened with their weekly or monthly wages, go with reps who will work on a percentage basis. Ineffective reps are easier and less costly to replace than full-time salespeople, and they don't present the burden of benefits, which can run as high as 30 percent of the salary of a full-time employee. In many cases, reps have strong relationships with customers in their territory, which can translate into quick access and orders.

- **The factory.** I wanted to get this in relatively near the front of the book: You don't have to own a factory just because you want to make, assemble, store, and ship your product. Contract manufacturers are happy to do all this for you. (They're listed in the Yellow Pages under "Public Warehousing.") They charge either for the space you take up and the functions you call upon, or a flat percentage of your billing. Either way, this represents a huge saving in fixed and operating costs. Contract manufacturers also maintain insurance on your goods in their possession. They cover the cost of their employees' benefits. Yes, there are some downsides—including the fact that you may have to vie with their other customers for priority. Here again, persuasion and salesmanship are your best weapons. As soon as your volume warrants it, allocate a full-time person to cultivate the relationship with your "extended factory." At some point, you may even want to platoon your employee on their premises for more control (and reduced risk).

  You may have the type of product that would permit you to pay another manufacturer to make it for you under your brand. (This would be their "private label.") Products like beer, liquor, drugs, and computers are often made under this kind of arrangement.

- **Administration.** Guess what? Your billing, sales reports, commission statements, royalty statements, inventory reports, and aging reports can also be done on a percentage basis by your contract manufacturer. Of course, the more functions you outsource, the higher your percentage payment will be. But remember: everything that you're outsourcing is a function that you're not hiring a salaried body to perform. And it's not just bodies, either. Why should *you* pay for the latest computers and software to run them—especially if they'll only be used for a small fraction of the working day? Pay someone else to worry about that. Your customers will have absolutely no idea that these functions are being outsourced. (They probably wouldn't care if they did know.) And your company takes on the aura of a well-established business from the outset.

- **Creative.** I have great respect for creative talent. At the same time, there is an abundance of talented artists out there who are capable of creating any type of artwork you might need for your products or promotional materials. They can usually be compensated with a onetime fee, without residuals (unless they're already famous, of course). And by using a variety of freelancers instead of salaried creators, you can keep your products and other materials fresh and interesting. And guess what? Most of the really good people would rather work for you on this basis, anyway. Especially at the beginning, you won't have enough interesting challenges to keep a talented artist busy.
- **Personnel.** Once again: full-time employees get paid a fixed salary. But there's no reason why a portion of this salary can't be variable. Find a way to pay lower base salaries with the potential for large bonuses, or stock options. You'll have to spell out clearly the criteria whereby bonuses will be awarded, but this is almost always a good investment of time anyway. Make things *clearer;* people almost always work harder and are happier as a result.

You can also outsource certain job functions. For example, most small companies of between $2 million and $5 million in sales could use a chief financial officer, but feel they can't afford one. Such companies should consider hiring a CFO part time, perhaps beginning on a day-a-month basis. As the company grows and learns more clearly what it needs and wants from a CFO, it can begin the transition to making this a full-time position.

GETTING OUTSIDE ADVICE

One of the best ways to minimize and mitigate risks is to get expert advice. I'm not referring here to paid consultants, a luxury that most early stage and small companies can't afford. (When you can afford the right ones, by the way, they can be an excellent investment.) Instead, I'm referring here to getting a *mentor* of one kind or another.

In the majority of my interviews with successful entrepreneurs, my interview subjects attributed their success in part to the existence of a mentor. Bud Pironti of NSI, a direct response company, was particularly passionate on this subject, and he credits a great deal of his early and continued success to the mentors he's cultivated over the years. (His wife accuses him, jokingly, of "collecting antique men.") Bud stresses that you have to *work* at these relationships. If you're sincerely humble and solicitous, he says, you'll get back your investment five times over.

What does this mean? It means simple things like saying thank you to your mentor, and following up to let that person know what happened when you followed up that lead he gave you, or when you tried out that idea she suggested a few weeks back.

Where do you find mentors? The answer is, "Lots of places, including unexpected ones." They come in all flavors. The senior managers of your suppliers may be fertile ground, or maybe people you've worked with in the past, or college professors, or publishers of industry magazines. Entrepreneurs who own their own businesses are ideal mentors. They're easier to approach than many corporate managers, and they've already been through much of what lies in store for you.

"Surround yourself with people," entrepreneur Earl Peek of Intellectual Technologies, Inc., advises, "people who you can call upon for different things. Get someone you can bounce things off of—someone you trust. Get someone with scrapes on his knees, someone who's lost something. The best advice you can get is from someone who's been through something bad."

Again, mentors are everywhere. Think about the people you look up to. Can you call upon one of them for advice? Could you build on that relationship over time?

When I talk to young people at business schools who want to start their own companies, I often feel their intense frustration at not having experience and having no way to *get* the experience they need. (You have to have a job to get a job, as the old Catch-22 goes.) But I tell them that youth and inexperience are actually great cards for them to play. There are *lots* of experienced, successful business people who are more than willing to help young entrepreneurs if they are approached respectfully. They want to help, and they know that in many cases, teachers learn as much as students.

Another mentoring possibility is SCORE: the Service Corps of Retired Executives. SCORE is a non-profit, founded in 1964 and funded in large part by the Small Business Administration. Today it's a substantial operation, with almost 400 chapters in communities across the country, and more than 12,000 business counselors volunteering their time to small businesses. Their services are entirely donated (no fee to you). To find the SCORE chapter nearest you, call 1-800-634-0245.

SCORE's Web site (www.score.org) has many pages of useful content. One of its most popular features is "Get e-mail counseling." An entrepreneur in need of help can search on a key word to find an e-mail counselor with industry-specific knowledge. This service is available seven days a week.

Another source of free advice is a board of directors—or the equivalent. I use that qualifier because if you're a small business, you probably don't want to incur the cost of directors' insurance. (This is a must if there are other stockholders involved.) To get around this, call it a "board of advisers." But this name change doesn't mean you should take the creation of such a board lightly. No, this board doesn't have the right to get rid of you and hire your successor—as does a formal board of directors—but you should consider it a serious obligation, nevertheless. Run it in a formal way, and make sure it deals with matters that a traditional board of directors would deal with. (In most cases, this means policy-level questions rather than operational issues.) Share the numbers. Put together a binder of relevant materials, perhaps including both historical information and forward-looking material, and prepare an agenda; then mail it well in advance of the meeting.

As board members, you can solicit retired executives or entrepreneurs, suppliers, or anyone else whom you respect and who might have skills or knowledge that would complement your own. Offer to pay their expenses and—when you can afford it—a nominal fee. (If you make products, think free samples!) But do everything that you have to do, personally, to make this work for you. It's a great discipline, and it can help keep you focused on tomorrow's problems. Be prepared to take criticism. Remember: that's why you invited them.

TALKING WITH OTHER ENTREPRENEURS

This is an extension of the mentoring approach, but more on a peer-to-peer basis. One of the biggest problems in the small company setting is that the CEO/entrepreneur has no one to talk with about troubling issues. Many entrepreneurs aren't comfortable talking about certain issues with employees, and some subjects aren't appropriate for this audience.

I've found talking with other entrepreneurs about my problems to be extremely helpful. It didn't matter if they were in other businesses (which they almost always were). Many issues are common to all small companies. I regularly had lunches or dinners with my entrepreneurial friends, and those relaxed, informal discussions meant a great deal to me. As a result, I always tried to build and maintain these kinds of friendships, with people in and outside of my specific industry.

I also found it helpful to join Joe Mancuso's Chief Executives Club, a non-profit organization of small company CEOs dedicated to improving the quality and profitability of their enterprises, through personal growth and the sharing of experiences. The organization has chapters in twelve cities, which run meetings, seminars, and lunches, sometimes featuring high-quality guest speakers. Again, I found these interactions with other entrepreneurs to be helpful and stimulating. You can contact Joe for details at CEO Club, Inc., 180 Varick Place, New York, NY 10014 (phone: 212-633-0060; fax: 212-633-0063; e-mail: ceoclubs@bway.net). I also recommend Joe's *Small Business Resource Guide,* which contains the name, address, and phone number of almost every conceivable niche business association, as well as government bodies that are supposed to help small businesses.

Depending on where you're located, there may be other similar resources available to you. If there aren't, try thinking a little "sideways." Is there an inventors' club in your city? Maybe you'll find some kindred spirits there—or at least, some original thinking. Find people to talk to!

GETTING "INCUBATED"

Reducing risks often means lowering your costs and getting good guidance. A very useful resource to help achieve both of these goals at once is an innovation called an *incubator.*

The National Business Incubation Association (NBIA) offers the following definition of the "incubation" process:

Business incubation is a dynamic process of business enterprise development. Incubators nurture young firms, helping them to survive and grow during the start-up period when they are most vulnerable. Incubators provide hands-on management assistance, access to financing, and orchestrated exposure to critical businesses or technical support services. They also offer entrepreneurial firms shared office services, access to equipment, flexible leases, and expandable space—all under one roof.

NBIA's explanation needs a little elaboration. Most incubators are run on a non-profit basis, often by state or local governments. Their primary mission is to foster economic development, which translates into more local jobs and tax revenues. Many are affiliated with universities or colleges. For the beginning entrepreneur, the incubator can provide resources as lofty as expert advice (e.g., accounting, legal, marketing, and finance) and as mundane as fax machines, conference rooms, telephone systems, and so on. By and large, an incubator's client pays only for services that it uses—and often pays at less than the going rate.

According to NBIA, an incubator's goal is to "graduate" businesses as soon as they are able to stand on their own two feet—commonly within two or three years. Some incubators impose selection criteria on their prospective clients, in the same way that venture capitalists pick and choose among their portfolio companies. Some incubators focus on a particular industry niche, while others are more broadly based. Some take on existing small businesses, in addition to start-ups.

NBIA statistics show that there were 587 formal business incubator programs nationwide in the spring of 1998. Each of these programs housed and provided guidance to an average of twenty entrepreneurial firms. Some 30 percent of the clients of a given incubator "graduate" each year. According to NBIA (Web site: www.nbia.org), North American incubators have nurtured nearly 19,000 companies that are still in business (as of this writing), and that have created more than 245,000 jobs.

An example of this resource in action is the Ohio-based Edison Incubators program, created and funded by the Ohio Department of Development. The Edison Incubators are a network of ten facilities across the state. The Youngstown Edison Incubator Corporation, for example, works in collaboration with the faculty at the Cushwa Center for Entrepreneurship at Youngstown State University. The Youngstown incubator's Web site stresses that for "true start-up companies," everything is negotiable. (Companies that are still in the R&D stage may be given space rent-free for short periods of time.) In Akron, the Akron Industrial Incubator serves as the temporary world headquarters for twenty-four young companies, ranging from a market research firm to a distributor of landscape lighting products.

I never used an incubator, mainly because (to my knowledge) they weren't around when I was launching my various enterprises. It may be that given the nature of your particular business, an incubator wouldn't serve your purposes. But I include this brief discussion of incubators to make a broader point: If someone out there wants to give you free and expert advice, and wants to offer you flexible space at below-market rents and access to a host of subsidized goods and services—well, that's worth looking into. If Ohio is where you want to be, and if the state of Ohio is offering to assume some of your risks in the earliest stages of your venture, it may be a good deal for you.

The Ohio network claims that "95 percent of Incubator tenants have graduated and become viable businesses in their communities." I'm sure the jury is still out on some of those businesses, but if using an incubator reduces your risks and shifts the odds in your favor, I'm all for it.

———

The not-too-subtle point of this chapter has been to rub your nose in the subject of risk. Think of it this way: Why wouldn't you be as creative about risk management as you are about developing and marketing your products? Why wouldn't you be *more* creative about risk management, in fact?

As you ask yourself these questions, also ask yourself: How much risk can I tolerate? This varies from person to person. Know your own comfort level, and rather than fight to change it, try to work with it. To some extent, it's a built-in part of your personality. Don Bakehorn admits, "I'm a pretty conservative guy. I'm not a high risk taker. I invest my earnings in direct-mail companies and in businesses that either I can manage or I can get other people to manage for me. I like things that are concrete, that I can see, that I can look at and see what's going on."

So you can be an entrepreneur without always being on the edge. And keep in mind that this comfort level may vary as your life circumstances change. "I think risk is different as soon as you have young kids," television producer Jonathan Axelrod told me. "You look at what colleges are going to cost, and you look at their future.

"Mostly for that reason, my wife and I are never going to take a risk with the fundamentals. And we sleep better at night. I drive my accountant nuts because I won't take out a mortgage on my house. He says, 'You're crazy—that's the only thing left you can deduct!' In a sense, he's right, in terms of the government getting more money. But for me, *I'm* right, because I want to own my own home. You do what's comfortable."

There's no such thing as a "risk-free" business, just as there's no such thing as risk-free skiing. But there *is* risk minimization, risk sharing, and other very helpful approaches to risk management.

Don't let the process of risk assessment itself become a risk. In most business settings, you're going to have to *act,* and usually in a hurry. Yes, do your homework; then *jump.* You can keep your eye out for new risks, and resurgent risks, at every stage of the life of your business.

Now that I've got you focused on risk, I'm going to ask you to put your best idea on the table.

4

THE IDEA

The starting point for any new venture is *the idea*. What product or service will our business offer?

A great many people can't get past this first requirement. It seems to me that many of them stall out because they are waiting to hit upon some kind of revolutionary new idea—a concept of such power that it will appeal to everyone. They want bells to go off in their heads. They want *brilliance*.

Most of the time, though, most of us aren't brilliant. There's a great story about how Mark Twain was accused of plagiarizing a passage from Oliver Wendell Holmes. Twain was incensed at this accusation—until he checked it out, and discovered that he had indeed written something that was almost identical, word for word, to something Holmes had published years earlier. Twain immediately wrote an embarrassed letter to Holmes. He explained that he must have been so impressed by Holmes's writing that he had committed it to memory—and then unwittingly plagiarized it.

Holmes wrote a very gracious note back. "Don't worry about it," he said, in effect. "I've always thought creativity was a measure of the obscurity of one's sources."

The fact is, there's not a lot that's new under the sun. Most businesses, even highly successful businesses, are founded on a very ordinary, very mundane idea, pretty far removed from brilliance. It's luck, timing, and execution that transforms a ho-hum idea into a good business. (And by the way, it's also luck, timing, and execution that transforms that rare blockbuster of an idea into a good business.)

Take Chuck Burkett, CEO of Monogram Industries. In 1971, at the not-so-tender age of forty-two, Burkett invested his entire life savings in an idea he had for a new company. He and his wife sold their California house, packed all their worldly possessions and their two children into the family car, and moved to Florida.

What was this idea that the Burketts were willing to stake everything on? Get ready: *novelty key chains.* Monogram had landed a contract to make key chains for a new enterprise then starting up in Orlando—an East Coast version of a West Coast institution that was to be called "Disney World."

Yes, as it turned out, Burkett had started with a good account, and he had thoroughly researched the economics of key chains well before he decided to take the plunge. And yes, he deserves a lot of credit for growing a great company. He built a sophisticated infrastructure and assembled a loyal, highly motivated workforce. He executed brilliantly—so well, in fact, that when Disney went looking for a licensor to produce other Disney goods, they went to Burkett first. Today, Monogram—which has recently been sold—employs more than 130 people, is a dominant supplier of licensed key chains, and (according to Burkett) is a great place to work.

But can you imagine a more ordinary product?

All of us would like to come up with a show-stopper of an idea, especially if we're going to bet the farm on that idea. The bad news is that show-stoppers are a rare commodity. The good news is that—as Chuck Burkett and countless other entrepreneurs have demonstrated—you don't necessarily *need* a show-stopper.

THREE KINDS OF IDEAS

Let's divide the Universe of Business Ideas into three galaxies. They are:

- tinkering at the margins
- old ideas into new markets
- new ideas into old markets

"Tinkering at the margins" is what most businesses—including entrepreneurial businesses—are really all about. It involves taking someone else's idea, working it a bit, and making it just a little bit better. (And, as Oliver Wendell Holmes might have put it, making the sources of your creativity that much more obscure.)

I like to point to the example of the Japanese electronics companies, which have more or less conquered the world of consumer electronics. Once in a blue moon, one of those companies comes out with a dramatic new technology that changes everything. But 99 percent of the time, companies like Sony, Mitsubishi, Panasonic, and Hitachi make only tiny, incremental improvements on someone else's proven winner of an idea. This is something like adding a few letters to the beginning or end of an existing word on a Scrabble board and getting credit for all the letters.

I'm not saying that this is the only, or best, way to win at Scrabble. I'm just saying that there's no shame in piggybacking on someone else's formula for success. Look for existing products or services that you can do better than they're currently being done. Tinker at the margins.

John Korff, the events entrepreneur, is a whiz at tinkering. He knows how to improve on something. When a young friend with a degree in "ornamental horticulturalism" complained to him about the lack of a flower show in New York City (all the while confessing she had no idea how to get one started), he replied, "Let's do it together." Korff admits, "I don't know beans about flowers. They're pretty and I'm allergic to them. But I know who might go to this kind of thing, and what kind of company that profile might appeal to. And I understand that there's no Jimmy Connors flower; there's just a lot of flowers. So you don't have to worry about disappointing people on Sunday who came to see Jimmy. And you don't have to pay the flowers to show up—the flowers pay you." It's not like New York had never tried a flower show before. "The New York Horticultural Society used to run one, and messed it up. They didn't understand that it was more than a love of flowers; it was a *business.*"

Of course, when you tinker with someone else's idea, be prepared to handle some hostility. Korff is trying to get the NYHS to sanction *his* flower show, but if they don't, that won't stop him. "We'll do it anyway," he says, "under the sanction of the American Horticultural Society, or we'll just start our own society"—which is an option he has exercised in the past. When the International Chili Society tried to restrict Korff's chili cook-off event, he told the ICS rep that his event was sanctioned by the World Chili Federation. "'Who are they?' the guy asked. I said, 'It's me, and I just started it.' And we did it. We called ourselves the North American Tour Championships of the World Chili Federation, and all these companies were saying, 'Whoa—this is a big deal!'"

The second category—"old ideas into new markets"—is what Chuck Burkett did for Disney World. Key chains weren't new; but selling Mickey Mouse key chains to Mickey Mouse fanatics at Mickey Mouse's place of business *was* new, and smart.

The third category is putting "new ideas into old markets." Say there's an established market and distribution channel for widgets. You study how widgets work, and why people want to (or have to) use them. You think about this phenomenon for a while. And one day, maybe in the shower, you realize that if you could come up with a widget holder, you could piggyback on the existing market and channels.

Dan Blau, while working with a publisher who was focused on the general market, saw some opportunities in a specialized segment of that market: children's books. "I brought the opportunities to the publisher," he told me, "but I felt like we were two ships passing in the night. We weren't communicating. The new ideas I brought to him fell on deaf ears." It's no surprise that Blau decided to start a business of his own that would build on the opportunities he had discovered.

Again: You don't have to be Einstein to dream up children's books or widget holders. Good ideas can come from anywhere. The curious mind spots problems that need solutions (widget holders). Most important, I think, is to get into the mind-set in which you *want* to find an idea. If you get into that mind-set, you've already got a leg up on those around you who are not so mentally attuned.

Kettle Cuisine's founder, Jerry Shafir, likes to use the Snapple/Nantucket Nectars story as an example of being *tuned in* to the right time for a product. When Quaker Oats bought Snapple, they pulled the rug out from under the Snapple distributors by deciding to distribute the juices through their Gatorade distribution network. "Along comes Nantucket Nectars," Shafir says, "and all of the distributors *jump* on this product. It had come out locally and had done pretty well in Massachusetts. But now the Nectars guys couldn't even *make* the stuff fast enough. The blockbuster idea was the detection of the market opportunity, and not necessarily the development of the product. They'd tapped into hundreds of distributors who had just lost tons of revenues *and* were dying to get back at Quaker."

Notice that there's a fourth category missing from my list: "new ideas into new channels." Myra Hart (now on the Harvard Business School faculty, and formerly one of the key figures in creating the Staples empire) points out that it's unusual for entrepreneurs to jump into a *new* stream with a *new* product. That situation creates much higher risk, which would have to be justified by (1) good research, and (2) higher potential rewards.

TESTING THAT IDEA

Once you get an idea that you think you can embrace, it is essential that you do some homework. (You've probably already done some; now you'll have to do some more.) You need to assess the feasibility of the idea, and understand the risks you'll have to manage—and the resources that you'll have to commit—in order to turn the idea into a reality.

Each idea generates its own list of questions, but here are some generic questions you ought to be able to answer:

- What is unique about my product, approach to market, strategic alliances, packaging, customers, etc., that will differentiate me from my competitors, and increase my chances of success?
- Who will buy this product? (And how big is that market?)
- How will I reach the buyer? (What are the potential channels of distribution?)
- What competition am I likely to encounter?
- Why should someone buy my product rather than some competing product?
- How will I make this product? (Can I sell it profitably?)
- Is timing of entry critical to my success?
- What other factors may be required for success?
- How will I sell this product?
- How sustainable is this idea? (How easy is it to copy?)
- Are there any barriers I can erect to prevent imitation?
- What risks can I mitigate?
- Who are the key people, inside and outside my company, who can make key contributions to the successful execution of my idea, and how can I get them to participate?

Ask, analyze, study, enquire. Poke and probe. Learn as much as possible about what you're getting into. Don't let your love of the idea blind you to its realities. Test out your ideas on a trusted friend or mentor, and ask them to play devil's advocate. Think about the front end of low risk, high reward. Your job at this stage of the game is to get out of the starting gate on a horse that's good enough to carry you; don't focus too much on whether you're headed for win, place, or show. Limit your risks, mainly by understanding them. Just like a marriage, you'll never know everything in advance; but the time you spend checking out an idea on the front end is time well spent.

At the same time, *believe in yourself.* This is something that the heads of very successful companies tell me all the time: Trust your gut. Do your homework first; test it against your gut; and then trust your gut. If at this point you still have a passion to forge ahead, then forge ahead. Don't let naysayers discourage you.

Also: Don't give up on your idea just because you don't have the money you need. Almost nobody starts out with all the money they need at their fingertips. As we'll see in the next chapter, one way or another, persistence, smarts, and good planning eventually will get you your seed capital; or you'll find a way to get started without it.

STILL NO IDEA?

Look: Assuming you've got access to enough capital, there's absolutely nothing wrong with buying *someone else's* idea. You may be the kind of entrepreneur who accomplishes great things by making sense out of somebody else's vision. The kinds of brilliant people who come up with esoteric technologies often need help from someone who is savvy about marketing, level-headed, and can talk "investment bankerese." Maybe someone like *you,* for example.

This is a short chapter for such an important topic. If I haven't given you enough guidance, I'd recommend that you look back to the remarks on creativity in chapter 1. I'd also suggest that you keep reading. I'll be introducing many more entrepreneurs in subsequent chapters, and many of them have ideas to share about creativity and innovation.

Meanwhile, keep your eyes open!

5

GETTING STARTED

Getting off the ground: This is where the challenges of entrepreneurship separate the men from the boys, the women from the girls, and those who "walk the talk" from the posers. Pulling the trigger—actually doing it; starting your own business—turns out to be very difficult for many people, and particularly the first time out of the box.

Most people hesitate for good reasons. They don't want to fail, especially if the stakes are high. Can they live without that regular paycheck? Can they cut back dramatically on their standard of living? If they do, will they damage their family relationships? How will they feel—about themselves, about their lives—if their loved ones have to start giving things up as a result of this strange entrepreneurial passion?

Even would-be entrepreneurs without such weighty responsibilities tend to blink when they hear the starter's pistol. In my informal survey of budding entrepreneurs at leading colleges and graduate schools, for example, the single biggest factor holding these young people back is their fear of failure.

I think this fear is misplaced. "Failing" is mostly in your mind. I talked about mental toughness back in chapter 2, but let me revisit the topic here. Think about all the times, back when you were a kid, when you didn't want to try a new sport or other activity because you didn't want to look foolish. You didn't want to *fail*, and that fear kept you from acting.

I bet that if you think about it for a while, though, you can remember at least some occasions on which you overcame your fears, and you ventured forth. Maybe your parents pushed you, or your peers; or maybe you just decided that you really wanted to *try* that thing, whatever it was.

What happened next? Maybe you were one of those rare kids who could do something perfectly the first time you tried it. But if you were like most of us, you probably discovered that you were really bad at this new thing—in fact, you were downright *terrible* at it. Horrible. Hopeless.

And guess what? First of all, to your great surprise, it turned out that most of the world didn't even *notice* that you had tried and failed. And among those who did notice, the good guys (the ones you wanted to hang around with) tended to give you a lot of credit for trying this difficult thing. By and large, it was only the jerks who gave you a hard time for trying and failing.

Maybe as a result of this experience, you decided that the consequences of failing weren't so bad. Maybe you applied yourself to this particular thing, and got better at it. Or maybe you never tried it again, but the next time you faced a new experience, you found yourself much more willing to jump in. You were less worried about what other people thought, and more interested in the potential rewards of that new experience.

Entrepreneurs go through exactly this same learning process. Many of them fail in their first ventures. Some go bankrupt, and yes, some lose everything. But the process of failing, and *surviving that failure,* tends to do good things for them. They learn very specific lessons about what not to do next time. More important, they learn about their own resiliency. They learn who the good guys and bad guys around them are.

Think of it this way: Who learns more, the quarterback who wins the Super Bowl or the one who loses?

Not everyone is cut out to be an entrepreneur. Some people simply wouldn't be able to sleep well enough at night when they started thinking about all the risks (or perceived risks) that they faced. Other people wouldn't be happy making the trade-offs that come with entrepreneurship. They love the perks and bennies that come with life in a big corporation, and they would be miserable in any circumstance that required giving up those p's and b's.

By the way, I think it's perfectly okay *not* to be an entrepreneur. In my mind, there's no moral judgment attached to any way of making an honest living. But even big organizations have come to expect some degree of initiative and "intrapreneurship" from their employees. If you want to reinforce the supposed "security" that comes with life in the Fortune 500, you should probably learn to take the kinds of calculated risks that may benefit both you and your company.

Back to the main theme of this chapter: getting started. The biggest obstacle to getting started is in your head. You've got to overcome your fears, take off your shoes and socks, and dive into the deep water. Do it! The good things that will happen to you will only happen after you get started. Opportunities arise that never would have come your way if you weren't already in business. Getting started takes you out of the grandstands and puts you in the ball game.

STARTING YOUR OWN COMPANY VS. BUYING AN EXISTING ONE

Should you start from scratch, or buy someone else's company?

There's no one correct answer to this question. A lot depends on your own style, on the particular idea or opportunity that's sitting there in front of you, and—of course—your ability to come up with the dough.

I talked about "the idea" (or the lack of it) in the last chapter. Many people who decide that they want to be in their own business have no preconceived idea about what that business should be. So they look for an opportunity to buy an existing company that they are comfortable with, which in some way has already proven itself and which also seems to lend itself to improvement.

There's no such thing as a perfect package. The company that has a skilled management team may lack capital. The well-capitalized company may have lost its manufacturing edge. A company with great manufacturing skills may be facing the expiration of a critical patent. If you decide to go this route, your job is to understand the company's strengths and weaknesses in its competitive context—and also how you can add value to the situation. If the answers keep making sense, then your decision will hinge on your resources.

In many cases, it's easier to take over an existing company than to start a new one. But some people—myself included—enjoy the special challenge of starting up from scratch. (I would call this healthy ego.) Instead of seeing a mountain of detail in front of them, they see an un-plowed field full of potential. They think it's a luxury, rather than a burden, to create a workforce from scratch and inculcate those for-merly unrelated individuals with a common vision.

Jerry Shafir once said to me, "When you're starting from zero, one of the hardest things to deal with is the complete lack of infrastruc-ture. Things you might take for granted elsewhere simply don't exist. For example, there's nobody cleaning the bathrooms. Doing a new venture, even with funding, means that you're going to be doing an amazing array of stuff, day to day. You're gonna be surprised at how much time you'll spend on things you don't think are important, things that have to get done if your business is going to get off the ground. People think they're gonna be sitting there wheeling and dealing, and making decisions. But I remember when we moved into the new facility, we had to wash and paint the walls ourselves. It's not as glamorous as people think it is. You've gotta be prepared to get your hands dirty. You're gonna clean the bathrooms yourself until you make the money to pay someone else to do it."

When you start from scratch, there is both more to do and less to undo—especially in terms of people. And of course you may *have* to start from scratch if you have a passionate commitment to a product or service that no one has done in just this way before. (You can't buy it if it's not out there.)

FRANCHISING

A third option is to buy a franchise—an approach to entrepreneurship that lies somewhere between buying a business and starting your own.

Franchising involves signing a contract with a *franchisor* (e.g., Mc-Donald's, MailBoxes, or Subway) to use its corporate name and expertise, almost always in a specific geographic area. In return for the uses of these resources, as well as continuing support from the parent company, you (the *franchisee*) usually pay up-front fees and/or continuing royalties. In effect, you are buying into someone else's proven business format, and—unless you choose a franchisor that's dishonest or is itself on shaky financial ground—you can substantially reduce the risks involved in going into business for yourself.

The franchise choice is very popular, and that popularity is growing. Some figures compiled by the U.S. Department of Commerce (DOC) in 1992 may be of interest here:

- There are more than 3,000 franchising companies in the United States, which in total have established more than 600,000 franchises.
- Collectively, these franchises register more than $800 billion in retail sales each year, accounting for 40 percent of the gross national product. This total sales volume is expected to exceed $1 *trillion* by the year 2000.
- According to the DOC, franchised businesses on average survive longer than independent businesses. A DOC study showed that 97 percent of franchised businesses were still in existence after one year, as compared with only 62 percent of independent businesses. The gulf widens from there on out. After five years, 92 percent of franchises were still in business, compared with 23 percent of the independents; after 10 years, it was 90 percent compared to 18 percent.

Unfortunately, there have been no reliable statistics assembled since 1992. But according to the International Franchise Association, franchising has been growing between 10 and 14 percent a year in the last decade. Based on these kinds of numbers—especially those survival rates—it might sound that franchising is the way to go. But are franchises really the slam-dunk solution? Are they really the secret formula for low-risk, high-reward entrepreneurship? Jeffrey Tannenbaum, the *Wall Street Journal*'s expert on franchising, offers a mixed verdict. "For many people," he writes, "becoming a franchisee is the shortcut to prosperity. But for others, it is the shortcut to hell."

I agree with Tannenbaum's assessment. As with almost everything else in life, becoming a franchisee involves trade-offs. For example: as a franchisee, you will be giving up a lot of your independence. You will be expected to follow a thoroughgoing and sometimes burdensome set of rules which are designed to ensure that the product (or service) you offer is exactly the same as that offered by another franchisee of the same company. (A McDonald's french fry is not supposed to reflect the personality of the franchisee who fried it.) You will most likely be told where to buy your supplies, how to advertise and otherwise promote your product, which products you can and can't offer, what kind of sales volumes you're expected to hit, if and how you can expand your business, etc., etc., etc.

Independent business owners are far more free to invent their own answers (and, of course, to make their own mistakes). If a given product begins to falter in the marketplace, the independent can quickly change it, or dump it altogether. If a locale becomes less desirable, the independent can simply pack up and move to a better spot. Franchisees usually don't have the right to make either of these choices. Remember, too, that if your franchise is in a declining category, your franchisor may be experiencing diminishing profits, and may be tempted (or even forced) to cut back on the support it provides to you. Conversely, if you're in a hot category, the parent corporation

A FRANCHISING SAMPLER

The variety of companies that have franchised their operations is amazing, and the franchising phenomenon comprises both products and services. Here are only a few examples, borrowed from the January 1999 issue of *Entrepreneur* magazine:

McDonald's	fast food (burgers, etc.)	16,319 franchises
7-Eleven	convenience stores	14,549
Mrs. Field's	cookies, etc.	4,722
Arby's	fast food (roast beef, etc.)	3,105
Taco Bell	fast food (Mexican)	2,977
GNC Franchising	vitamins	1,290
Merry Maids	cleaning services	1,128
Lawn Doctor	lawn care	356
Jenny Craig	fitness	138

may be tempted to license additional franchises that will be in a position to compete directly with you.

This brings up the money question. For sure, you'll make more as a good franchisee than as a failed independent. But you're likely to make even more money, and *keep* more of it, as a successful independent. Remember that a choice franchise may require an up-front, onetime fee of at least several thousand dollars—money that goes off to the mother corporation forever. (Franchises like McDonald's can run as high as $45,000.) And the real hit comes in the start-up costs, which range from $20,000 to $2 million, with a lot of start-up costs exceeding $100,000. You're going to have to sell a great many burgers (or cookies, or vitamins) to earn back these initial costs, and this is money that you could have invested in your own idea.

Meanwhile, of course, you're likely to be paying substantial royalties to the mother corporation, and this is the real financial rub. These royalties are based on gross sales rather than profits. This means that you can be losing money, and still be paying out full royalties to your franchisor. Take the fast-food business, for example. This is a low-margin business, but as a franchisee, you'll be expected to pay between 1 and 16.5 percent royalties, with a median of something like 7 percent. (McDonald's is extremely high, at 12.5 percent.) There will almost certainly be moments when you'll wonder whether you're getting the short end of the stick.

I'd also advise you to think carefully about the "end game"—that is, how you're going to get *out* of business, many years from now. (See chapter 10 for more on harvesting.) Do you hope to pass something on to your kids? Do you want to build and retain value in the business? If so, then you should understand that in many cases it is much more difficult to sell or transfer ownership of a franchise that you've built up than to transfer ownership of your own business. You should also be aware that when your franchise contract is up, its renewal is not guaranteed, nor are its original terms. Of course, it's most often in the best interest of the franchisor to renew franchisees who do a good job.

All of that having been said, you may be tempted by the relative security of a franchise relationship. (And as someone who endorses low-risk entrepreneurship, I wouldn't argue with that impulse!) In that case, I'd recommend that you think of your prospective franchise relationship as a *partnership,* a topic which I'll explore in the following section. In the franchise context, however, the partnership is very unequal. Your partner has far more power than you do, especially when it comes to structuring the deal. This means that you had better make sure that you're signing on with a high-quality partner.

Fortunately, you can learn a great deal about your potential partner in franchising. The Federal Trade Commission requires all franchisors to prepare an extensive disclosure document, which the franchisor must provide to every prospective purchaser of a franchise. When the time comes, get this document, and study it carefully with the help of a lawyer or an accountant who specializes in franchises.

The disclosure document happens relatively far down the road. Before you get to that point, you should definitely talk to current owners of franchises. (The parent company must supply you with names.) Also talk to people who have abandoned their franchise. Again, the parent company has to supply you with these names, if the franchise has changed hands in the recent past. Former owners are likely to give you a very interesting perspective on franchising in general, and on relationships with this particular oversized partner.

Don't have a specific partner in mind yet? I'd start on the Web under "franchise" and "franchising." Among other things, you'll come across consulting firms that specialize in helping people get into franchising. This may or may not be a promising avenue to explore; I'd go to the Better Business Bureau in the consulting company's home region and see if there's any information available on them. If you're still interested, pick up the phone.

I'd also pick up a copy of *Entrepreneur* magazine, which publishes an annual issue ranking the 500 best franchise opportunities in the United States. This special issue is an excellent introduction to the nitty-gritty of franchising. It provides contact information for each franchisor; states how long each has been in business and in which geographic region(s) each currently operates; lists the number of franchisees each has; specifies franchise fees, start-up costs, royalty arrangements; and details what kind of financing is available, if any.

The Small Business Administration (SBA), which is discussed at greater length later in this chapter, may also be a useful resource when it comes to financing. The SBA, which guarantees bank loans to small businesses, has pre-approved certain franchisors, and if you're dealing with a company on this list, you may get a relatively fast response from SBA (which sometimes moves slowly). Don't be discouraged if your prospective partner isn't on the SBA list; SBA will consider loans against any legitimate franchise opportunity. Call them at 800-827-5722.

Don't overlook the professional franchise associations, which represent groups of franchisees. The Chicago-based American Franchisee Association (312-431-0545, skeziosAFA@aol.com) represents more than 7,500 franchisees. The Washington-based International Franchise Association, which represents some 800 franchisors and 300 franchisees, is also a great resource (202-662-0770). Its Web site (www.franchise.org) includes an excellent resource center, which gives much more detail than I've given here about the whys and hows of franchising.

In summary, franchising is a very viable option for getting into business for yourself. For some, it represents a first step—a transition toward owning one's own, independent business (whether acquired or started). In a sense, it's a learning experience in a relatively low-risk environment, with the franchisor as "mentor."

I will admit that I never considered franchising, mainly because (1) I didn't know enough about them, and (2) what little I knew struck me as too restrictive and confining. But I'll also admit that I've heard of people who put together a string of Taco Bells (or KFCs, or whatevers), and managed to retire rich, happy, and relatively young. If you can pull this off, too, more power to you!

DIRECT SELLING

This is a fast-growing sector, which in 1998 accounted for more than $23 billion in U.S. retail sales, and employed more than 9.7 million salespeople in the United States alone. These are salespeople who are in business for themselves, and are their own bosses.

The Direct Selling Association defines the activities of its members as "the sale of a consumer product or service in a face-to-face manner, away from a fixed retail location." For many people, direct selling can be a good way to embark on an entrepreneurial career. The reasons?

- The field is open to everyone. There are no educational, racial, or gender-based barriers to entry.
- Getting in is cheap—much cheaper than getting into franchising, for example. Starter kits range from $50 to $250.
- Your time is your own. You set your own hours and don't have to make a full-time commitment.

- Bookkeeping and other detail work is mainly done by the manufacturers, who want their salespeople to spend all of their time selling.
- Thinking more broadly, the sales skills you hone in the direct-selling industry can be an important asset in other business settings.

Some of the leading product categories are home/family care products (cleaning, cookware, cutlery, etc.), personal care products (cosmetics, jewelry, skin care, etc.), wellness products (weight loss, vitamins, etc.), and leisure/educational products (books, toys, encyclopedias, etc.). Some of the leading companies in this industry are Amway, Avon, Excel Communications, Mary Kay, Rexall Sundown, Tupperware, and Herbalife International.

The direct-selling industry is sometimes referred to as "multilevel" or "network" marketing. The latter two terms are interchangeable, and differ from direct selling only in the compensation structure they involve.

Traditional salespeople are paid on a commission basis for sales they generate themselves. But multilevel or network salespeople are paid not only commissions on their own sales, but also "overrides" on sales made by other people whom they have brought into the business. (An override is essentially a commission on someone else's commission.). Eighty-five percent of the salespeople in the industry get paid this way. Rexall Sundown defines multilevel marketing as "an innovative distribution channel through which independent distributors move products directly from the manufacturer to the consumer. Distributors have the opportunity to generate income from their own efforts, and from the efforts of other distributors whom they recruit and help develop."

Most sales distributors work part-time to supplement income derived from another job. The attrition rate is relatively high: About half of the people who enter the field leave it within five years. On the other hand, those who work full-time at it—approximately 10 percent—make a very good living.

For more information, contact the Direct Selling Association in Washington, D.C. (202-293-5760, info@dsa.org, www.dsa.org).

WHAT KIND OF COMPANY STRUCTURE IS BEST?

I won't go into great detail on this question, because there are plenty of books and articles out there on the subject. I'm also going to point out up front that this is a decision you shouldn't make alone; you should definitely involve your attorney and accountant. That having been said, let me make a few observations about company structures in general, and also about the options in front of you.

Before deciding on the company form you want, I would urge you to give careful thought to the kind of *company* you want, and how you want that company to function. As my lawyer-entrepreneur-teacher-friend Joe Rubin preaches, "Form should follow function." So here are the kinds of questions you should address before deciding on a particular company structure:

- How do you want to run the company? Do you want to "go it alone" and make all the decisions, or will you share the decision-making authority?
- Must you control the company—in other words, own 51 percent or more of its stock? Do you feel you need to own all 100 percent of the stock? (Why?)
- What other expertise do you need in the company to supplement your own? Do you plan to hire it, or rent it? Can you hire it without sharing ownership?
- If you have partners, how will you resolve disagreements?
- How much capital do you have access to, in relation to your known needs? Is it enough?
- How wealthy are you personally, and how much of your capital are you willing to expose in this venture? If you're taking in partners, how wealthy are they? Is there any chance that disparities in wealth (if any) will have an impact on the business?
- If ownership is shared, which types of decisions will require unanimous agreement, and which will require a simple majority (or some other percentage)?
- How much risk are you comfortable living with? If others are involved, what's their risk tolerance?
- How will profits be split?
- How will the responsibilities of key people be defined, and what authorities will be assigned to them?
- What kind of company do you want? Is it important for you to be in a workplace where you know everyone, and everyone (including you) is in a hands-on role?

- Do you want to build a company that you can pass on to other family members?
- What kinds of exit strategies (if any) are you contemplating?

Once you get a handle on the answers to these and other personal questions, then you are ready to explore the pros and cons of the various company structures, looking for the one that best suits your needs. In reviewing those options with your accountant and lawyer, you might want to set up a simple spreadsheet "scorecard" to help you make comparisons. Along one axis of your scorecard should be the following topics:

- tax implications of each form
- personal liability to which you will be exposed
- ease of transferability
- costs to set up and administer
- associated governmental restrictions or oversight
- flexibility
- ability to raise money, and from which sources
- ability to change forms at a later date
- paperwork/administrative detail required
- continuity of management
- management control (who has the final say?)
- fringe benefits
- relative ease of getting out

On to the specific forms that you may want to consider:

The sole proprietorship

In this form, the individual and the business are one and the same. It is the simplest form, most commonly used in small start-ups in which one individual owns and operates the business. The proprietorship does not pay taxes as a separate entity. Instead, the individual reports all sources of income and expenses on his or her personal income tax return. All after-tax profits belong to the owner.

The sole proprietorship is quick and cheap to form, and it's relatively free from regulatory or legal entanglements. If you adopt a trade name rather than your own name for the company, it is generally required that you file some kind of business certificate with the local government, mainly intended to let creditors know you are doing business. Most home-based businesses use this form, as well as small retail stores, small consulting firms, and so on. The business can easily be sold at any time (providing, of course, that there's a buyer!). The proprietor controls all the decision making.

The big disadvantage to this form is that the proprietor has unlimited liability. This means that if the business makes a mistake that results in a legal claim, the proprietor's personal assets are fair game. Another disadvantage is that the sole proprietorship is entirely dependent on one brain, one set of eyes and ears, one reservoir of stamina and energy, and so on. When the proprietor dies, or quits, the business dies too.

The partnership

There are two forms of partnership: the *general partnership* and the *limited partnership*.

A partnership is a business form that is basically a contract between two or more people who share in the ownership of and profits from the business. The division of the spoils doesn't necessarily correspond to the respective investments of the partners, since—for example—the expertise of one partner may be assigned a value in lieu of a cash investment.

The partnership is similar to the sole proprietorship, with the key exception that there are more owners and (probably) a larger management base. It's easier to attract better and more highly motivated people if an equity (ownership) position is on the table. A partnership may be the best way for a cash-poor "ideas person" to get the funds he or she needs to get ideas transformed into realities.

In terms of taxes, partnerships must file tax returns, but they are not taxed. Again, the profits or losses are passed through to the individual partners, even if distributions are not made, and are allocated according to the partnership agreements.

Like sole proprietorships, partnerships are relatively easy and inexpensive to set up. Unlike proprietorships, they tend to tie into a larger universe—of contacts, expertise, and access to cash and other resources.

The major disadvantage to the partnership is that the partners have unlimited personal liability. (Again, their personal assets are on the line.) And they are also liable for the actions of their partners. As a friend of mine once said, "Pick rich, healthy partners who never make mistakes."

In a limited partnership—which consists of "limited" and "general" partners—the limited partner is not actively involved in the management of the company, and has liability that is limited to his or her investment in the company. (If a limited partner becomes involved in the day-to-day running of the company, he or she loses the "limited" status.) The general partner is actively involved in the business, and has general liability. (The general partner can be a corporation, as well as an individual.)

General partnerships involve no limited partners. They lack continuity, because the partnership terminates upon the death or withdrawal of one of the partners. In a limited partnership, the entity has a better chance of surviving the departure of a limited partner, whose stake may be able to be sold according to some agreed-upon procedures.

Up to this point, I've talked about the formal and legal characteristics of the partnership. It may be worthwhile to consider partnerships from another perspective: that of people working together toward a more or less common goal.

Going into business with a partner can either be a huge plus, or a huge minus. On the plus side, you have someone with whom you can share the risk. You can minimize the capital you need to come up with personally for the start-up. You can sign up somebody who has skills that are complementary to your own. You can have someone to cover for you when you go on vacation (important!).

On the negative side, a partnership is a lot like a marriage. (And remember, you can't know everything about that partner, no matter how much you've studied him or her ahead of time!) You could very easily wind up disagreeing on key issues, being uncomfortable with each other, and having different visions and goals for the company. And it's these kinds of problems that can paralyze and kill a company—even one based on a great idea, and otherwise well run. Breaking up, by the way, is almost always costly, and sometimes downright nasty.

"I had a partner with whom I was fifty-fifty," Jerry Shafir told me, "and we had big problems. As relationships broke down, we were paralyzed. It was a horrible situation. Now I can't imagine having less than 67 percent of the stock. In the future, in order to grow, I might take on a financial partner. But that would only be strategic. Financial partners have to be minority partners. You've *gotta* have control. I think you could have four partners, as long as they were all minority investors to whom you had to report on a quarterly basis. You don't want to have to run to them for management issues."

So before starting a partnership, you should ask yourself some key questions:

- Do we all have the same moral compass? (Listen to that little voice inside you that's expressing some doubt here.)
- Do we all have the same vision for the company?
- Are we all in agreement—preferably committed to writing—on a specific division of responsibilities among the partners?
- Is one person clearly in charge? (This is hard to do, especially if one partner brings the experience and the others bring the money; but it's almost indispensable for the success of the business.)
- Are the spouses compatible? You might well ask: "Do they *have* to be?" Not always, but I've seen partnerships break up over this issue. I've also seen partners who agreed, at the outset of the venture, not to socialize, in order to prevent spouse problems from interfering with their business.
- Do we have a written buy/sell agreement in place at the outset? This is extremely important, even though it never seems like a priority in the rush and excitement that surrounds a start-up. The way to think and talk about it is as a prenuptial agreement—the kind of deal that well-to-do people often strike to keep existing fortunes unentangled.

Why go through this potentially embarrassing process? Because there are a million things that can go wrong with a partnership. The business can outgrow the abilities of one of the partners. A partner's individual goals can change, meaning that key people are now on different tracks. One partner's comfort with risk may change, or the bigger risks associated with a new stage of development may be too much for another partner to stomach. Your individual work ethics may be very different—or may change over time—and therefore your respective contributions to the business may be disproportionate. And, as suggested above, you may simply disagree on the best course of action for the business.

No matter what the cause of the disagreement, it's *far* better to talk things through while people are still optimistic and committed to each other, and to the success of the enterprise, than to wait until matters get tense. Take advantage of the fun and passion that characterizes those early, heady days, and talk about a tough issue like splitting up. (I guarantee you'll learn something interesting about your partner, and maybe even about yourself). Set up a mechanism for breaking apart, and thereby avoid the kinds of expensive, crippling legal actions that really can destroy a company. And if, God forbid, you ever find yourself in one of these situations, don't linger there. Find a way out. Life is short.

I've wound up implying that partnerships are full of complications and troubles. I didn't mean to wind up there. If you find the perfect partner for you, your life will be relatively perfect. It's just that perfection is hard to find.

The corporation

A corporation is a legal entity owned by stockholders and managed by a board of directors, who are elected by and responsible to the stockholders for appointing the operating officers. (Of course, if an individual entrepreneur controls more than half of the voting stock, he or she in effect controls the board.)

The individual stockholders have limited liability. With a few exceptions, they cannot be sued personally, unless they have participated in illegal practices. There is continuity of ownership. Corporations are not required to dissolve upon the death or departure of a founder or stockholder. Stock can be sold, assigned, or inherited.

It is often easier to raise money within the corporate format. Corporations have certain legal advantages, at least for the time being. Health insurance, for example, can be deducted as a business expense, which is not currently the case for sole proprietorships or partnerships. (This distinction is in the process of changing, though; this corporate advantage eventually may well disappear.)

The major disadvantages of a corporation are that it is more expensive to set up; it is subject to more governmental regulations; must keep more extensive records; and—in many cases—must pay more state and local taxes. (These taxes will vary by locale.)

For tax purposes, a corporation may elect to be treated in two ways: as a *C corporation* or as an *S corporation*. A third type of entity, the *limited liability corporation,* or *LLC,* is also discussed below.

C corporation. All public companies choose this form. The advantages of the regular (or "C") corporation are those stated above. Once a company adopts this form, it can't convert to another form without going through legal hoops and risking tax consequences. (Generally, you can go in the other direction, however—e.g., from a partnership or LLC to a regular corporation—without tax consequences.)

The major disadvantage to this form is the federal "double taxation" burden. C corporations are taxpayers, and pay income tax on their earnings. They then distribute the after-tax income to stockholders in the form of dividends, which are not deductible expenses. The stockholders who receive the dividends are then taxed on these dividends at individual income tax rates.

Many entrepreneurs with private corporations try to minimize this double taxation by increasing their salaries, or by giving themselves big bonuses and not declaring dividends. To a certain extent, this is a workable strategy. But if the IRS audits the company, it may determine that some of the individual's pay should have come in the form of dividends, and therefore be subject to corporate tax as well as personal. There is also something called an *accumulated earnings tax.* This was designed to prevent companies from accumulating profits instead of distributing them as dividends.

Losses incurred by a regular corporation are accumulated as an offset against profits in future years. This can be a great advantage to companies that are investment-intensive in their early years.

S corporation. A corporation may make an "S election," which means that it elects to be taxed at the federal level as a partnership. The advantage to such an election is that there are no federal corporate-level taxes, and therefore, no risk of double taxation. All profits and losses flow through personally to the individual stockholders based on their ownership share. The limits on liability, however, remain unchanged from the "C" structure.

"S corps" must operate on a calendar (January to December) fiscal year, which is not the case with a regular corporation. This restriction might present a problem if yours is a fast-growing company with seasonal cash flow problems.

Remember, too, that the direct flow of profits to the stockholders can create challenges for fast-growing companies. Stockholders must pay taxes on their profits at ordinary tax rates, *whether or not cash distributions have been made.* Fast-growing companies tend to have their cash tied up in expanded receivables and inventories, and may not be able to distribute cash. This can create cash flow problems for shareholders who can't lay their hands on the necessary cash to pay their taxes. The corporation may be able to limit this problem by borrowing against a bank credit line and distributing the necessary cash, but (as noted earlier) bank money can be difficult for a new or non–asset-based company to obtain.

Beyond this, the major disadvantage of an S corp is a set of restrictions on stock ownership and structure. An S corp can have no more than seventy-five shareholders. No foreign nationals, corporations, or trusts can be shareholders. (If you're looking for a big investment by an industry giant, the S corp is not for you.) Only one class of stock can be issued, which means that voting rights and ownership cannot be separated—not a problem for most new and small companies, but worth thinking about ahead of time.

The LLC. The limited liability corporation is a relatively new form. It was created mainly to provide the liability insulation of a corporation and the tax treatment of a partnership without the restrictions of the S corporation election. There are no limits on the number of shareholders. Corporations and non-U.S. nationals can be LLC members.

Even though LLCs are basically equivalent to other types of corporations, they require the use of a different vocabulary. Corporations issue shares, while LLCs have "units of membership interest." Corporations have stockholders; LLCs have members. Corporations have boards of directors; LLCs have boards of managers.

I'll close this section with the same advice I opened it with: figure out what *kind* of business you want to be associated with, according to the parameters that you define as most important. Then go see your lawyer and your accountant, and together design or select the structure that is likely to get you to that kind of business.

One last caution: The United States is one of the most litigious countries in the world. If only for this reason, I'd think twice before I entered into a business form that held me personally liable. Even if you're convinced that there's no practical liability associated with your particular product or service, you should probably think through the implications of the worst outcomes. (Get your lawyer talking about those circumstances.) Remember that jurors are a lot like buyers, at least in the sense that they have been known to make decisions based on emotion rather than reason.

THE BUSINESS PLAN

The next logical step is to put together a plan of action. Common sense tells you that some kind of planning is required. If your company is just you and your idea, your plan can be sketched out on the back of a napkin or even just stashed in the back of your head. If your company is (or gets) bigger, a written document is a very good idea.

"I never wrote a business plan, not for one of those businesses," admits John Altman, who has started up and sold six companies so far. "In fact, I can remember saying, 'What's a business plan?' But in fact, I had the business plan in my brain—every single part of it. And now I realize that's not enough. If you're going to empower the other people, and have them be partners in this flat organization, guess what: You'd better give them a map to the highway you're on! Otherwise, they can't share that vision in your brain. Especially when you're changing it every three and a half seconds."

Generally, if you're looking for outside financing, you'll need a detailed business plan. Creating a business plan can be an awesome task the first time you take it on. It can be intimidating. It may look like a trip to the dentist—something you'd rather put off forever. But it doesn't have to be that way. There are many people who make a living writing these plans for others, and there are many books out there that map out the steps in putting together a business plan.

And it doesn't have to be a weighty tome. Venture capitalist Michael Hsieh told me, "We work with our portfolio companies to try and develop business plans, but not the kind that are an inch thick. We want to help them build a cash flow model. It comes down to what are your assumptions, how are you going to grow revenues, what margins can you realistically expect, what are your expenses going to be, where are your finances coming from. That's the business plan. The numbers matter less than understanding the business in terms of market position, customers, potential for growth, strategic growth, and necessary investment. In our own due diligence, we'll do a competitor analysis and so on. We don't want the company to spend time doing that and writing it up. We've already covered all of it, and it'll take them two months and distract them from running the business."

Most business plans that I see, and especially those that are generated for small businesses, are far too long. But don't be so brief that you sacrifice thoroughness. Your plan needs to cover such topics as:

- an executive summary, summarizing what's in the plan
- your basic idea for the company
- a description of your product or service
- the backgrounds of your key employees (including you, of course)
- your anticipated customers
- the potential size of your market
- your strategy to reach and sell this market
- the competition you will face
- how the product will be made, where and by whom
- the financing you will need (and how much of that you will supply, and how you plan to spend the money)
- a cash flow statement showing your monthly cash needs, projected sales, and your ability to pay back any loans you may be taking out
- a projected profit and loss statement and balance sheet for the next three to five years

Think of your plan as a work-in-progress—something that explains what you're about, at least as you understand it today; something that will help you manage risk better; and something that will help you measure progress. It is, in some cases, a necessity. (If you go beyond friends and family for money, you'll need a business plan.) So find a way to make the business plan your ally, rather than your albatross.

SCORE (described in chapter 3) can be helpful in putting together a business plan. There are also plenty of good books on the market that can give you tips on writing a plan.

THE MISSION STATEMENT

The *mission statement* is something very different from the business plan. Mission statements set the moral and human goals to which your company is supposed to aspire. In many cases, they also state higher-order business goals, such as a corporate commitment to maintaining an annual compounded rate of growth of a certain percentage.

Mission statements are most often associated with large corporations—an effort to get thousands of people to pull in the same direction, across a far-flung corporate empire. But I think a mission statement is a good thing for a small business as well, and it's something that should be developed at the outset.

The mission statement clearly tells employees what behaviors are expected of them, and describes the kind of treatment they can expect from their employer. Most people have a strong desire to know the rules of the game. In addition, they want to be proud of the company for which they work. The mission statement gives them at least one piece of the puzzle.

This is also the best reason *not* to have a mission statement: if you don't intend to follow it. There's nothing more poisonous in a corporate setting than to have the management thumping away on some ethical tub, and at the same time acting in ways that directly contradict the espoused values. If you can't walk it, don't talk it!

The mission statement, like the business plan, is a useful tool for triangulation and mid-course correction. Take it off the shelf, every once in a while, and see if you're living by it. (Better yet: look at the framed version on your office wall.) And when you face a tough choice—under resource pressures, or in a personnel dispute—look at that statement again for guidance. To the extent that your mission statement contains concrete business goals, make sure that you either (1) achieve those goals, or (2) acknowledge that you aren't achieving them, and take steps to bring the company's performance into line with its aspirations.

You may not spend a lot of time on your mission statement, but you should clearly set the tone for the kind of company you're trying to create and sustain. Culture comes from the top—that is, from you. How accessible will you be to your employees? Will you truly listen to their input, or will you just pay lip service to their ideas? What are your expectations from everyone, especially in the realm of building trust? How will your company treat its customers? What are its attitudes toward quality?

Part of the point of the mission statement is the *process,* as well as the product. If you involve other people in the development of the mission statement, you're already sending a signal about your culture. If disputes arise, how are those disputes resolved? Do people walk away feeling that the resolution was fair, smart, and efficient? Again, your personal example is extremely important here. One of the best ways that you can inculcate values into the fabric of your company is to *embody* those values.

GETTING THE MONEY

Aside from developing the idea for the company, the most troublesome issue that most entrepreneurs wrestle with is *getting the money*. Before looking at some of the financing options, you should try to think about all the ways you can operate on less money than was specified in the original plan.

Have you really thought through all the so-called fixed expenses? Aren't there *any* that can be converted to variable expenses (see chapter 3)? Are there certain necessary investments that can be staged, so that you don't need as much cash up front? Can you do some kind of market test, which can prove (or disprove!) your ideas about the power of this product? (If the results are good, by the way, lenders may be more responsive to your pleas.) Ask yourself honestly: Am I being too ambitious here? Is there a baby step I can take before I take my first giant step? As I suggested in the last chapter: Is there any good reason not to start locally rather than nationally?

Most entrepreneurs will work with less money than they think they need, particularly in the early stages. This can be a very good form of discipline. Good habits for preserving capital get established early, with every detail of spending and resource allocation being scrutinized carefully. The converse is also true: Start-ups that begin with a plentiful supply of cash often slip into wasteful habits that in the worst cases lead to their demise. Steve Gordon, founder/CEO of Restoration Hardware Stores, feels that if sufficient capital had been available to him in the company's early stages, he might not have been as successful as he is.

On to the money sources:

Your own savings

It's very important, in almost all cases, that you put a good percentage of your own savings on the line. Investors of all stripes will be reluctant to come through with money if you don't have your own money at stake.

If you have little in the way of savings, that's okay, as long as what you do have is put on the table. If you have expertise in the field of the enterprise, proven entrepreneurial experience, a blockbuster idea that's clearly a protectable idea, and a large and untapped market, you probably will get the financing you want without putting up a dime. Take it from me, though: this kind of scenario is very rare. Most start-ups are funded by the entrepreneur himself/herself, with the help of friends, and family.

Friends

The most common source of initial capital in bootstrap start-ups is friends. If you have friends with deep pockets, you should definitely consider going to them for support.

A word of caution: If your business doesn't work out the way you planned, you may be putting your friendship in jeopardy. In my experience, though, this is at most a limited risk. We start with the assumption that this is a friend who knows you well. We go on to assume that this friend has seen you struggle like a galley slave to make this business work—and understands why it hasn't. In cases like these, your friendship is likely to survive, or even be strengthened.

Another problem with hitting up friends—and this is a problem that I take seriously—is that it's very hard to go back to friends for a second infusion of cash. Even if you go to friends first, you'd better be planning an alternative source of financing for the next crunch.

Family

Family members are right up there with friends as the most common source of seed money for start-ups. The advantage of calling on family members is that you probably won't have to prepare a business plan, and that the money—if it's there—can be accessed quickly.

You can guess what I'm going to say about the downside here. If the money is lost, a very valuable relationship may be put into jeopardy. Before I took family money, I'd make sure the lender could afford to lose it. I'd also resolve to break my butt in working hard to protect their money. The absolutely *worst* scenario would be to lose their money—and to have them think that I hadn't worked very hard to protect it.

Banks

Don't plan on leaning on banks until you've developed a successful company. Are you surprised? It's true. In fact, you may not extract any money from a bank even *after* your company is up and running. Banks usually are willing to loan only against a company's assets. They most often want you to sign personally for the loan (meaning, once again, that your house is on the line).

My own experiences with borrowing from banks has been very frustrating and disappointing. To put it mildly, I don't think of banks as my friends. Maybe my own case is an extreme one, since our profile could never be made attractive to them. Our plan was *never* to invest in physical assets like real estate, machines, buildings, and so on, which meant that we never had much in the way of assets to pledge.

All this having been said, think of banks as potential sources of conservative money once you've got buildings, machines, and money in the bank. Generally speaking, banks like to lend you money if you've been in business a number of years with proven and steady profits. They are one of the cheapest sources of money, and that is of course a good thing. But take care! Your bank may very well choose to call in (or refuse to renew) your loan *even if you've performed your end of the loan flawlessly.*

Why? Lots of reasons. Sometimes a change in loan officers leads to a new direction for the bank's loan portfolio. Sometimes your bank merges with another, in which case all bets are off. Sometimes a crash in an entirely separate part of the bank's overall loan portfolio—say, the real estate loans—gets the regulators on your bank's tail, and the bank retrenches at your expense.

I have no advice here, except to invest the time necessary to build a strong relationship with your loan officer. And his or her boss, if possible. Be aware, too, that under certain market conditions, banks may be more willing than usual to take risks. Competition from other banks or lenders, imbalances of supply and demand, and aggressive bank growth strategies may lead them to adopt higher-risk strategies. This could work to your advantage.

Leasing

Why tie up precious capital in buying things that you can rent? When you go looking for space, you don't usually start by buying the building; you rent what you think you'll need, for the time you'll need it.

Learn to think about your equipment and other capital-intensive stuff in the same way. Computer, fax machines, photocopiers, phone systems, cars, office furniture—you name it; it's out there to be leased.

In many lease agreements, you will be offered (or you can negotiate) an option to buy at the end of the lease period. This means that a portion of your "rent" is applied to the ultimate purchase of the machine, at a point in time when your cash flow may allow you to buy the thing outright.

Another benefit of leasing is that you avoid obsolescence. Leasing is more expensive than financing, as a rule. On the other hand, at each renewal period, you can exchange your leased product for the latest, state-of-the-art version. And finally, you have no maintenance costs. If it breaks, call the place that leased it to you.

Credit cards

How many times have you received unsolicited offers for credit cards, at a special introductory rate? The same thing will most likely start to happen to your business. In most circumstances, you throw these offers away, because this is one of the most expensive sources of money.

But many small businesses—not necessarily those in early start-up mode—take out multiple cards, use them as cash sources, and pay them off on an installment basis. As long as you pay at least the minimum, the sponsoring bank will love you. You'll even develop a good credit record, which may help you secure a more formal line of credit later.

Factors

This is a world that lots of people—even lots of business people—know little about. *Factors* are companies that operate a little bit like banks. (In fact, some banks have factoring divisions.) But rather than loaning against your track record or your personal guarantee, they specialize in loaning money against your receivables and inventory.

For companies like mine have tended to be—light on assets, heavier on receivables and inventory—this has been the way to go. Depending on the quality of your customers and the strength of your company, you can expect to receive cash advances of between 60 and 80 percent of your receivables from a factor. (The remainder is paid to you when your customer pays.)

Inventory loans from factors can usually be on a basis of 50 percent of the wholesale value of your inventory. Factors must approve of both the accounts you ship to and the dollar amount of these shipments. Once they do so, you are guaranteed payment. In effect, factors are an excellent way to buy insurance on your receivables.

There are other pluses to using factors besides getting access to money. For example, by pre-screening your customers, they eliminate the cost to you of having a person checking credit on those customers. They can create a lot of very useful reports for you. And most important, they exert great leverage on customers who are slow paying their bills. This is leverage that you, as a "little guy" (and here I'm contrasting you to Wal-Mart) will never have on your own, and it's increasingly important vis-à-vis today's huge retailers.

One downside to factors: If your customers are mainly small retailers, they may be turned off to your company because of the aggressive tone that some factors employ in their collection methods. In some cases, you can get around this by arranging to do the collections yourself, rather than the factors. You lose one of their services, to be sure; but you still get access to their money.

Factors can't be free, right? Right. You can expect to pay between 1 and 4 percent over prime for the advance monies they give you. You may also be subject to minimum monthly and other fees. Read your contract carefully, as your total costs in some agreements can run as high as 25 percent, after all the extras are figured in. On the plus side, you should not have to personally guarantee advances from factors. And this can be a big, big plus.

Venture capitalists

Venture capitalists are those guys you read about in the *Wall Street Journal,* backing the latest hot high-tech start-up from Silicon Valley. And in fact, they do a lot of that. They also do a lot of other less sexy work. Basically, they place bets on a number of companies in whom they have some confidence—most often because of the quality of the management. Most of these bets, perhaps nine out of ten, never pan out. If the tenth one hits big, then everybody makes out great.

Venture capitalists are a major source of capital for new and emerging businesses. Some specialize in giving seed money to start-ups. Most will invest only in new companies that have launched and proved themselves. Businesses that require heavy capital investments, or investments over a number of years (such as high-tech and drug companies) almost always go to the VC community for funding.

How can you get the attention of a venture capitalist? Michael Hsieh told me, "We're looking for a person who knows the industry.

Not someone with a great idea for a toy or mousetrap but with no experience in the industry. We're looking for people who have spent at least five to ten years in the industry, who have learned the trade, usually under the tutelage of someone else or in a company."

Maybe you fit this profile. So, does this funding option sound great? Well, sort of. The downside is that as the entrepreneur, you have to be prepared to give away a substantial portion of your equity in the business—in many cases, more than 50 percent. This sticks in the craw of many entrepreneurs, who have no intention of giving up voting control of their companies. And by the way: venture firms will usually put provisions in their agreements stating that they can take over the operations of the company—and even oust the founder—if the company fails to meet its agreed-to goals.

When you contemplate going to the VC community, it's a real good idea to keep in mind what their ultimate goals are: either to make a substantial profit by selling the (appreciated) stock in the company, or to conduct what is sometimes called euphemistically a "liquidity event." In most cases, this means going public. If these outcomes are okay with you, and if you're comfortable with the five-year time frame that most venture capitalists work within, then VC may be the funding source for you.

Angels

Maybe you didn't expect to read about *angels* in a section on getting the money. This is a specific use of the word. It means wealthy individuals who play the same role as venture capitalists: looking for promising managers with good ideas, and then bankrolling them in return for a piece of the action.

I'm told that angels are sometimes more personally involved in deals than venture capitalists, but that's not something I've experienced personally. (You can certainly find venture capitalists who are willing and able to play an activist role in your business!) And from my point of view, having an investor who's actively involved in your business can be a great thing, or it can be a terrible thing.

Angels can be difficult to find. (They're never in the Yellow Pages.) Calling on the widest possible range of friends and business contacts increases your odds of coming across one. Jeff Armstrong, a venture capitalist, told me he sometimes found angels through contacts at university business schools. He would make a special effort to meet the members of a school's board of advisers, many of whom were success-ful and wealthy entrepreneurs themselves, and had a soft spot for young entrepreneurs with passion and a good plan. Jeff also met with some success by making contact with business school deans, who sometimes steered him toward angels.

Small Business Administration (SBA)

The SBA is a federal agency set up back in the 1950s to assist small businesses. It doesn't loan money directly to businesses, but will guar-antee a portion of the money that banks loan to businesses. Its maxi-mum loan, in most cases, is $750,000. On loans under $150,000, it will guarantee 80 percent of the loan; for loans over $150,000, it'll guaran-tee 75 percent.

Many banks have preferred-lender status, and can handle loan ap-plications expeditiously. You can contact the SBA for a list of banks near you who work closely with the agency. If you decide to go after one of these loans, be prepared to come in with a business plan, which should include a cash flow statement for the first year of operations. Also be prepared to pledge your company's assets against the loan, and also to sign personally. In the case of start-ups, the SBA won't consider backing a loan unless the principal comes up with at least 20 to 30 percent of the required capital.

People sometimes grumble about paperwork and bureaucracy when they talk about the SBA. Nevertheless, in 1995, the SBA guar-anteed more than 60,000 loans totalling $9.9 billion to small busi-nesses in the United States. If you're willing to do the necessary homework, this may be a great source of financing for you. (And be aware, too, that SBA can also be helpful in securing financing of ex-port orders.) To locate the SBA office nearest to you, call 800-8-ASK-SBA. The fax number in Washington is 202-205-7064, and the Web site is www.sba.gov/aduo.

Barter

Barter is the exchange of goods or services for other goods or services, with little or no cash involved in the transaction. It dates back to pre-historic times, when the tribe that controlled the hides traded with the tribe that controlled the fish. It goes on today in much the same way, in lands (such as parts of the former Soviet empire) where the econ-omy is in a state of chaos.

But there's another kind of barter that goes on today, and this trade is far different from the primitive scenarios I just described. This kind of barter is run by sophisticated, worldwide enterprises that serve huge corporate customers. Relatively late in my career, I discovered that barter works for the little guy, too.

Why is barter included in this "getting the money" section? Because if you can limit your cash outlays, you effectively create another source of cash.

Here's how it works: You sell your excess inventory—including the worst of your dogs—to the barter company. For this inventory, you receive the full wholesale price. You get this "money" in the form of other company's goods and services, which they have brought to the barter market just like you. (Think of a huge outdoor bazaar in Marrakesh, but with pinstripes and telecommunications.)

Meanwhile, your accounting department grows ever fonder of you. Instead of showing all this hopeless inventory on your books—or writing it off as a loss—you're transforming it into a *prepaid asset*. This asset is then expensed as you draw down your credits for whatever goods or services you receive.

In my experience, the best deals are often to be found in magazine advertising. Instead of paying full price for an ad in your favorite magazine, you can get huge discounts. Of course, many companies have no use for advertising. Well, okay; why not trade for printing, hotel rooms, fixtures, furniture, or whatever? Surely there's something out there that your company needs. If there is, you can probably barter for it.

Barter is an intensely competitive business, and you should be prepared to engage in some tough negotiations. On the other hand, the people you're negotiating with are sophisticated business people who know how the world works. You're within your rights to restrict the barter company from selling or trading your inventory to classes of trade or geographic areas that might disrupt your normal channels of distribution.

Don't be put off if this all sounds too exotic. Peter Benassi, CEO of the MRI barter firm in New York City, worked very productively with me and my watch company on several occasions. He tells me that he enjoys working with small companies, and my own experience with MRI backs him up. Find MRI and other leading barter companies at the Web page of the Corporate Barter Council, Inc. (www.corporatebarter.com).

Suppliers

This is a source of money that's often overlooked—which is too bad, because it can be an important source.

Suppliers know you, and—if you've treated them right—have an interest in seeing your business succeed. What you need most often from your suppliers is *time*. If a supplier will give you sixty days to pay, rather than ten days, this may result in a significant reduction in the amount you have to raise or borrow. Even if you pay interest on the owed money, you'll almost certainly get a better rate from your supplier than from your bank.

Key suppliers can also be persuaded to invest in your business if they feel that you have the potential to become a significant and long-term customer. Remember when I made a pitch for sales in chapter 1? This is only one of the countless cases in which salesmanship can make a huge difference to your company—and again, it's *not* a case of selling snake oil; it's a case of getting another person to see the world the way you see the world.

I like to cite the case of Bud Pironti, who started a direct response company called NSI. He was running NSI as a division of a larger company, which chose to sell off that division. Pironti decided that he wanted to buy it, but had nowhere near enough money to pull that off. What he *did* have, though, was a reputation for competence and integrity. He went to a few of his key suppliers and got them to loan him the money he needed to buy the company. He was able to borrow without giving up equity. He proposed that, in exchange for a loan of $1.5 million, he would give his suppliers a three-year exclusive. They agreed, and the deal was struck. Pironti paid them back the full $1.5 million, with interest, in less than a year.

"In a sense, your vendors are your bank," Pironti told me. "There have been times when I've gone back to our five or six key vendors, when we've been expanding into a new activity, and asked our vendors if they could take their payments over ninety days, rather than thirty days. That has worked, on a couple of occasions. You can't do it on a regular basis, but sometimes, your vendors can be a 'line of credit' for you. And when things are tight, you can call up your vendors and tell them what's what. Let's say you owe them $100K and it's due on July 15. You're gonna pay that $100K 50 percent on July 31, 25 percent on August 10, and the last 25 percent on August 20. Then you've gotta *deliver*. You gain a lot of trust by volunteering this kind of schedule. And you've gotta take all the vendors' calls on payment issues! I have my CFO field those calls. You can't push that down into the organization."

Another interesting angle was developed by my friend Jerry Shafir, the soup magnate. He financed his business in part by offering incentives to his customers to pay quickly—a 2 percent discount if they paid within ten days—and paying his vendors in thirty days. "That twenty-day float was a big source of capital," Shafir recalls, "which grew along with the company. It was expensive, in terms of margin, but it was very helpful."

Pironti's and Shafir's stories aren't as unusual as they may sound. Many entrepreneurs find mutually beneficial ways to collaborate financially with their suppliers.

Strategic alliances

Is your idea really a good one, and does it really have a market? If so, there are probably other kinds of companies that will benefit from helping you get off the ground. Here's an interesting example supplied to me by Johnson & Johnson's Bill Doyle:

> *Question:* Back when General Motors was being pulled together by Alfred Sloan, which industry stepped forward to help Sloan most enthusiastically?
> *Answer:* The paint industry, which couldn't wait to sell G.M. the many coats of paint that would go on all those cars.

Maybe you're not yet G.M., but try to think of existing companies that might make you a loan, become equity partners, give you special credit terms, or otherwise invest in you. Will you be storing goods in a public warehouse? (Don't build your own warehouse!) Maybe that warehouse is only using 65 percent of its capacity, and its managers are gloomy about their near-term future, and they'll see you as someone with real potential for growth. If so, they might well give you extended dating on your bills—say, from ninety days to a year. This is just as good as cash, and it's a lot better than your average bank loan.

Is there an existing company out there that has a great distribution system that you could piggyback onto? If so, this would certainly keep your costs down and accelerate your market penetration. It might also bring your partner's distribution costs down, and justify the expansion of their existing network into new regions.

To summarize this quick run-through of the potential sources of money: Dig into your own pockets first, and as deeply as you can. Then go talk to your uncle Bob. Then see if you can get your spouse to work hard enough to support the family, so that you can avoid taking much-needed cash out of the business in its infancy.

Meanwhile, *hang on to as much of that equity as possible, as long as possible.* Venture capitalists and angels are great resources in some situations, but the sooner you go to them, the more it's going to cost you in terms of equity. Jerry Shafir was told by his friends in the venture capital business to stay away from them in the early stages, because a relatively tiny loan (on the order of $100,000) would most likely cost him at least half of his company. (Jerry stayed away.) So go to these resources for second- and third-round financing, when you look less risky and therefore won't have to give up as much.

But above all, *get started.* Fifty percent of something is better than 100 percent of nothing. And after you get started, *keep in regular touch with your investors or lenders.* You should keep them abreast of new products, management coups, sales triumphs—and also disappointments and failures. Educate them constantly about your industry and opportunities. You definitely want to keep these good allies on board.

Why? Because there's almost no circumstance under which you *won't* need them. If you get in trouble, you'll need them not to pull the plug on you. And if you succeed beyond your wildest dreams, you'll need them to fund your next round of growth. So don't take their money and run. Take their money, and bring them along!

One last thought on "getting the money": Historically, most start-up companies wind up needing more money than they have budgeted for, even in their most conservative (read "pessimistic") scenarios. What this means is that in some part of your brain, you'll probably always have to be asking yourself a key question: *Where am I going to get more money?*

GETTING THE RIGHT PEOPLE

Okay, let's assume that you've got your idea, your business structure, and your money in hand. The next thing you've got to get your hands on is good people. In many ways, this is the scarcest commodity of all.

Before you hire, you have to figure out:

- what skills you're looking for, and in what combinations
- what type of people are likely to have these skills
- how much time you can allow for individuals to begin to produce
- how much you can pay
- how much responsibility and authority you are *really* willing to give up (even to the most talented people in the world)

You've certainly heard the axiom that *your people make or break your business.* In my experience, that's almost always been true. But keep in mind that your business will need different kinds of people over its life span, and the people who are most valuable at the beginning may be less valuable as time goes by and the business changes into something new. For example, at the outset, *you* are the indispensable employee. But as we'll see in later chapters, there's a very good chance that in another decade or so, your company will find compelling reasons to ease you out the door.

At the outset, you may very well need some "sharpshooters"—people with very specific and targeted skills, who are themselves a key competitive edge for your company. There are manufacturing people, and creative marketers, and salespeople, etc, etc., who fall into this category. Figure out what you need, find a way to compensate them (see below), and then sign them up.

But for most jobs in most start-ups, you're far more likely to need multitalented people who are willing and able to take on all kinds of tasks. You need people who either aren't accustomed to all the perks and support systems of corporate life, or who are consciously making a trade-off that they think will be good for them. But even these people, who are more or less going in with their eyes open, are likely to be astonished at the realities of life in a small business. If they spill their coffee, they have to clean it up themselves. (Did anyone remember to buy paper towels?) If a nut falls off the bottom of their chair, they have to find a wrench and put it back on—and by the way, they should check the rest of the chairs while they're at it.

Compensation can be a critical issue. There's almost no way a small company can compete in terms of salary, so to get talent, you'll need to offer other kinds of incentives to key employees. Equity—a piece of the company—is something that lots of people are looking for today, and it is a tool that's available to you. But what I said earlier about hanging on to as much equity as long as possible still holds here. If you give away equity, it should be tied to sustained individual and company performance.

Equity can be given up front or in the form of options. Options can be exercised on certain measured performance levels of the individual or the company, and may also be contingent on other factors (such as number of years employed at the company). Be creative with equity. Structure options to meet the needs of both the individual and the company.

An alternative to high salaries or pieces of the action is bonuses. These can be based either on objective or subjective measures, but you're likely to create less unhappiness if you can point to some benchmarks that the individual has hit. John Korff, the events impresario, hires young people with a predetermined bonus figure in mind—a sum that he builds into his budget as if it were deferred salary. If the individual *doesn't* earn that bonus, John knows he's made a serious hiring mistake.

The opportunity to learn *many* aspects of business can be a strong lure for many potential employees of entreprenurial companies.

Recruiting, like almost all other aspects of business, requires *salesmanship*. When you spot a great potential hire, figure out what he or she needs from you, and—within the bounds of practicality—give it to him or her. Maybe someone needs to leave a big corporation because that company's hours are too inflexible. It's not that they won't work lots of hours; it's that they sometimes need to be out for two hours in the middle of the day. Well, if you can afford to offer flexibility, offer it. Stress the things that your little company does do, rather than the things it doesn't (yet) do. Maybe your 401k plan is still entirely funded by your employees. But, hey, at least you *have* one; and maybe you have a timetable in mind for starting corporate contributions to that plan in the future. Are you willing to pay for certain kinds of training, so that your future employee can make himself or herself a more valuable commodity? If so, mention it, see what kind of response you get, and move forward from there.

Is the person you're talking to a techno-wizard? Can you honestly say that you're committed to providing the best technology possible— or, alternatively, that you'd be willing to back that person in a large-scale effort to upgrade your company's technology base? How can you sketch out an attractive future for this individual in the context of your company? How will your vision be liberating, empowering, and financially rewarding for that person?

When doing due diligence on an entrepreneurial company he's interested in investing in, Mike Hsieh always makes a point of meeting with the key people working for the entrepreneur. He feels that if the company's personnel are high quality, then most likely the entrepreneur is high quality, as well: quality people want to work for quality people. So, recruiting and developing great people may also have a bearing on your ability to attract the capital needed for growth.

We'll return to the subject of developing your personnel in later chapters. Meanwhile, don't think you're alone, or that you're a bad person, if you absolutely dread the prospect of dealing with personnel issues. The personnel function is the Great Black Hole of business. People can be complicated, unpredictable, and demanding, and they can suck up all the energy that's available out there. You don't have enough time in the day to make everything right and everyone happy. You'll drive yourself crazy if you set that kind of unrealistic goal for yourself.

But you *do* have to make as big an investment as possible in your people, and this begins with an effective recruitment process.

LOCATING YOUR BUSINESS

This is a question that's not always addressed in an explicit way. Very often, people take location as a given: "I'm here, so that must be where I should be." But this isn't usually true for businesses. In fact, location can be a most important decision.

Some of the key factors to consider are:

- **Labor supply.** Are there enough people around with the skill sets you need? If so, will you be competing for them with large and profitable companies that can outbid you for their services? Is there another place with the same kinds of good people and less big company competition? If you need a supply of non-skilled labor, many communities will pay and subsidize you to train and hire such people, and this can prove to be a good deal.
- **Suppliers.** Are they there? Are they already as good as they need to be, or are they willing to get better? If you grow quickly, can they grow along with you?

- **Taxes.** How much will your business have to pay, and to which government entities? Are there any hidden taxes? (A friend of mine was astonished to learn that the city of Boston had the right to charge his tiny business more than $2,000 per year as a tax on personal property, which consisted mainly of a dozen computer workstations and the software programs needed to run those computers.) Is the state income tax so high that talented people would rather work in a neighboring state?
- **Governments and agencies.** How will the various levels of government treat you? Is anyone offering a tax break? (What's it worth? Would you move there if it *weren't* offered to you? Why not?) If you do enough research, you'll discover that there are absolutely huge differences in the ways that various states and communities treat businesses. Some are very business-friendly; others range from indifferent to nasty. I can say from personal experience that the state of New Jersey is unfriendly to small business. (Sorry, Governor.)
- **Incubators.** I mentioned this little-known resource in chapter 3. If there's a quasi-governmental agency out there that's willing to do things for you at below-market rates, why not take a hard look at that deal?

If you have a choice when it comes to locating your business, then take advantage of that flexibility. You may well decide that you want to stay where you are now—because you want to be near the mountains, because your friends and family are there, whatever. But I'd encourage you to get a good handle on what a given locational choice is likely to cost you. If there's a premium, maybe you'll choose to locate your *second* facility somewhere less costly.

THINKING EARLY ABOUT INSURANCE

No one except an insurance agent likes to think about insurance, but—! Once you know what your business is going to make, where it's going to be located, and who's going to be involved in it, you should start thinking about protecting it against disasters of various kinds. In chapter 7, I'll emphasize the importance of product liability, but much earlier in the game, there are lots of other kinds of insurances you need to examine, including:

- property
- business interruption
- transportation
- premises liability
- operations liability
- contractual
- errors and omissions
- workers compensation (required in many jurisdictions)
- "key man"

Get a good insurance agent to sit down with you and figure out which kinds of coverage you need, and when, and how much. Think creatively about how your insurance may be put to work serving more than one purpose. (For example, so-called key man policies purchased as whole-life insurance can accumulate value, and can be used to fund a buy-out agreement.) Revisit these coverages on a regular basis—say, once a year—to make sure your coverages are adequate.

There's one more kind of "insurance" that you need to think about as soon as you set up a computer network—even a network of one. How are you going to back up your electronic records, and where will the backups be kept? There are all sorts of solutions to this problem, many of them expensive. As soon as you establish a good relationship with a network expert, explore the possibility of automatic and re-mote backup. That way, if your building burns down in the middle of the night, you can start putting the pieces back together the next morning—with your electronic memory intact.

GETTING STARTED: MINORITY ENTREPRENEURSHIP

I didn't want to end this chapter without pointing readers toward a special resource available for minority entrepreneurs. This is the U.S. Department of Commerce's Minority Business Development Agency (MBDA), which is the only federal agency specifically set up to en-courage the creation, growth, and expansion of minority-owned busi-nesses in the United States.

MBDA administers its programs through five regional offices (in Atlanta, Chicago, Dallas, New York, and San Francisco). It provides business development services through a number of different kinds of programs. Separately, these programs focus on opportunities in specific target markets; collectively, they form a national business service network.

You can find MBDA through its Web site (www.mbda.gov) or write them at 14th Street and Constitution Avenue NW, Room 5055, Washington, DC 20230. A second MBDA Web site (www.turnharp.com/capital) directs would-be entrepreneurs to financial resources for minority businesses, including grants and loans.

I haven't used this resource myself. (It's brand-new, and I'm not a member of a minority.) But I'd recommend that minority entrepreneurs push this button—and any others like it that you can find—as part of your overall effort to get started. You're building your network, and this is a piece of that larger challenge.

Many large retailers and corporations have programs that set aside purchasing dollars for minority-controlled businesses. If you fit their description (which may vary), you should definitely look into these set-asides. That having been said, let me give you a sneak preview of chapter 9's main message: It's the quality of the product (not your minority status) that will get you *reorders,* and it's reorders that will keep you afloat in the long run. No reorders, no business.

ARE YOU STARTED YET?

Maybe after slogging through this chapter, you've decided that getting started is just as difficult as you suspected it was.

I hope not. My goal here has been to give you a sense of the key decisions that you may have to face as you get started in your business. Not all of these decisions will come at you at once. To some extent, at least, you can pace yourself. If things start to seem overwhelming, get help. Take "seven habits" guru Steven Covey's advice, and focus on what's both *urgent* and *important.* (You'll be surprised at how much of what you're dealing with is both urgent and unimportant.)

And as soon as time allows, study the next chapter: Building the company.

6

BUILDING THE COMPANY

Think of the material in the last chapter as covering the gestation and birth of your company. This chapter focuses on getting your company through infancy and adolescence—fun and challenging stages of development, especially for low-risk, high-reward entrepreneurs.

Building your company, like getting your company started, begins with planning. It continues with managing the suppliers and professionals upon whom you'll have to depend, with gaining credibility in the marketplace, and with building competencies.

Great products and services are equally important, of course. They are so important that I've pulled them out and put them in their own chapter (chapter 7).

PLANNING FOR A BETTER (AND MAYBE BIGGER) COMPANY

Planning is a critical tool for building your company. Perhaps your main goal is to run a small company brilliantly—or perhaps you're aiming for the Fortune 500. In either case, you'll need to *plan*.

Sometimes I think it would be simpler for every company to have only two executives. Their titles would be "vice president for today" and "vice president for tomorrow." This would sure help in keeping the emphasis on *both* time frames. The problem is that in most small businesses, the entrepreneur has to wear both hats. So life is always a juggling act: putting out the fires, getting orders, surviving today, and planning for tomorrow; so we can grow and maybe not have so many crises. As much as I believe in the validity of "going with your gut," your decision making will be greatly enhanced with good, consistent planning, including changes of the plan as needed.

Even a sole proprietor, bootstrap, start-up entrepreneur needs some type of planning. It can be in your head, on a napkin, or an elaborate business plan for investors. Whatever your style, you should get in the habit of writing your plans down. This way, you can revisit them to measure your progress, or to make the requisite changes. It also helps your employees or partners learn the game plan.

Your planning process, which is an ongoing process, should include at least ten key factors:

1. Goals

These can include things like dollar profits desired, when to exit from the company (if at all), style of life you want, non-profit contributions you wish to achieve, the extent of the risk you will embrace, and so on.

2. Strategy and tactics

Which strategies will you follow, and which tactics will you employ, to achieve your goals? Will yours be an upscale product with limited distributors, or will you go for more popular prices and solicit mass movers? How will you promote your product or service in light of your resources? How will you differentiate yourself from the competition?

3. Timing

The timing question is often overlooked in the early life of a company. How critical is timing in your launch? Do you have a good idea and plan, which may be hurt because you are too late (or too early) to market?

4. Risk

How much risk are you willing to take? How much can you afford— today, and tomorrow? (Look back to chapter 3 for more thoughts on risk and risk management.)

5. Managing your people

After you get the right people on board, the company's growth is going to be closely related to their performances. You can't do it by yourself. This is something that founding entrepreneurs often find difficult to accept. Well, *accept* it! You need to multiply yourself through your people. And to do this, you'll need to put lots of energy into managing and motivating them.

There are a wide variety of approaches to this challenge. Here are three specifics that illustrate that variety. Don Bakehorn says, "Yes, we provide them with decent wages and fringe benefits. But mostly we give them *independence,* and in my experience, that's what's important."

Bud Pironti offers his own version of the same advice. "Simply saying, 'It's my way or the highway' never works," he says. "You've got to spend the time getting your staff embracing your ideas. Or even better, in a lot of cases: You've got to embrace *their* ideas."

"I try to hire well and then let them fall off the cliffs," says John Korff. "I figure you've got to make your share of mistakes. I just tell them, 'Make your mistakes once, and make them quickly. Try a lot of things, and assume that half of them won't work. But make sure the other half *does* work. Keep looking for new ways to do things. Figure out what went wrong with the bad stuff, and don't do that again.'"

Of course, money is very important to your employees. But in my experience—and in the experience of most entrepreneurs I talk to—it's not the main motivator in doing a great job. People want to be listened to, respected, and given responsibility. They want to know clearly what you expect of them. If they're good, they want to be given tasks and they want the authority to carry them out.

Money can be a major source of conflict, and usually needs to be handled in different ways at different stages of your company's life. When you have few employees, you can be flexible, and you can handle everything personally. I liked to pay average wages and gave large bonuses based on company profits. In some cases, bonuses were based on measurable performance; in others, they were totally subjective. (Striking the balance between individual performance and high performance as a team member may be important in your particular business setting.) Of course, when business was good, people were ecstatic with their financial rewards. When times got tougher, they were less ecstatic, in part because they had come to depend on those large bonuses.

As implied above, non-financial issues are at least as important as financial ones. Remember to make a priority out of talking to your people regularly, giving them feedback, and *getting* feedback. These don't have to be formal reviews (although those are necessary at regular intervals, preferably on a different cycle from compensation reviews). Use the opportunity of an individual success to pat that individual on the back; and if relevant, use this opportunity to suggest things that might also be improved.

Don't let poor performance go uncorrected. You owe it to yourself, your coworkers, and your company to keep people on track. Be assured that your other employees know who's slacking off, and who's incompetent—and they're not happy about that, and they're watching to see how you handle the situation.

There's no magic bullet. Many poor performers simply don't know how they're doing in a relative sense. Tell them early and succinctly. Keep notes on these meetings in case an unhappy worker later decides to file a lawsuit.

Firing people can be the most difficult management task you'll ever experience. Sometimes it can be avoided by straightening things out. But if a sincere effort to straighten things out fails, cut the cord. (Your prior efforts to make things work may help you feel okay about this.) Remember that keeping someone in an unhappy situation is no favor to them. If they can't do better with you, they deserve the opportunity to do better somewhere else.

6. Money

After you have your initial financing, start to plan for how you will get more. Odds are that you'll need it. Either you miscalculated your needs, you've come up against unforeseen crises, or you've developed faster than you anticipated.

It is important and desirable to stay ahead of the curve on your money needs. The time taken to focus on money needs is usually well rewarded. When you are short of money, your total focus will be on it, to the exclusion of other things needed to properly run your business. You can't effectively sell or create new products when your time and energies are drained on scrambling to get invoices paid, stalling creditors, and hustling to get cash to meet the payroll or the rent.

7. Culture

I wrote at some length in chapter 5 about the mission statement. If you took my advice in that chapter, you already have a strong and specific statement hanging on the wall in conspicuous places, and this statement is going a long way toward defining your corporate culture.

CULTURE IN YOUR WALLET

A key challenge in culture building is to make your company's "cultural goals" *real* to your employees. The first step, of course, is getting to the right statement of what you're all about. But the next step is keeping those ideas in the front of people's minds.

To help solve this challenge, Hamid Moghadam of AMB Property adopted a technique used by Johnson & Johnson and other progressive companies. He printed the seven points of his company's mission statement on a wallet-sized card, which is given to all new employees. It reads as follows (note the attitude toward "risk" in the last entry, and note the phrase spelled out verically):

I The structure of our business must rest on a foundation of INTEGRITY. Our word is our bond.

C If our CUSTOMERS' needs are met, we will prosper.

R All of our actions must be directed to achieving concrete RESULTS. We will not engage in process for process' sake.

E Our mission for today is producing work of EXCELLENCE. Our mission for tomorrow is improvement.

A Each and every member of the organization must be ACCOUNTABLE. Each and every member of the organization will have our respect and trust.

T We are a TEAM. We will communicate openly and value diversity of outlook and opinion.

E We are ENTREPRENEURIAL. We add value by taking calculated risks. We are prepared to make mistakes, acknowledge our mistakes, and learn from them.

Consult it whenever "cultural" issues arise.

Corporate cultures emerge in different ways. Sometimes the corporate culture is simply a personification of the entrepreneur, which obviously can be either a good thing or a bad thing. In other cases, the entrepreneur is so buried in problems that a culture gets created that does not reflect his or her values, or the values that he or she wants for the company.

Remember that *it is very difficult to change established cultures.* Better to anticipate cultural issues, and spend an appropriate amount of time on them, than to undo bad habits that have already emerged. For example: How will you build trust? How accessible will you be to your employees? (Don't talk about an "open door" policy unless you mean it!) How much information are you willing to share with your people? How will you truly encourage your people to be innovative? Will you tolerate office politics? Is continuous learning for everyone important to you, and if so, what will you do to foster it? Is being a good citizen in the community on your radar screen? If so, what actions will you take to be one?

Managing suppliers

Of course, your approach to managing suppliers needs to be part of your strategic plan. But I'm calling this out as a separate topic here because of its critical importance. Almost every company, whether product or service oriented, is dependent on suppliers. Many people seem to get this supplier issue wrong. They feel that because they write the order, they are in the dominant position and can act in unkind and unfair ways toward their suppliers.

Please let's get this right! You need good and reliable suppliers. When you find them, treat them like gold. I personally don't want gifts from suppliers. For every lunch or dinner they buy me, I want to match it and buy them. Work as hard on building a supplier relationship as with any other one.

Be loyal to your good ones. They are essential to your good health, and your growth.

How suppliers impact you

Let's briefly look at all the ways they can impact your company:

- **Quality.** Whether you purchase a component, finished product, or service, suppliers can positively or negatively affect the quality of your product.

- **Timeliness.** Their timely deliveries are crucial to your reliability to your customers. Their quick turnaround becomes the key to your minimization of inventory, which in turn translates to less risk of inventory obsolescence and lower cash needs.
- **Competitiveness.** They can keep you competitive, and one-up on your competition, based on their pricing, quality, reliability, and technological breakthroughs. They can keep you abreast of these and other industry trends.
- **Innovation.** They can make major contributions to your new product development. Remember, they live their product more than you do. They are also working to be on the cutting edge of innovation of their product. The good ones will understand your company, its industry, and your needs, and help you accordingly in your new idea execution.
- **Finance.** They can be a major and constant source of financing for you. I mentioned this earlier: Your payment terms to them can be an important source of money. Their extended terms don't usually carry interest. If over a period of time you've proven to be a considerate, loyal, and growing customer, you may be able to tap into your suppliers for additional financing in your growth mode—or if you run into a cash crunch. It may take the form of postponed debt, extended terms on new purchases, a loan, or an investment in your company.

To maximize the benefits your supplier can deliver to you, it is important that you be open with them. Include them in some of your strategy meetings, invite them to break bread, visit their offices, invite them to meetings with your people, including companywide ones or office parties or picnics. In other words, work hard on building a good relationship with them.

Having said how valuable and important a supplier can be to you, I'll now say that you should not be a patsy. You can be a demanding customer—just be *fair.* State your quality and time needs clearly. Hold your suppliers to their agreements. Make sure they stay competitive. Tell them you expect never to pay higher prices than other purchasers.

Let them know you are there for the long term, as long as they perform and can keep pace with your growth. There are times you need to replace a supplier, because you have outgrown them and they can't perform to your new expectations. Before dropping them, however, I would try to educate or help them change to keep up with you. Failing that, you might be able to throw them some bones, in the hope that over time, they can change and grow to meet the needs of your new business model.

As you grow, you may find that it's not prudent to rely on one supplier. If that supplier has a strike or a fire, you don't want to be in a position where you'd be shut down, too. So develop a second or multiple suppliers, and don't be embarrassed to tell your key supplier that you're doing so. They will appreciate your honesty. If they are savvy, they will also know you need backup suppliers on key products or services, if you are to raise money. The lenders are sure to ask this question.

Imagine, for example, that yours is a mail-order company that ships all its products to consumers. Your sole supplier is UPS. What happens if UPS goes on strike? Well, it happened recently, and many companies that were overly dependent on UPS are now well acquainted with Federal Express and other shippers.

Assume that you have two competent suppliers, and that each knows about the existence of the other. In most such situations, you can encourage a healthy competition between the two, which may well lead to better and cheaper service to you.

Hamid Moghadam carries this one step further. He does a modest but structured "performance review" on each of his suppliers—including an overall grade—and then sits down with each company and goes over its review. He tells them where they stand in the bigger picture of suppliers, and promises them that a better performance will earn them a bigger piece of the pie.

10. How to be a valued customer

These ideas assume, of course, that you are a customer that somebody out there *wants*. Don't take this for granted! In order to be a valued customer to your suppliers, here are a few good things you should do:

- **Pay your bills on time.** For the sake of emphasis, I'll repeat this one: *Pay your bills on time!* You can negotiate for favorable payment terms before you place an order, but once the order is placed, don't renege or attempt to change the rules.

  Always pay on time. If for some reason you can't, call up your suppliers and tell them why, and then tell them when you *will* pay. Don't play games with suppliers' cash. You'll be absolutely amazed at the goodwill and benefits you will earn by observing this simple rule.

Don't let your bookkeeper or comptroller think he or she is a hero if he/she succeeds in stalling payments. In fact, I personally would come down hard on anybody who tried to do that as a general rule. My question to that person would be, "Who do you think is going to get deliveries when there is a shortage of product? The prompt payer or the staller?"

- **Provide adequate lead times.** Try to give suppliers as much lead time as possible on your orders. Unless there's a good competitive reason *not* to, share with them your *honest* projections of your needs, and then keep them abreast of any significant changes in that estimation. In developing your lead times, try to be knowledgeable about your supplier's production methods and needs.
- **Share information.** Keep your good suppliers aware of what's going on in your company. Tell them about changes in key personnel, new products, special promotions, new markets, and so on. Many times, you'll find that good suppliers can be helpful to you in developing new business.

Developing good suppliers and dealing with them effectively is not a complicated process. Tell them of your needs and standards, treat them fairly, be demanding, be loyal, be communicative, and *pay them on time.*

MANAGING PROFESSIONALS

From the outset, and increasingly as you grow, you are going to need an array of professional help: lawyers, accountants, bankers, perhaps even consultants. In all cases, I'd advise you to remember that *these professionals work for you,* and not the other way around. They are, in effect, extensions of your staff, hired to provide technical assistance in their particular area of expertise in order to help you make better business decisions.

Yes, they can sometime be intimidating, especially if you feel like you or your company is on unfamiliar ground. To compound this problem, many consultants want to offer not advice, but *decisions.* But remember that some of these resources are legends mainly in their own minds. (How many consultants are actually running a business, like you are, or have ever run a business?) So, ultimately, the critical business decisions are yours to make. This means you have to separate the expertise from the business.

A few words on a some of the key categories:

- **Lawyers.** We need them, but not for everything. In a subsequent chapter, you'll read about copyrights and other legal protections. This is a good illustration of a larger point: you'll probably find that you want to use a lawyer the first time you secure a copyright. After you learn these kinds of ropes, though, you may conclude that legal advice is unnecessary when it comes to securing copyrights.

  After using lawyers on license contracts a number of times, I decided that I could save a considerable amount of money by working out those contracts myself. Think this through on a case-by-case basis, and play it safe. When it comes to international licensing agreements—for example—I *always* get local counsel involved.

  I prefer to do my own negotiating on the business end of a deal, and keep the attorneys more or less away from those negotiations. After I reach an agreement in principle with my counterpart across the table, I then bring in an attorney to write it up in a way that protects (1) the agreement, and (2) my legal interests. Of course, there are circumstances in which a good lawyer is a better negotiator than the entrepreneur. If that's true in your case—for the moment, or forever—by all means bring in the lawyers at the outset, but *tell them what you want, and what's important to you.*

  Give the lawyers guidelines. If time is a factor in getting a deal done, you must play an active role vis-à-vis your attorney, telling them what absolutely has to happen by what date. Some attorneys are inclined to drag things out (sometimes an outgrowth of being paid by the hour). They can also get caught up in ego games with the lawyer(s) on the other team. Your job is to keep your lawyers on track, and on task.

  As for fees, don't be embarrassed to ask ahead of time. I always try to put a cap on a potential legal fee. If you can get a lawyer to handle something on a contingency basis, that's great, but it's very rare, outside of high-stakes personal liability cases.
- **Accountants.** Most people—including me—need accountants for general tax guidance and for specific onerous tasks, such as filing tax returns. But they can do a lot more for you, particularly if you are a smaller company and don't have a bookkeeper or comptroller. They can be an outsource supplier to you for setting up sys-

tems, doing cash flows, running product costing, etc. As I stated strongly earlier, however, you *must have a handle on the key numbers* behind your company's operations.

So know how these numbers are obtained. Know the relationships between certain numbers, and how to use them. It's *your* job to see that the numbers are current. (Stale numbers are worse than useless, since they imply a precision that absolutely is not there.) Your accountant can be extremely helpful to you in performing these vital management tasks, but they remain your tasks.

One last thought: Accountants record history. You make it.

• **Bankers.** I wish I could say equally positive things about bankers, but by and large, I can't. Most don't take the trouble to understand either your business or your industry. Their business advice is usually designed to protect their interests, which *very often* are not the same as yours.

Beware of restrictions that bankers may try to put on the way you run your business. Think of it this way: very few bankers have entrepreneurial training or experience. When bankers make up rules for the conduct of your business, they almost certainly aren't aware of all the ways that those rules may affect your business—including some bad ways. It's your job to tell them how what they're proposing may be harmful to your competitive position.

Again, *don't be intimidated.* Banks, too, operate in a (more or less) competitive marketplace. You *can* negotiate the terms of that loan—either on its own merits, or as part of a bigger picture. Do you keep other accounts in that bank? (Would they be easy to move out?) Do you have other business, such as 401k money, that you could credibly steer in the direction of this bank, assuming the talks go well?

A major, major caution about banks: Try to get assurances *in writing* that they can't call in your loan, or refuse to renew it, if you perform according to your promises. On this issue, I'd be as friendly as necessary, but also very tough. You're perfectly willing to bet on yourself, and you're willing to be called to account if you don't keep your commitments. On the other hand, you don't want your loan called if the United States decides to bomb some Middle Eastern despot. (Not your problem!) You don't want your loan called because the Feds are scrutinizing the bank's real estate investments, or because the bank's investments in Latin America are going sour. (Not your problem!) You may not prevail on this one, but it's definitely worth a strong push on the front end.

Mike Hsieh recommends that you develop a relationship with more than one bank. He says that this is the best way to keep your bankers competitive and service-oriented, and I agree.

• **Consultants.** Many people, when they hear the word *consultant,* think of high-powered strategy wizards whispering in the CEO's ear. And yes, these types exist, but if your business is like most early stage companies, you won't have much to do with the "strategy boutiques" of the world. There are at least three good reasons:
  - You don't need the kind of advice they offer (yet)
  - They don't offer the kind of advice you need
  - You can't afford them (yet)

I'd emphasize the second point: many general consultants have surprisingly little real-world experience in business. As a result, they don't have much understanding about the kinds of problems you're dealing with every day. They can describe what life may be like for you if and when your company gets to the next stage of growth, but not necessarily how to get there.

The kind of consultant I'm willing to spend good time and money on is the person who has deep and specific expertise. The guy who designs, installs, and maintains your computer systems, for example, is worth his weight in gold. The woman who figures out the best health plan for your company is indispensable. Two general pieces of advice for dealing with these kinds of consultants:

1. Don't be overly impressed by the senior salesman for the consulting firm. (He pays himself well to be impressive.) If you like what this salesman tells you, ask to meet with the people who will *really* be working on the account. This is particularly important in creative work, such as advertising, where it's the writers and designers who will make or break your account. Get to know these junior people before you sign on the dotted line.

2. Make sure that your consultants have only one motivation: giving you the best possible solutions to your problems. Under no circumstances should your consultants realize any financial gains from a supplier as a result of having steered you toward that supplier. Don't be shy about this. If you think it's happening, ask.

GAINING CREDIBILITY

In the early and building stages of most companies, one big challenge is how to gain credibility in the marketplace, particularly with those whom you want to give you orders. You've developed a good internal business plan, your product is of a high quality and fills a need—but nobody knows who you are. Customers prefer to buy from a familiar face, or at least a known quantity. This is one reason why companies spend a lot of time and money "building brand equity"; in other words, transforming themselves from an unknown to a known quantity.

Here are three basic ideas for building your company's credibility:

1. Be a publicity hound

Publicity is the great wild card for small businesses. Certainly, advertising and staged events serve very useful purposes. But a legitimate story in the media about you, your product, or your company generally carries far more weight than any sales pitch or stunt. Such a story is likely to reach both consumers and any intermediate customers, such as retailers. And because management generally has more time to read than buyers and other middle-level people, a news story or human interest feature may have disproportionate impact on decision makers. And finally, the cost to you can range from minimal (an investment of your time) to more substantial, but is usually lower than the cost of "equivalent" advertising.

So, you like the sound of all these benefits. How do you get started?

If you have the money, hire a public relations firm. Try to retain a company that has prior experience with (1) your kind of products or services, and (2) the kind of media you want to reach. If you are inclined to hire a large PR firm, ask to meet with the person who will be working directly on your account. In all cases, ask to see a proposed plan or approach to the job before you commit. I'd recommend interviewing more than one company, and I'd definitely ask for, and check, references. This may surprise you, but I'd be suspicious of any PR people who "guaranteed" results. Unlike advertising, there are no guarantees either that something will appear in the media or that you'll *like* what appears.

You don't have to make a long-term commitment; you can hire a PR firm on a trial basis—say, ninety days. (Remember: *low risk, high reward*.) Once the firm is retained, plan on being an active participant in their activities. In general, reporters like to meet with the person who started the company, or who is running it today. If that's you, be available and helpful. Make sure you understand and approve of the "angle" that your PR firm is pitching, and to which the media are responding.

If you can't afford a PR firm, or don't like the approaches you're hearing, you may be able to get the ball rolling yourself. One way is to go after your local newspaper. Think of that paper as a giant furnace that needs constant stoking, and think of your story as tomorrow's (or next Sunday's) fuel. They may not know it, but they *need* you. Read the paper thoroughly, and decide which department or columnist is the best fit with your product, service, or company. Make a phone call or write a letter to that department or individual, asking for an in-person meeting.

In this initial overture, and also in the follow-up meeting, your job is to pique their interest. Give them the kind of material they need. What's interesting about you? Is it the way you came up with the idea for the business? Is there something unusual in your background, or the way the company is structured? Are you providing good jobs locally? Is your product indicative of a new trend?

Of course, this is harder to pull off if your local newspaper is the *New York Times* or the *Washington Post*. But these media giants, too, need stories every day, and they generally have an informal quota of locally oriented stories that they want to include. Think creatively about the different sections of your targeted newspaper, especially if it's a big and complicated paper. How many could you possibly be of interest to, in addition to the business section?

Another interesting but generally difficult approach is to solicit the wire services (Bloomberg, Reuters, AP, Knight-Ridder, etc.) directly. These companies are also in the "fuel-providing" business, but on a large scale—a story from one of these services can appear in hundreds of newspapers around the country. The farther you get from home, of course, the tougher this sell gets, but it's worth a try. *They need you,* in some cases as much as you need them.

Remember, too, that this pipeline goes both ways. Stories by individual newspapers can get picked up by a wire service and garner national attention. There was a famous 1973 incident in which poultry magnate Frank Perdue lost a critically important yellow legal pad—one that contained the results of a month-long survey of butchers and retailers in the Boston area. Perdue, determined to retrieve his invaluable data, wound up going through mountains of garbage on a pier in South Boston. Against all odds, he found the pad. The story was written up by a local reporter, and within a week had shown up in literally hundreds of papers. Perdue went from being an unknown quantity—just another guy selling chickens—to being a known quantity ("that fanatic who was willing to go through piles of garbage to find his notes").

Don't overlook the other media that are out there, either. Many consumer magazines, for example, run "new product" sections. Someone in your company should regularly submit pictures and short descriptions of your new products to these kinds of outlets. You may be surprised at how many of these descriptions get picked up verbatim, and at how that translates into good orders. Similarly, most medium-sized and larger cities have at least one locally oriented magazine (*Boston, Philadelphia, New York,* and so on) that can be fertile ground for your story idea or new product description.

Industry magazines, newsletters, and papers are almost always excellent prospects for free publicity. In many cases, they will run your releases about new products. Most have reporters on staff who are on the lookout for good stories for the next issue; get to know them. There's a common misperception that you only get coverage in these trade publications if you also buy advertising space; but in my experience, that's not true. If you want to buy advertising, fine; it can't hurt your chances. But your immediate goal should be to sell them on your bright prospects. This is the news story they're looking for. And incidentally, the brighter your prospects look, the more likely it is that these media will look at you as a potential advertiser.

In many ways, TV is the most powerful medium of all. It's visual, visceral, and far better at evoking and implying things. But the economic stakes are much higher, and it's therefore that much harder to get attention from the TV crowd. On a more mundane note, remember that print stories can sometimes serve your subsequent purposes better than a TV feature. Mailing videos to people doesn't have the same impact as mailing photocopies of newspaper or magazine stories. (So far, it seems, people just don't play unsolicited videos, whereas they definitely seem to scan unsolicited news clips.) So send those story ideas and new product descriptions to your local TV stations, and follow up—but don't do so at the expense of other, more accessible media, including radio.

Above all, be persistent and tenacious. Don't be shy about tooting your horn, or about calling the same elusive person for the fiftieth time. Be the pit bull of publicity hounds!

2. Trade on someone else's good name

You are known for the company you keep (as well as the company you are). There are several ways to bask in reflected glory. For example, you can run an ad for your product featuring your most prestigious customers. There's some chance that those customers will kick in some money to support your ad, but don't count on it, at least in the early stages.

Even better (and certainly cheaper) is getting your customers to build you into *their* ads. When we were building our game company in the upscale market, we looked to run ads for our products with stores like Bloomingdale's and Brentano's, which were then dominant game retailers. We worked hard to get them to put our name in the ad: ". . . By Reiss Games!" It was amazing how many other retailers bought into our products after we showed them these ads.

The good news was that we didn't need a lot of money to pull this off. We (like our competition) built a sum of money for an "ad allowance" into our product. In other words, we rebated to our customers 10 percent of their purchases toward advertising. If the opening order wasn't enough to cover the ad cost, we would advance the balance to ensure our ad with these strategic customers, at the outset. Similarly, you can encourage a key targeted customer to run an ad with your product and your name by giving them an exclusive on the product for an agreed-upon period—say, thirty days.

Another good tactic is to use established sales representatives (reps). Trade on the good name of these sales reps to get orders from your targeted accounts. In the next chapter, I'll go into greater detail on how reps work, and on how to get orders, in general. But it makes sense to introduce reps here as part of your larger credibility-gaining strategy.

Be aware that you'll probably have to do a substantial sales job on the good ones to get them to take your line. But this investment is well worth it. First, and most important in the short run, your fixed cost for employing these established reps will be zero (they mostly get paid on commission). And in the long run, once you've established a mutual rapport and proven that your company has talent and staying power, these reps can help you hire on additional reps in other territories.

Partnering with established entities, preferably with a tie to your products, can also be a good credibility builder. When we produced a line of magic-related products, we approached the Society of American Magicians, a prestigious national organization, and offered to help them promote National Magic Week by sending local magicians into J. C. Penney stores around the country to demonstrate magic.

The Magic Castle Club in Beverly Hills features highly skilled magicians (in addition to good food). One weekend, we paid their magicians to demonstrate our products in all thirty-one Broadway Department Stores (a prominent Los Angeles chain). In return, Broadway ran full-page newspaper ads and radio spots about the event, which included a drawing at each store for a dinner for two at the Magic Castle. (Broadway paid for these ads.) So it was a win–win–win–win. The Magic Castle and Broadway got good publicity at an affordable price. A group of magicians got the chance to make some good money doing what they liked to do, in front of mostly appreciative audiences. And we got our products into a leading chain, and also had our name publicly associated with two respected institutions.

Last but not least, don't overlook the power of endorsements. Certain products and services lend themselves to endorsement by celebrities and other prominent individuals. The relationship can be direct (athletes endorsing breakfast cereals, doctors endorsing health products) or more tenuous (athletes endorsing high-end wristwatches). Somewhat more difficult to pull off, but often less expensive, is the man-on-the-street endorsement: "Down at Joe's Diner, here's what they're saying about the new all-night cough medicine."

3. License something

Licensing is another way to gain credibility—instantly—by trading on someone else's good name. I've licensed things throughout my professional career. Here's how it works:

Licensing is the process whereby one company uses the trademark, property, or brand name of another company in return for some form of compensation. In most cases, the licensor grants the licensee some sort of exclusivity—perhaps geographical, perhaps by product, perhaps by distribution channel. Most often, the compensation involves some sort of up-front fee and a percentage of sales (a *royalty*).

For instance? Let's take one of the most famous and successful of all. When someone buys a watch featuring an image of Mickey Mouse, you can be sure that the manufacturer of that product is paying the Walt Disney Company a royalty for the use of that image. Similarly, a company that makes Bugs Bunny Clocks pays Warner Bros. a royalty, and a capmaker that makes Dallas Cowboy caps pays a fee to NFL Properties.

There's an amazing range of products for which licenses are issued. They include, for example, limited-run automobiles, perfume, plates, cereals, vitamins, clothing, jewelry, and beverages. The number and volume of licensed products seems to grow each year, and in 1998 amounted to something like $144 billion at retail worldwide.

Why go this route? There are at least six good reasons:

- *More credibility in selling into established distribution channels.* This is particularly true for start-ups. The right name of the license on your product will get you in the front door with your target customer. If this particular licensor's goods have performed well in this distribution channel in the past, your product is less risky for this retailer. Your potential customer may not have heard of you, but they most likely will have heard of your licensor.
- *Better profit margins.* A license takes your product out of the commodity class—it's not just a watch; it's a *Mickey Mouse* watch!—and simultaneously protects your product from being knocked off. This, in turn, means that you can build and maintain higher profit margins, despite the higher selling price that is necessitated by the pass-along of royalty charges.
- *Better sell-through.* Because consumers recognize and (hopefully) like this brand or image you've licensed, they will pull your product through the distribution channels, and this will lead to the re-orders that will keep you in business.
- *Better products.* In some cases, a licensee licenses a process or a technology, which permits the licensee to make a more valuable product, and get into markets that he or she otherwise couldn't penetrate.
- *Access to capital.* A good license will assist you in getting capital (whether invested or loaned). Smart "money people" know the value of an appropriate license.
- *More company value, more quickly.* A successful licensed product builds the value of your company, which will help you if you sell, go public, or merge.

In light of all these benefits, licensing may sound like a gold mine. In many ways, it is. (I know lots of people who have gotten wealthy producing licensed goods.) But as in all other realms of business, there are questions to be answered, rules to be followed, and obstacles to be overcome on the road to success.

The first question you need to answer, *honestly,* is whether your product is good, and whether there is a demand for it. Just as great advertising can't sustain an inferior product indefinitely, a good license can't rescue a bad product. Don't pay somebody else money for the right to produce a product that nobody wants.

The second thing to be aware of is that licensing is a competitive field. Lots of people want to use Mickey Mouse's face. As a result, Disney can afford to be choosy and expensive—and it is.

What does a potential licensor want to see, when he looks at you? One major licensor, Peter Van Raalte, former VP of Turner Entertainment and currently VP with Scholastic Entertainment, Inc., told me that he looks for six things when evaluating a potential licensee:

- distribution
- distribution
- distribution
- creativity and quality
- appropriate positioning of the property; and
- financial responsibility

In my experience, *all* licensors put an overwhelming emphasis on distribution. They are granting you a valuable right in the expectation that you can get enough orders in markets where they think their products should be available. This means that you are likely to be asked about your distribution capability. Although this is in many cases an obstacle, it may also be an opportunity. Licensors with strong properties are increasingly inclined to award licenses by *channel of distribution.* If your company is new, and inhabits an unusual niche—say, downloadable Internet games—a channel-specific license may present a special opportunity.

When licensors appraise you as a potential licensee, they will check your references with retailers and other licensors (if any). They will want to know your market strategy, point-of-product differences, quality, and on-time delivery record, and they will want reassurances that you have the financial strength to do a good job with the property. And finally, they may want to explore whether your corporate philosophy and culture fit well with their own. (Here's another good reason to be able to speak concisely and compellingly about the mission of your company.)

Looking at licensing from the other end of the periscope: As a licensee, you have to choose your licensed product with care. Here are some sensible questions to ask:

- Does this relate to the consumer of my product? (Do I want a Big Bird license for my watch company, if I'm convinced that most preschoolers can't tell time and don't wear watches?)
- Is this a good fit with my product? (If I make farm implements, how valuable is a ready-to-wear designer brand name?)
- Do the buyers in my major channels of distribution think highly of this license? (How hard will they work for it if they don't?)
- Can I afford the guarantee, advance payment, and other commitments related to this product? Are the royalties too high for the product? Is this license strong enough to make up for the higher retail price it will have to command?
- Is this a license I want to put resources into and build for the long term, or is its value short term or tactical—e.g., to sell one account or one channel of distribution?
- What's the reputation of the licensor? Will they renew my contract if I do a good job? Will they award too many licenses to competitors in my category? What type of artwork will they provide, and at what cost? How long is their approval process? Is their contract fair, and can I live with it?
- What is the licensor's policy when major national retailers come to the licensor to give them exclusive product? (This is a growing trend.) Will they work through their licensee on the product category of interest, or will they do a direct deal and circumvent the licensee in this case? Most licensing contracts are non-exclusive, and would therefore allow the licensor to make these deals directly with a retailer.

Contracts deserve a closer look. While every licensing relationship is different, here are the eight broad topics that may come up in negotiations for a license:

- *Geographic territory covered.* This may be, for example, a regional or national slice. Because people around the world are beginning to place a high value on American licenses—the Japanese, for example, are fans of the NFL, Elvis, and anything Tiffany—many large licensors will attempt to restrict your license to U.S. domestic sales. They are less likely to restrict you if they can be persuaded that your company is competent to sell your products internationally. What evidence can you produce to make that case?
- *Products to be covered by the license.* Again, the licensor is naturally inclined to define this narrowly; your effort should be to define it broadly. Think carefully about product extensions when you negotiate your first license. If you're a wristwatch manufacturer, make sure mantel clocks and pocketwatches are also covered by the license. (Your contract should refer to "timepieces" rather than "watches.") Keep in mind that it's far easier to get broad definitions in the initial contract than in a later contract—especially if you do well, and thereby underscore how valuable the license is.
- *Rates of royalty.* Unfortunately, this is not usually open to creative negotiations, except in the case where you (as the licensee) are dominant in your product category. Royalty rates range from 2 percent to 20 percent. They are generally paid on wholesale sales, but in some industries, they are paid on retail. In some cases, royalties are a flat fee per year (or some other time period).

  Make sure that your contract explicitly defines what constitutes a "sale" on which royalties will be due (and at what rate). If a customer fails to pay you, are you still responsible for the royalty? If you discount your goods, are you responsible for paying royalties on regular prices or discounted prices?
- *Length of contract.* Most licensors want to give two years to new licensees. (This is long enough to provide a fair test, but not so long that the licensor will give up too much opportunity.) In very large or unique deals, five years or more is appropriate, especially if you will be required to make a large investment to make your licensed products. You should definitely try to get automatic renewals of your license—preferably without qualification, but if necessary based on performance.
- *Guarantees.* Most licensors will demand a guarantee of a specified number of dollars, either for the duration of the contract or for

each year of the contract. Licensees should seek the former, to avoid hard times as a result of a poor selling year.

- Guarantees vary greatly, depending on the perceived potential volume of the product, competitiveness within the product category, strength of the licensee's distribution network, the patentability of the product, the licensee's track record in this product category, the licensor's level of promotional activity, and so on. Currently, most big-name licenses have a $25,000 annual minimum floor, but this

LICENSES: TAKING THE FIRST STEPS

The first step toward getting a license is to find out who is authorized to grant it to you. In many cases, the name of the licensor of a brand that you're interested in can be found on products already in the marketplace. Beyond that, here are some good places to look:

The *Licensing Industry Merchandisers Association* (LIMA) is the industry trade group. They put out a resource directory, which includes licensors, licensees, and support services such as license agents and consultants (see below). Contact them at

LIMA
350 Fifth Avenue, Suite 2309
New York, NY 10018
212-244-1944
212-563-6552 (fax)
www.licensing.org

The *Licensing Report,* an informative newsletter about the licensing industry, is published weekly by

Adventure Publishing Group, Inc.
1501 Broadway
New York, NY 10036
212-575-4510

Continued on next page

EPM Communications produces a semi-monthly newsletter, and an annual sourcebook which includes licensors, licensees, agents, and consultants. Contact them at

160 Mercer Street
New York, NY 10012
212-941-0099

Once you've determined who controls the property that you're interested in, you can go one of two ways:

1. *You can hire a licensing agent (or licensing consultant).* These are people who make their living securing licenses for manufacturers. As in all trades, some are good and some aren't so good, so you'll have to do due diligence before signing on with an agent. By and large, though, licensing agents have good access, and can usually get you an appointment with the right people. (Some licensors also use agents to sell their licenses.) They can be extremely helpful, especially for novices in the licensing game. They can guide you in preparing your presentation, and tell you more or less what you'll be up against in your efforts to secure the license—royalty rates, guarantees, competitors, etc.

   Compensation for these agents can be a fixed fee, a percentage of the property's wholesale sales (usually 1 to 5%), or some combination of the two.

2. *You can contact the licensor directly.* In most cases, your initial contact with a potential licensor will generate an application that you'll have to fill out. You'll be asked for information regarding your yearly projections for sales of the licensed product for the next three years, the channels of distribution into which you sell, the other licenses you currently hold, the number of salespeople you use, your marketing plan for the product, how much you plan to spend promoting the product, the proposed retail price point, where the product will be made, your financials, and so on. In other words, they want evidence that you've got a sensible plan. If your application gets over the licensor's initial hurdles, you can then arrange a meeting to further plead your case.

minimum can go up into the millions of dollars for an established, high-volume product.

- *Promotional dollars.* In many cases, licensors today are demanding promotional dollar assessments from their licensees. These dollars may be for ads to consumers, or to the trade. The rationale is that their promotions are helping you, so you should kick in for this service. You can try to negotiate this one, but the tide is running against the licensee. You may also be asked by the licensor to commit a specified amount of money to promote the licensed product.
- *Advances.* After the guarantee is established, most licensors will ask for some sum of money in advance. The advance generally ranges between 10 and 50 percent of the guarantee. Licensors believe that high cash advances motivate licensees to invest more of their resources in the product, to stay focused, and to come to market sooner. (Sometimes they're right.) But I would make the case that

13 TIPS FOR EFFECTIVE LICENSING

Here are some nitty-gritty tips intended to help you get a good license on good terms, and then to perform successfully as a licensee.

1. *Get in the deal stream.* There is an annual national licensing show in New York City in early June, and most major licensors exhibit there. It's an excellent place to meet people in the industry.
2. *As always, do your homework.* Check with other licensees about the character of this particular licensor. Many licensors will let you build the category and then, when you seek to renew, attempt to increase their royalties dramatically. Some will add other licensees in your category, creating direct and unplanned competition for you. For these reasons and others, get a good feeling for the "ethics quotient" of the licensor you're planning to partner with.
3. When considering a new license, *get a list of current licensees to see the kinds of companies with which you'll be associated.* (This is also a key piece of doing due diligence on a licensor.) Most licensors will give you this list if you ask for it.

Continued on next page

4. *Be fully prepared for your first meeting with the prospective licensor.* You have to demonstrate that you know the product, the market, and your own strengths. Good sketches or samples of how you will apply the license to your product can only enhance your prospects.

5. *When projecting your sales, be very careful in establishing estimates.* Using high estimates to woo the licensor will quickly come back to haunt you (they will use them to demand high guarantees). On the other hand, lowballing your estimates may cause you to lose out on a license in a competitive environment.

6. *Negotiate hard.* If you have a totally new product category or patented item, you should negotiate for more favorable terms.

7. *Negotiate smart.* There is a recent trend in retailing, particularly on the part of mass merchandisers who hold the balance of power, to have suppliers guarantee the sale of the products they sell. This is happening with licensed goods as well. Therefore, when working out your license contract, negotiate to pay royalties on sales, net of returns. Currently, many licensors insist on royalty payments based on shipments only, which means that returns from a guarantee sale are not credited.

8. Try to include a time factor in your contract governing approval of new products or artwork, and *try to make the default favor you.* For example: "If no approval or disapproval is forthcoming within two weeks of submission of the new product request, that product shall be deemed to be approved."

9. If the license involves artwork, *find out in advance what art is available for your use.* Find out, too, what process will be involved in creating new art work to meet your current or future needs.

10. *Think on your feet if that first meeting seems to be going off the rails.* Most licensors are reluctant to grant a license to new companies. Be prepared to overcome this resistance by demonstrating the uniqueness of your product, the depth of your management, your financial strength, your dominance in a given channel, your commitment to building their property, or whatever. If they're still negative—and if you *really* want this license—propose to take the product to a limited market, or for a limited time, to prove your abilities.

Continued on next page

11. Remember that once you get your license, *your work has just begun.* Develop relationships with as many people as possible in the licensing company. Stay in close touch with the account manager with whom you closed the deal, but also open up lines to art department employees, retail coordinators, top management, and so on. They can all help steer you to good accounts and new product ideas, and help you get approvals for your own new ideas.

12. *Keep the licensor fully informed about your activities.* Send them copies of your ads. Tell them about your successes. Run new ideas past them at an early stage. Get and keep them involved!

13. *Do a great job with your license.* Remember the deal stream in tip #1? This is a surprisingly small world for a $150 billion industry. Licensors talk to each other, follow each other's lead, and figure out which licensees (and manufacturers) do good jobs. In addition, individuals move from one licensor to another, carrying their estimations of your skills with them into a new context. The moral: Don't take on a license unless you're convinced that you can deliver good results.

as a small company, I should pay the *lowest* possible advance, so that I'll have the cash necessary to promote the property.

- *Exclusivity.* An exclusive right to make a licensed product gives more value to the licensee, and gives them good incentive to put more resources into building and promoting the product line. But most licensors, reluctant to give up potential royalties, don't like to give exclusives. There is sometimes room for negotiation on this point, especially if the licensee is willing to go along with higher guarantees.

CLOSING THOUGHTS

In this "company-building" chapter, I've focused on planning, managing suppliers, managing professionals, and gaining credibility. There are some big holes in this list. For example, what about getting, conserving, and spending money? What about finding, winning, and holding customers? What about planning for the longer term?

These topics are covered in other chapters (5, 8 and 9, and 10, respectively). I hope you'll look forward and backward in this book, (and, of course, many other places, too!) as you steer your company through its infancy and adolescence.

A critical part of that adolescence is building your product line—a topic that is explored in depth in the next chapter.

7

BUILDING YOUR PRODUCTS

As I noted in the introduction, I don't like huge organizations very much, but I *love* products. Here and elsewhere in this book, I use the word *products* to comprise the broadest possible range of manufactured products and services. The most notable difference between a producer of physical products and a service company is that the former must deal with inventory and all its potential problems, while the latter is more or less free of these inventory-related challenges.

My own experience is mainly in the realm of manufactured goods aimed first at retail stores and their buyers (and secondarily at the consumers who buy those goods). But I've also worked as a consultant who priced his services, and as a manager who purchased a lot of services. So I'm fairly aware of how the service world works, and I hope that most of what I present here pertains to a wide variety of goods and services.

Products are inseparable from profits. I spend a lot of time in this chapter focusing on profits and prices, and the subtle relationships between the two. I examine issues like sourcing, packaging, extending, and knocking off your products. And finally, I spend a few pages being explicit about the product management challenge. Products are like children: They thrive on your attention and discipline.

PROFITS

Your ultimate goal is to make your product yield a profit. Obvious, right? So much so that it's not worth mentioning? Well, yes and no. I'm always surprised to discover how many entrepreneurs take their eyes off this ball, elementary as it is. So I'll go ahead and restate the obvious: The sustainability of your enterprise is wrapped around achieving profits. How much and how soon, of course, depends on your product and your resources, the competition, your strategy, and other factors.

If your cash is limited, you will need profits quickly—that is, before your company runs out of cash. As far as I'm concerned, "trophy" customers and market share are secondary considerations. If your product is unique, your competition is outgunned, and the economy is strong, you are likely to command high prices and high profits.

Profits, prices, and service: all are more or less jumbled together in a confusing bundle, and it's your job to find a thread-end and untangle it. For example, if you make your product overseas instead of at home, your costs are likely to be lower and your profits higher. But as a result, you may well have a longer lead time requirement in shipping re-orders. That raises the question: Can your customers accept this re-order time? If not, you'll probably opt for local manufacturing.

In looking at profit questions, as explained in chapter 2, you absolutely must *know your product costs.* And after you've determined your costs, you'll have to settle on the profit margin your product must yield in light of your company's overhead and sales projections. Product profit margins can be the key to your growth—and indeed, your survival. A lower overhead with high percentages of variable costs can sustain a lower profit margin, which may in fact be dictated by your product's competitors in the marketplace. High product profits may allow you to go after smaller niche markets which may have more long-term sustainability than, say, department stores, which see themselves as "fashion retailers" and thus change their products often. In fact, they sometimes change for change's sake, even if the current product is selling well.

There are many reasons why entrepreneurs get distracted and lose their focus on profits. Some of these are external. For example, the *Inc. 500* listing—that magazine's annual list of the 500 fastest-growing companies in the United States—uses sales as the sole measurement for their selection. *Profits* are nowhere considered. It would be very interesting to look back and see how many companies crash and burn within a few years of making the *Inc. 500* list, and to ask whether those casualties had failed to pay attention to profits.

I think the "Amazon.com" phenomenon has the same bad impact on many entrepreneurs. This Internet-based merchandiser was Wall Street's darling in 1998, with its stock soaring in large part due to meteoric sales increases. But Amazon has never made a profit, and publicly states that it won't break even any time soon. The company's strategy is to build a brand and establish a dominant position in "e-commerce," and—given its relatively deep pockets—it may well win at this long-term gamble.

Most entrepreneurs can't afford to think or live this way. Of course, it's very tempting to trumpet your soaring sales figures and downplay the importance of profits. Sometimes that's a strategic call. But at other times, it's an ego thing: "Look at us; we're growing like crazy!" Eventually, though, this falls into the same category as other ego excesses: measuring your business by the size of your showroom, by the quality of furnishings in your corporate offices, by the kind of car you drive, or whatever.

My advice, therefore, is to *put profits first.* Indulge yourself with ego trophies only after you've created substantial profits. If you're tempted to follow a market share strategy, make sure you have adequate capital to survive up to the point when you're finally making a buck. Otherwise, set proper profit margins and make them a high priority in your thinking. Revisit the issue of margins and overhead regularly, in light of all the changes that may occur. These changes can be in costs, competition, economy, supply, strategy, your own resources, etc. You should always be able to answer this simple question: Are we making money?

GETTING NEW PRODUCT IDEAS

There's no single best approach to developing new product ideas. As I've noted in earlier chapters, new ideas come from a multitude of sources. Every individual is different, and so are their sources of inspiration.

In chapter 1, we examined the skills associated with creativity, and the need to build a creative environment. This involves, among other things, giving a respectful hearing to the new ideas that your employees come up with, building the company's knowledge base, talking with a broad range of constituencies, and so on. In chapter 4, I wrote about the challenge of getting the idea with which to launch your company—or what to do if you don't have any ideas.

Much of this earlier advice pertains to getting new ideas in an on-going business. In addition, I want to put some other interview voices on the table, all of whom have wrestled with the challenge of idea-generation:

Todd: "Sometimes you see a piece of information, and then you see another seemingly unrelated piece of information, and then you put the two together in your mind and come up with something new. So you have to prepare your mind for that kind of serendipity."

Peek: "I'm not really blessed with the capacity to come up with new ideas. I work around that. I use PR and advertising to get people to come to me with new ideas."

Shafir: "I don't turn down phone calls. You never know: maybe a vendor out there has a great new idea. I also hear a lot from our salespeople."

Blau: "Our ideas are all market-driven. We spend a lot of time with our customers, who tell us what they want."

Benassi: "We have some innovative competitors. So one of them will do something wrong, and then we'll figure out how to do it right."

Pironti: "We're always looking for new items. Therefore, we've got to have an open door policy to anybody who wants to come in. They've got to know that we'll respect their ownership of the idea, and that they'll get a quick decision. That's critical."

As Earl Peek's comments imply, a lot of companies go outside to buy their ideas. There are many individuals out there who do nothing but represent inventors. Going up the ladder a few rungs, there are large companies like Johnson & Johnson, Microsoft, and Hasbro that simply buy innovative companies, either to get ownership of a specific product line, or more generally to buy access to the creative people who are making that acquired company so innovative.

I like Barbara Todd's notion of preparing your mind. As your company grows, put someone in charge of coordinating, seeking, and developing new ideas—the "vice president of tomorrow," as I like to call that position.

PRODUCT "CONSTRUCTION"

Should you make your product out of plastic, composites, wood, glass, paper, metal, fabrics, or other materials, or some combination of materials? In the case of a service, should your service offer free follow-up advice, toll-free numbers, personal visits, guarantees, etc.?

In most cases, there are endless options and variables that might be used in the construction of your product, and you owe it to yourself and your company to examine their pros and cons carefully.

If I go with plastic instead of wood, how will my customer perceive the overall quality of my product? Can anybody still afford wood? Is there a weight differential? How does a wooden product fit with my distribution strengths? What's the availability of, and lead time for, the specified raw materials?

Is there a threshold above which I'm going to have to switch over to plastic? If so, can the plastic version of my product still be made economically in small runs? Are there onetime costs (such as molds) involved in going with plastic? Which choice is likely to go farther toward differentiating me from my competitors, both known and unknown? Am I more or less comfortable offering a warranty (of what length and comprehensiveness?) on a wooden product or a plastic product? Which construction will allow me to turn goods faster—a major goal in satisfying customers, reducing inventory needs and consequent risks, and also reducing cash requirements?

I've only used wood versus plastic to illustrate a way of thinking and questioning. In my experience, there are almost always more ways to skin a cat than are apparent at the outset. A thorough analysis of your options can yield very positive long-term results.

WHERE TO MAKE THE PRODUCT?

I've already introduced one of the complexities inherent in this decision. Overseas may mean lower costs, but may also mean (1) longer lead times and (2) bigger quality challenges. All things being equal, I like being within driving distance of my manufacturing sources, but I don't want to pay through the nose for that kind of comfort. Past a certain point, I'll go to China myself, or make sure I'm well represented there.

Overseas suppliers (as well as some domestic suppliers) often require larger-sized orders. This may mean that more of your cash will be tied up than would be the case with a domestic supplier. In addition, overseas suppliers often demand full payment by letter of credit or wire transfer before they'll release a shipment to you. If your company lives on a tight cash flow, this may be a substantial disadvantage to you.

These trade-offs need to be evaluated against your needs, your customers' needs, risks, and your resources. You don't necessarily want to include your customers in the nitty-gritty of these discussions, but you definitely want to find out how their needs (including, for example, domestic content) fit together with your opportunities. The more important the customer, the harder you'll want to try to meet their specific needs.

If you plan to manufacture your own product or be a manufacturer for other people, then similar analyses should be made. Additional concerns will also be important, including proximity to suppliers and the customer base, access to raw materials, the local labor pool, community incentives (or disincentives), the transportation grid, and so on.

Service providers mostly have the luxury of not having to deal with this question—yet. I'd be willing to bet, however, that service companies will have to be more and more creative when it comes to thinking through where the service providers themselves will be based. If I'm headquartered in San Francisco, do I need to pay San Francisco wages to enable my key associates to settle in San Francisco and raise families there? Or can I pay Terre Haute wages and put more money into the travel budget?

PACKAGING

Many times, the packaging of the product is as important as the product itself. Of course, if you're making a product like industrial machinery, this may not be true. But in the case of consumer products, packaging can be an overwhelmingly important element. Perhaps the most extreme case involves products bought by collectors, such as limited-edition Swatch watches. In such cases, the product's resale value is largely determined by the condition of its packaging. Savvy collectors rarely even open the box.

Another case in which the package was as important as the product—maybe even more important—was the L'Eggs phenomenon. These women's stockings were designed for sale in supermarkets, and were packaged in a two-piece container that looked like an egg. In other words, the producers of L'Eggs took a commodity product with high purchase frequency and put it in a package that was brilliantly designed for a particular channel of distribution. Publicity and praise showered down on this relatively humble product—and the "buzz" was all about the package.

Most companies that produce packaging materials have in-house design departments and can make you prototypes at no cost. There are also plenty of independent package designers who can help you on a fee basis. Consider using this kind of resource if you've concluded that a radical packaging departure is what's needed to get you out of the pack, and to get you recognized for what you are.

It is imperative, before you settle on outside help in packaging, to provide this proposed vendor with clear guidelines as to what you can afford to pay, the quantities you will need initially, and the reorder cycle you currently anticipate. Some vendors may disqualify themselves as either too big or too small for you, depending on the information you provide.

Experts are great, and I never shy away from hiring a good one whose services I need. But you should be aware that there are many places to go for packaging ideas. I myself like to shop cosmetics counters in department stores. (Cosmetics marketers are very innovative packagers. How else could you charge so much for water and other humble ingredients?) If you don't relish the idea of hanging around a cosmetics counter, go to a packaging trade show or a related industry trade show. Remember that you don't necessarily have to see packages for products that are just like your own. An innovative packaging idea that sells socks may also sell clocks.

We shouldn't overlook functionality in this discussion. Remember that packaging should *inform,* as well as attract the consumer's eye in a crowded store environment. I've seen lots of examples of razzle-dazzle packaging that neglected to say what was inside the package. This is a mistake. One way or another, your packaging should communicate clearly the product's potential benefits to the prospective buyer.

In addition to flagging down the consumer and explaining the product's benefits, the packaging also has to protect that product. Depending on the nature of the product, functional needs may overwhelm aesthetic needs. If your product is glass, your packaging had first better protect something that's fragile. (Light bulb packaging comes to mind.) Point-of-sale considerations may also affect your packaging dramatically. If your product is generally sold from the box and not taken out (usually a lower-priced product), then colored labels on that box, showing the product to its best effect, may be the right packaging solution.

Be sure to put your company name and/or logo prominently on the package. This is a no-cost way to build your brand.

Is your product likely to be given as a gift? If so, that's likely to raise the packaging stakes. Will your product be sold in a display? If so, will that display be created by you or by a customer? If you're uncertain how to answer these questions, or why they're important, it's probably time to call in one of those experts I mentioned earlier. They'll have a list of questions that they'll want you to answer before they undertake the design of your package. Getting the right answers to these kinds of questions up front will save you time and money in the long run.

No, a great package can't save a lousy product. But sizzle sells, and packaging creates sizzle. Good product with sizzle sells better than good product without sizzle.

PRICING

One of the most important aspects of launching and growing a successful product is correct pricing. Pricing is one of the major components of profits. The right price gets you an order and maximizes your chances for reorders. The wrong price—on the low side—leaves valuable profits on the table. The wrong price on the high side may decrease your orders and your chances for getting reorders. In short, pricing is a key component of low-risk, high-reward entrepreneurship.

All too often, companies put a selling price on their product or service when they're under some sort of time pressure—for example, when they're dying to rush out there and *get some orders*. It's not until later that they discover they didn't account for some important costs in that selling price. These might include commissions (yes, people forget commissions), extra trade discounts in key markets, displays, servicing, advertising, or whatever. Now comes the trap: In many cases, *it's very tough to raise prices*. (We'll return to this shortly.) So they find themselves stuck with a low-margin item, or without the money to run a successful marketing program.

A PRICING CHECKLIST

Here's a list of the factors you may want to consider before you settle on a selling price—especially a price that you may not be able to change easily:

- *Determine and prioritize the channels of distribution into which you plan to sell.*
- *Establish what it takes to be successful in your key markets, and put a cost on each of these factors. For example:*
  - Will you need consumer or trade advertising? If so, to what extent?
  - Will your product require co-op advertising, and if so, what are the standard arrangements in the various markets you're pursuing?
  - Do distributors play a role? If so, what are their margin requirements?
  - What are the margin requirements of target customers in target markets?
  - Is servicing important, and if so, what is your service strategy?
  - Will you be using specialty reps? If so, what commission will you have to pay?
  - What inventory risks will you have to take? How will you handle guaranteed sales, stock balancing, backup stocks, and reorders?
  - What type of packaging will be required?
  - What displays (if any) will be needed?
  - What are the standard payment terms in this market?
  - What's the integrity level of this market, and of your target customers? (Are you comfortable with those levels?)
- *Analyze the uniqueness of your product.* What makes your product different? Are you unique, and in a hot classification? Or is yours a me-too offering in a declining category, which is unlikely to command good margins? Is it a commodity product?
- *Analyze the barriers to entry behind your product.* What's your sustainable advantage, if any?
- *Determine the up-front, onetime costs involved in coming to market.* What volume level will be required to recoup these costs, at what price?

Continued on next page

- *Think life span.* The shorter your product's expected life span, the higher your margins should be. Remember that "life spans" apply not only to products, but also to whole classes of products.
- *Think competition.* You're likely to have competitors, and maybe even skilled ones. Will you compete on the basis of product superiority, price, service, quality, advertising, sales coverage, delivery time, or some combination? What costs are associated with this strategy?
- *Know what your market will bear.* Is your product comparable in value to existing products, but able to be produced at a lower cost? If so, you might consider pricing close to (or just under) the levels set by your competitors, and thereby earning an above-average margin. Alternatively, you could price lower and go for more market share. Whichever way you go, don't make this decision solely on a *predetermined* margin over your cost. On products with short life spans, what-the-market-will-bear pricing can be very effective.
- *Prepare to be imitated.* Do you anticipate copies or knockoffs? If so, how much time do you have before they enter the fray? (You may want to start with a higher margin, and then either lower your margin when competition enters the field, or knock yourself off with a lower-cost version.)
- *Understand your legal rights, and what they may cost you.* For example: if your patent or copyright is infringed upon, will you have the resources needed to start and (if necessary) sustain litigation?
- *Think longer term.* Will the success of this product lead to successful spin-offs or follow-up sales? If so, you may want to consider selling this original product at minimal or no profit, in order to build and capture the after-market or add-on sales.

  The classic example is Gillette "giving away" the razor to capture blade sales, but there are many others. You can forego short-term profits to break into a new channel of distribution with good long-term growth potential, to help your company's image, to gain market share, or to send a strong message to your competitors.
- *Think strategically.* This is an obvious follow-on to the previous point. Is there some strategy aside from profit that this particular product may help advance? Is this a case where you know you have lots of good (and profitable) follow-up products to put into the pipeline? Will it help you break into a new channel of distribution?

- *Identify your costs at various volume levels.* Are there dramatic cost savings that come with volume? If so, what strategies and associated costs can you employ to achieve these volume levels?
- *Understand the implications of your (limited) finances.* If available finances limit your ability to produce and sell your product, then maybe you should opt for smaller, higher-margin markets. (Yes, there are bragging rights associated with "selling Kmart," or "selling Wal-Mart," but you shouldn't wind up paying for those bragging rights!)
- *Understand the implications of your (limited) manufacturing capabilities.* Again: if selling Target means you'll sell out your limited run at a relatively low margin, think twice. Shouldn't you look again at those smaller, higher-margin markets?
- *Examine the "spread."* What are your payment terms from suppliers as opposed to those you give your customers? The cost of money on the spread should be included in your overall costs and prices.
- *Keep your eye on that license.* If your product is licensed, you probably have both guarantees and royalties to worry about. If the guarantee is high, you may come up short, and you may want to price in light of this potential shortfall.

Think of pricing as a balancing act. If you have a unique product, a patentable product, a time advantage, a manufacturing edge, or some other kind of competitive advantage, you can and should get a higher-than-average margin. At the same time, your high margins may hurt your sales, and are very likely to act as a beacon for competitors or knock-offs.

In light of these many calculations, I suggest that you involve all the relevant constituencies within your company in initial pricing discussions. The accounting department may claim that this is their domain exclusively; if so, don't let them win this argument! Salespeople, production personnel, and even your key customers can provide valuable insights into the pricing decision. You, as the manager, have to balance these sometimes competing interests and arrive at an appropriate course of action. Notice that I didn't say the "right" course of action. In many cases, there's more than one legitimate pricing strategy that can be pursued.

Pricing needs to be revisited regularly. You may find that in order to maintain your margins, you are under pressure to raise your prices. Be forewarned, though, that you may have major customers who will not accept price increases, despite your increased costs. A good example of this was when Rubbermaid experienced a dramatic increase in the cost of resin—the major component of their products—and asked Wal-Mart (their largest customer) for a price increase. Wal-Mart refused to accept the price hike and gave parts of Rubbermaid's allocations to other companies. This affected Rubbermaid as a company dramatically: its stock plunged, employees were laid off, and hard times ensued.

My guess is that there was more to this interplay than meets the eye. It appears that with all the publicity generated by the proposed Rubbermaid price increase, the chairman of Wal-Mart felt this was an opportune time to send a message to all of its vendors not to bring them price increases. That message was surely heard among the community of vendors to Wal-Mart.

My main point, though, is that price increases are often difficult to obtain. One way around this is to change the product. Either alter its appearance, add value to it, change the package and give it a new style number, or whatever. Then tell your customer that you are dropping the old item and adding a new one. Technically, at least, there's no "price increase" involved in this. In many cases, this fig leaf makes life much easier for the buyer.

PRODUCT EXTENSIONS

It's never too soon to start thinking about product extensions. If your product becomes successful, then how can you capitalize further upon it? In the movie business, the James Bond series is probably the most dramatically successful example of product extensions, although the *Star Wars* movies and the *Star Trek* TV series aren't far behind. In the doll arena, Barbie's handlers have extended that product line into a $1.8 billion annual business.

You can do a number of things with your product. Like Mattel, you can keep coming out with new versions of your own "Barbie." (Recent versions include NASCAR Barbie and Harley Barbie.) You can add value and make a more deluxe version. Parker's Monopoly game—which traditionally has retailed for under $10—was very successfully upgraded to a $500 version, created for the Franklin Mint.

Going in the other direction, you can use less expensive materials or a smaller size for a lower-price version. Part of your extension thinking should be related to your channel of distribution. If you sell only to upscale retailers and now want to maximize your profits from this product by taking it to the mass merchandisers (Wal-Mart, Target), then make a different version for them. Part or all of the difference can be the package.

PRODUCT KNOCKOFF

If your product is very successful and if you have no legal way of protecting it—which is true, in most cases—then why not knock yourself off before someone else does?

Put yourself in the knockoff artist's shoes. How would he or she copy your product? In most cases, they will look to make it less expensive, in order to both build on your proven product and also undersell it. (And this can be a very effective strategy indeed.) Beat them to the punch. Ask questions like:

- Can I make it cheaper in other countries?
- Can I redesign it so that it's less expensive to make?
- What materials can I use that are less expensive?
- Who will I sell it to, and what kind of volume can they give me?
- What cost savings can I get by buying in much larger quantities? (This is one of the major ways the copiers are effective in their knocking off.)
- What internal cost savings can I achieve for the knockoff version? These might include, for example, lower sales commissions, less expensive packaging, higher packings to the master carton, better cash selling terms (like a letter of credit), etc.

By knocking yourself off, you beat the competition to the market and you discourage new competition. However, you also have to think through your new strategy. Will my original version continue? It can, if your knockoff is materially different and sold in different channels of distribution. Is my original version fading in sales? If so, then you might want to bring your new knockoff version to your regular customers. You might have to do so anyway and let the buyer make decisions about which to buy.

I'll return to the subject of knockoffs at some length in chapter 9.

BARRIERS TO ENTRY

In developing your product, give thought to different ways to erect barriers to competition. The first should be in legal protection, a copyright for design and a patent (if there is some new way this item functions).

Other strategies to discourage competition are to get to market quickly and sell to the major customers. Don't sell products that carry inflated profit margins (that only invites knockoffs). Maintain high quality, and in as many other ways as possible build your brand. Attach an appropriate license to the product. Create multiple price points. And finally, service your customers to death so they simply won't want to consider buying from anybody else.

PRODUCT LIABILITY INSURANCE

Don't forget: No matter what product you're in business with, you need insurance for product liability. Many large prospective customers will not give you a vendor number (a prerequisite for a purchase order getting cut) unless you send them proof of this insurance. Some types of products have higher insurance liability costs associated with them than others. These include, among others, ingested products, products that are applied to your skin, and products aimed at children. These costs have to be recognized and included in your overhead.

PRODUCT TESTING

Think of your favorite inseparable two-word combinations. *Soup and sandwich. Ham and eggs. Jekyll and Hyde.* Now add a new combination to that list: *risk reduction and testing.*

Not a very musical combination, but an all-important one. Market tests go hand-in-hand with risk reduction. If you want to keep reducing your product-related risks, keep testing their appeal in the marketplace.

Direct response companies know this lesson very well. They never advertise mail-order product on national TV without first testing the product—and the commercial promoting it—on a limited basis. This allows them to compare costs and benefits. How many orders did they receive, and what kinds of profits did they achieve, as a result of those ads? If the first test proves successful in a territory of size X, maybe their next step is a second test in a territory of size 2X or 4X. After enough of these staged tests prove successful, the company then commits lots of advertising dollars and purchases large quantities of goods in expectation of future sales.

"So many things that we do fail," Bud Pironti told me. "So we never make it very complicated to run a test. We get the tests done, determine if the activity will work, and then proceed."

There are lots of ways to test a product before assuming the risk of large inventory and overhead commitments. Many people fall into the trap of placing large initial orders so they can get the low unit cost that volume gives you. In most cases, I don't recommend it. Follow the example of the direct response companies, and build up gradually to high volumes.

Here are some ideas about different ways to test your product:

Commission focus groups

This is a favored method of many larger companies. You can hire professionals to do this for you, or—if cash is short—do it yourself as a sort of "kitchen research." The trick is to focus on a cross section of possible consumers of your product—a cross section that reflects the demographics of your target customers.

Now for my own biased opinion: I would not put too much faith in what a focus group tells you. Whatever situation you've put them in, it's got to be different from the circumstances of a consumer going into a store and putting their own money on the line by buying the product. In many cases, though, a focus group can give you clues about additional things you should be investigating—and this is essential to risk reduction.

Conduct market research

If you can afford it, market research can be a very valuable tool for testing the feasibility or appeal of your product, and for developing the best approach to marketing it.

This is another case in which you'll have to stay in charge of your consultants (see chapter 6, on managing professionals). I would conduct the same due diligence in selecting a marketing research company as I would in deciding upon a lawyer, accountant, or management consultant. If you're not yet at the stage where you can afford this research, you might consider approaching a nearby university and asking if they could assign a team of business students to conduct the necessary research. Many schools welcome challenging, real-world projects that their students can undertake.

Talk to people who sell your product

Whenever one of my companies was in the marketplace with a game, a watch, or some other consumer product, I made a point of going into stores that carried that product at around 10:00 or 11:00 a.m. Most days of the year, retail stores are relatively empty at that time of day, and the salespeople behind the counter have time to talk. I would tell them who I was, and say quite candidly that I hoped they could help me understand better what was happening "on the front lines."

Try it. And if you do, listen hard, because these people can tell you amazing things—things their own store buyers don't know. They can give you feedback from customers: why they decided to buy or not to buy your product, and what they liked or didn't like about it. They can tell you how your product stacks up against the competition, and which competing items are selling better than yours.

Most people like being recognized as expert at something (especially if they don't often get that recognition). For the most part, retail salespeople are flattered and pleased to get attention from the head of a company, and they'll willingly share what they know with you. And believe me, if you're out there asking these questions and your competitors aren't, you're giving yourself a considerable edge.

Talk to buyers

Think about the buyers you trust and are friendly with, and find ways to draw on their skills and experience. Show them your sketches or prototypes, and ask them for their candid reaction: If you made this thing, would they buy it?

Again, listen hard to what you hear. A dozen emphatic "no's!" in a row is surely a bad sign. "Maybes" are okay, because they probably mean that the buyer will give you a fair hearing when you come back with the real goods. "Yeses" are great, for obvious reasons. Also great are "provisional" yeses, by which I mean the circumstance in which the buyer says, "Look, Bob, I'd definitely take on this line if you made such-and-such a change." If you can actually make that change, you're a long way toward pre-selling the product. That buyer has become part of the process, and is very likely to make good on his or her implied promise.

One caution: Buyers may be dead wrong in their assessment of what their customers will buy. If you're good at what you do, your gut feeling is probably better than theirs. So don't take their yeses and nos as gospel, but listen for ways to make your product better, or ways to promote it more effectively.

And don't forget, meanwhile, that buyer X has told you that she wouldn't take this product under any circumstances. It makes absolutely no difference that your gut is right and hers is wrong if *her* gut keeps your product out of that store. (Her gut makes for self-fulfilling prophecies.) Eventually, you're going to have to change her gut and get that product into her store—or you won't be in the game.

Talk to consumers

Consumers are the ultimate test of your success. You can do reality checks with consumers in a variety of ways beyond focus groups. Unless your product is too specialized, start close to home. Your teen-aged daughter is likely to be a tough critic. How about friends and neighbors? True, these people may feel they have to sugarcoat bad news; but if your natural allies are all giving you bad news, your product probably needs some rethinking.

Going farther afield, find ways to talk to consumers who *don't* have to be nice to you. One of my favorite techniques is to go behind the counter in a cooperative store and try to sell my products for them. This kind of face-to-face contact is invaluable. Are they reluctant to buy this product? Ask them why. When you do make a sale, ask them for whom they're buying the product. (This almost always elicits useful information.) If you've got some product extensions in mind, this is a great opportunity to test them out: "Thanks for buying product X. By the way, if we came out with this variation on product X, do you think you'd be interested in that, too?"

"Every year at our balloon festival," John Korff told me, "I work in the parking lot for at least six hours, parking cars and taking money, because that way, you hear what people really think about you. You find out what they don't like about your ticket prices, how they're trying to beat the system, how many kids they've got hidden under their blankets, and so on."

In most cases, customers are very talkative, if you demonstrate that you're sincerely interested in what they have to say.

Market before you manufacture

Try to get an acceptable number of orders in hand before you commit to producing your product. How? One way is to run a coupon ad in a magazine or newspaper to test the waters. Certain kinds of products (including many magazines) aren't actually produced until a minimum threshold of orders is reached.

Make prototypes

Produce a quality prototype with a prototype package, determine a price that you want to sell it at (based on normal volume runs), and then show it to (1) key members of your sales force, and (2) key buyers whom you trust. Strong reactions either way can be most helpful in either giving you good reasons to move ahead, or, pull the plug.

Produce a short run

Take a partial plunge: produce a limited run of your product in its real package and try to sell it. This is the best test of all, because it's real. It's okay to lose money on a test like this, especially if that prevents you from making a heavy investment in a losing proposition.

One great place to test a product is on a home-shopping TV channel. This is a medium that gives you instant feedback.

Test in a store

Not only will you control the environment (displays, etc.), but you may be able to move excess inventory. Dennis Boyer says that his first tests were "strictly experimental. We were given the worst locations in the worst towns in Wyoming. If it would work next to a video machine in Casper, Wyoming, we had strong evidence that it would work in downtown Denver." You may have to guarantee the sale, but the information you gather will be well worth this cost.

PRODUCT TIMING

The success of a product launch often can hinge on its timing. When I was in the game business, lots of buyers wanted to run an ad on my new products for Father's Day. They felt that the response to such an ad would tell them whether or not to put that product in their Christmas catalogue (or to feature the product in major displays at Christmastime). For the buyers, of course, the stakes were high: for many stores, 50 percent or more of their annual sales volume can come in the weeks leading up to Christmas.

Well, we learned the hard way that Father's Day was a dreadful season for a product launch. (We eventually referred to it as a "mythical holiday." People who make neckties probably do okay on Father's Day, but I bet nobody else does.) We learned not to do any introductory advertising before the fall—*period*. Working with a friendly buyer or retailer, we might put together a counter display in July or August just to get some kind of early reaction from consumers, but by then we all knew that in the dog days of summer, it made sense to keep our expectations low.

So, too early to market can be a disaster, but too late to market can be even worse. This is especially true for "fad" products, where you absolutely have to catch the wave of consumer demand. My *TV Guide* trivia game (see Appendix 3) was by all accounts a big success, in large part because it met a consumer demand for trivia games that the makers of Trivial Pursuits were unable to meet at that time. But had my product been brought to market even three months later, it most likely would have failed. By that time, the bigger game companies would have been flooding the market with their own trivia games, and we would have been lost in the crowd.

Successful product timing, then, means taking advantage of the factors that you do control, and working as best you can within the constraints of seasonality and consumer demand.

And once again, I should mention the importance of *luck*. Do your best to be in the right place at the right time, and try like crazy not to be in the wrong place at the wrong time! A friend of mine was booked to promote his new book on a national cable network—a degree of exposure that probably would have sold thousands of copies of the book, and generated some major buzz—on the day the Monica Lewinsky scandal broke. My friend got preempted for Monica; he never got another shot at the national stage.

Do your homework, and *be lucky!*

PRODUCT MANAGEMENT

Some products—Grape-Nuts, Ivory Snow, and Scrabble come to mind—seem to live forever. Most new products, however, hit the market, have their run, and then get closed out. In most cases, therefore, it helps to think of your product as having a natural life span, within which the product needs to be managed. I'll define three stages in that life span: the *introduction, ongoing support,* and the *closeout.*

Introduction

What special marketing efforts will you make to introduce your product? A press conference? Press releases? Demonstrations at key customer sites? Celebrity appearances on your behalf? Consumer and/or trade advertising? Bonus commissions to your salespeople (or to your customers' salespeople, if you're selling stores)? Some kind of special offer with an initial purchase, such as a onetime premium, a two-for-one deal, or something of the kind? A special event that you've created or tied into?

I throw all these ideas out just to make the point that a new product deserves *some* kind of special introduction. Think of how much time you've spent coming up with this thing, whatever it is. Think of how happy everybody involved will be if this product catches on. And, on the negative side, think of how rare it is for a new product to succeed. (Very few do.) You have to *help* this infant take its first steps in the world!

The introduction doesn't have to be a blockbuster. Use your tried-and-true techniques, perhaps with a new spin. Master chicken pitchman Frank Perdue had long used his own face to promote his products. When his company first launched a line of all-chicken hot dogs, Perdue's PR firm decided to stage a very visible hunt for the kid who bore the strongest resemblance to Frank Perdue himself. The search was successful, and Perdue and the odd-looking kid then promoted the hot dog product together. Old story; new wrinkle.

Ongoing support

What will you do to support your product, maximizing its sales and longevity?

The answer lies, in part, in what kind of product you're promoting. Some products—particularly lower-priced ones—are intended to sell primarily to impulse buyers. When you're supporting these kinds of products, you need to emphasize packaging, display, and "real estate" (positioning in the store).

Other products need very different kinds of support. Does your product seek to replace an established product, or does its purpose need some explanation? If so, you'll need to put more of your promotional dollars into regular advertising (and perhaps cooperative advertising) over the longer term, building awareness and understanding of your product.

Does your product lend itself to extensions? There are cases in which a product extension "cannibalizes" the original product, and others in which the success of an extension gives new life to the original product. You should have a good idea ahead of time which way your product line is likely to break, and tailor your advertising accordingly.

I'll return to the subject of product support, and particularly advertising and promotional strategies, in later chapters.

Closeouts

Even if your product has a long and happy run in the marketplace, it's likely to reach the end of its run eventually, and leave you with a pile of inventory on hand. Welcome to your first closeout! Think of this as an entrepreneurial rite of passage: If you're in the game long enough, you're almost sure to go through it.

Keith Mirchandani, president of a TV direct response firm, once said to me, "Manage your inventories, and there's no risk. Unfortunately, you don't necessarily know when to stop. You don't have a crystal ball. I think that no entrepreneur wants to lose that last 10 percent. I'd probably make a lot more money if I learned to capture 80 or 90 percent of my sales and not get stuck."

The key thing in closeouts is to spend as little time as possible in assigning blame. (Yes, it makes sense to figure out what went wrong so that you won't make the same mistake again, and you should do that; but scapegoating never made a nickel for anybody.) Move quickly! Get that inventory out of your warehouse, and—one way or another—turn it into cash. Among other compelling reasons for acting decisively, you absolutely don't want to have an unsuccessful item in your offerings. If a buyer sees one dog in your lineup, he may suspect there are others there.

Think of your closeout options as rungs on a ladder. If you can stay on the upper rungs of that ladder—for example, by offering a sale to your regular customers—great. But if you can't, be prepared to start climbing down, *quickly.*

If you're sticking with your established customers, don't think about cutting your turkey's price incrementally; it won't work. Go for dramatic price cuts. These will not only help move the product, but will get the buyers' attention (and underscore in their minds that you understand how the game is played).

Who else can help? Can you go overseas? Is barter a possibility (see chapter 5)? Is there somebody out there who might be able to use your product as a premium? These kinds of options usually require some advance planning, which illustrates an important point: It's good to have some idea *early on* about how you may close out this particular product, when that almost-inevitable day finally arrives. If you start these conversations when your product is still riding high in the marketplace—assuming, of course, that it ever got there—you'll have more negotiating power.

Toward the bottom of the ladder, in terms of dollars returned to you, look to *liquidators.* This is an industry that thrives on the bad bets made by people like you and me. Liquidators will try to buy your product at 5 to 10 cents on the retail dollar. This hurts, but on the plus side it frees up needed cash and warehouse space.

In general, I try to get my raw costs back when I close out a product. But at the end of the day, I'll take what I can get, and move on. Closeouts are a natural cost of doing business. They're like a trip to the dentist—better done sooner. Get it over with, and concentrate on your next great product.

———

I reiterated at the beginning of this chapter that I love products. That's absolutely true. I believe a great product deserves to be loved and coddled, especially in the early stages of its life. It's a tough world out there, and even the best product that a smart person like you can come up with requires care and feeding.

But don't let your commitment to your product blind you to reality. Count on it: *There will be products that you love that just don't sell.* When that happens, and after you're convinced you've done absolutely everything you could have done to make this product a success, it's time to throw in the towel and move on to another product. Close it out!

"When I buy stocks," mail-order king Don Seta told me, "I spend a tremendous amount of time in research and sometimes I blow it, but I can tell you, I have the discipline so that if I make a mistake, I don't live with that mistake. I immediately switch or correct it. You have to do the same thing in business."

Try "falling in like" with your product, rather than falling in love. Love is a commitment that can be carried to an unhealthy extreme. At least until recently, high-tech companies (for example) have been notorious in this regard. In high-tech, the product—and the engineer(s) who created it—is king.

I hope your product is king, too; but I also hope you're prepared to anoint a few more kings, in and around your organization. For starters, I'd nominate your corporate culture, your employees, your quality control processes, your planning process, and—of course—your customers and consumers. All will have to make contributions if you are to secure that all-important order, which is the subject of the next chapter.

8

GETTING THE ORDER

At the start of this book, I described the act of *selling*—securing orders for your company's products or services—as one of the most critical skills for the success of your enterprise. In this chapter, I want to make that point again, this time in a much more detailed way.

In a very real sense, everything you've read up to now has been only the warm-ups. Now the vital work begins: Now you have to get your first *orders.*

Orders drive the company. Your ideas, your structures, your planning, your strategies and implementation—all will go for naught unless you get those orders. "Sales is everything," says John Korff. "You can cut costs and watch expenses, and that works for two years, and then it's over. If you're not selling, you're cooked."

In this chapter, we'll look at how to get your initial orders. For companies that sell direct to consumers, this means solving a particular set of problems. For companies that go through middlemen, it means solving an additional set of problems related to those middlemen.

Marketers distinguish between *pushing* and *pulling* strategies. Pushing is the same as selling in: you go after your identified customers or consumers and pitch your products to them. Pulling is the process whereby you create demand for your product among consumers, who then go to the appropriate outlet and pull it through the distribution channels. I call that process *selling through,* and that's the subject of chapter 9.

Despite the importance of selling to all businesses and all occupations—yes, even to those professions that we sometimes think are "above the fray"—there is little or nothing taught about selling in our schools, at any level. This continues to amaze me, and I always bug my friends on business school faculties about this glaring deficiency. For the most part, they agree with me that selling is critically important, but maintain that it's not an easy subject for academic institutions to get their arms around.

I listen to this politely, and then I say, "Yes, Professor X, but that's what they used to say about entrepreneurship, too, and now there's hardly a business school in the country that doesn't brag about their entrepreneurship courses."

Well, that's my own personal battle, which I intend to keep fighting. Meanwhile, of course, this huge vacuum in business education hasn't gone unfilled. There is a plethora of books, videos, software programs, and seminars on the subject of successful selling. Some of them are great; many of them aren't. I recommend that you start with people who sell successfully, and ask them if they can suggest ways for you to improve your own selling skills. I suspect that most people will tell you either that they learned the hard way, or they learned at the foot of a master. But when someone gives you a lead on a particular sales-oriented book, video, or course, follow up on it and see if it can be helpful to you. Be optimistic. In many cases, if you *think* something is going to be helpful, you're halfway home.

I'm not going to attempt a complete selling tutorial in this short chapter. Instead, I'm going to focus on six key topics:

- Who should sell?
- Preparing for the sale
- Effective selling techniques
- Selling and selling again
- Tips for dealing with sales representatives
- Selling without a sales force or reps

WHO SHOULD SELL?

I insert this question here in order to give me the chance to reiterate a key point from chapter 1. In an entrepreneurial company, *everyone* has to sell. Most likely everyone in your company won't be out there on the streets with a sample case, but if you're smart, you'll be encouraging all your people to do their own skilled brand of selling, no matter where they sit in the company.

Let's start at the front desk. The receptionist who answers the phone and deals with customers is a key sales agent. Don't believe me? In my experience, many customers' *overwhelming impression* of a company is formed through their phone contact with that company. In many cases, most of those contacts go through one or two receptionists.

A friend of mine employed a young woman once who was without a doubt the world's greatest phone answerer. According to my friend, it was no exaggeration to say that people fell in love with her on the phone. First of all, she recognized voices instantly (well before the advent of Caller ID). She conveyed warmth, interest, and a determination to *solve that caller's problem,* no matter what it took. And even though she wasn't managing accounts in any formal way, she somehow had a rough idea in her head as to where her company stood in relation to that particular person or company. She often was able to recall and refer to a recent company-to-company contact, and also (when appropriate) to something personal in the caller's life. For several years after she left that company, people still asked my friend about her, by name.

Why am I rattling on about a long-departed receptionist? Because I'm convinced that if everyone in a company acted as she did, there'd be no stopping that company. Yes, the head of the company is positioned to be the most effective salesperson for the company, especially in its early stages. And yes, customers are flattered to have the CEO involved in the sales process, and it gives them confidence that their needs will be looked after. But at the end of the day, the CEO is a limited resource.

And meanwhile, while the CEO is out beating the bushes, someone is back home answering the phone, answering technical questions about the product, taking warranty calls, answering the mail, directing visitors in the parking lot, getting coffee for and taking the coats of visitors, and so on. All of these people are either reinforcing the work of that traveling CEO, or they're undermining it.

So my answer to the question, "Who should sell?" is, *everybody.* Selling will take different forms, depending on where an individual sits in your organization, but there are really very few people who don't have at least the occasional opportunity to help sell your products or services. I think that *everybody* in the company who has contact with the outside world should have the benefit of some sort of training, designed to help them deal effectively with these outside constituencies.

I came across a copy of the *Chief Executive Officer's Newsletter* recently, in which a Dallas-based business person, Dodee Frost Crockett, advocated for replacing the "receptionist" title to "Director of First Impressions." Sounds right to me, in light of the all-important sales imperative.

Moving on to the more formal sales function, there are four basic ways to make sales and get orders:

- sell it yourself;
- hire salespeople;
- use sales reps; or
- sell without a field-based sales force.

I'm a great advocate of "selling it yourself," and I'll devote most of this chapter to that topic. As for the second approach—hiring and managing a sales force—I won't spend much time specifically on this one. (Of course, the selling tips that follow apply equally to members of a large salaried sales force.) In my experience, it's usually unwise for a small company to strap on the expenses associated with a salaried sales force. Hiring salespeople is not "LRHR": It builds in fixed (rather than variable) costs, increases your risks, and in some cases diminishes your rewards.

For that reason, I've tended to use sales reps, which I'll have more to say about later in this chapter. The fourth approach—selling without a field-based sales force—is in some ways the wave of the future, and I'll also devote a number of pages to the various techniques under this broad heading.

PREPARING FOR THE SALE

Let's assume that you and/or other people in the company are going to be spending time selling your products or services in person. You (or your crack salespeople) are responsible for bringing in those orders. How are you going to do it?

The first step is to identify and prioritize who it is that you want to sell to. Unless you already know who your customers are—lucky you!—this involves starting with a broad perspective (the channels of distribution) and then getting increasingly more specific (from the business type to the specific account to the specific person at that account).

Pick a channel.

If you have a consumer product and you want to sell to retailers (for example), you should first identify the channels of distribution you're going to go after. Decide if they have to be tackled in a particular sequence. Are your selling resources limited? (The answer is almost always yes.) Will success in one channel make it easier to be successful in another channel subsequently? If so, then go to that first channel first.

Pick a region or regions

Once you've got your channel(s) down, figure out which *regions* might be good jumping-off points. Frank Perdue of chicken fame originally went after specialty butchers (his first channel), because he knew that it would be extremely difficult for him to crack the supermarket chains (his second channel). He concentrated initially on the New York metropolitan area, figuring that New Yorkers were already accustomed to paying a premium price for a premium product. It's a little bit like going to war: throwing all your resources into the right battle is a whole lot more effective than opening up along five fronts at once.

Pick specific accounts

Next, figure out which specific retail accounts are most important to your sales effort. The same general rule about concentrating your resources applies here. I always find it helpful to draw up a list of target accounts and then go after those accounts diligently. Review the list each quarter, and amend it as necessary (but don't quit too easily).

Above all, *keep your list short.* Go for the gold. In my industries, there were always accounts, such as Bloomingdale's, that were seen as trendsetters. Selling Bloomie's often meant that you were selling a whole flock of retailers who watched and mimicked Bloomie's innovative moves. Remember the old E. F. Hutton ad campaign: "When E. F. Hutton speaks, people listen"? This herd mentality is especially dominant in fashion-conscious industries, but you can find evidence of it in almost any industry. Take advantage of that by going after the trendsetters.

CHANNELS OF DISTRIBUTION

Channels of distribution are simply the pipelines that get products from the producers to the consumers (and sometimes to wholesalers and retailers along the way). But "pipelines" is too rigid a metaphor. These things change all the time, and there are always new ones emerging. So keep your eye on the distribution side, and think creatively about your most promising channels.

What does "promising" mean? In your analysis of channels, you may discover fierce competition in some, and none in others. (I'd avoid fierce competition whenever possible, unless it's a high-volume channel and you have a unique approach to it.) Marketing strategies, too, tend to vary according to channel. Which channels match your resources and strengths the best? Where are your targeted customers most likely to be found?

A partial list of channels of distribution (in alphabetical order) would include:

Ad specialty
Airport and hotel shops
Bookstores
Bridal shops
Catalogue showrooms (e.g., service merchandise)
Clothing stores (including men's, women's, and infant's)
Collectible retailers
Comic book stores
Company-owned stores
Computer stores
Confectionery stores
Convenience stores
Department stores
Direct response television (including infomercials)
Direct selling (network marketing)
Direct to consumer (mail/phone)
Discounters (e.g., Target, Wal-Mart)
Door-to-door sales

Continued on next page

Drug chains/drugstores
Duty-free shops
Electronics stores
Export channels
Fast-food outlets
Flea markets
Florists
Furniture stores
General merchandisers (e.g., Sears, J. C. Penney)
Gift stores
Golf/tennis/ski shops
Gourmet shops
Hardware stores
Hobby/craft stores
Home improvement centers (e.g., Home Depot, Rickels)
Home-shopping cable networks (e.g. QVC, HSN)
Houseware and home furnishing stores
Internet/Web sites
Jewelry and watch stores
Learning stores
Luggage stores
Mail-order companies (e.g., Spiegel, Potpourri, Fingerhut)
Media
Military post exchange
Music stores
Office supply superstores (e.g., Staples, Office Depot, Office Max)
Party plan (e.g., Tupperware)
Premium outlets
Resorts
Specialty stores (e.g., Things Remembered, Linens 'n' Things, Brookstone's)
Sporting goods stores
Supermarkets
Toy stores (ranging from Toys "R" Us to game stores)
Variety chains (e.g., McCrory)
Video rental outlets
Warehouse clubs (Sam's, Price Costco)

And at the same time, of course, you need to be flexible enough to depart from your strategy to pick up immediate orders, if your targeted accounts are slow to materialize. Don't forget that *survival* is your overriding goal.

Zero in on the right people

Once you've got your key accounts targeted, then find out the name of the person at that company whom you need to sell. Sometimes this is as simple as calling the appropriate office and asking who the lamp buyer is (assuming you're selling lamps). Sometimes, it's harder to find out who's making the buying decisions for your service or product. In some cases, it's a committee that makes these decisions. Assume it's going to take some time to get to the right person (or people), and also assume that it's worth it.

Remember that you're looking for a *decision maker.* A major challenge for sellers today is that, in many cases, they must make their first pitch to a designated buyer who is only authorized to say no. The ability to say yes resides one level higher in the organization—and this is the person you're ultimately trying to get to. But you have to accomplish this without aggravating the "naysaying," first-screen buyer. (You definitely don't want this person down on you!) Think of legitimate reasons why you need to go to higher-ups in the organization—and why you'd really appreciate being introduced to those people by the gatekeeper.

If all else fails, run around the gatekeeper. Find a way to get a call in to the higher-up buyer. When you succeed, you can either ask for an opportunity to make your pitch directly to him or her, or you can ask for something else. One thing that has often worked for me is to inquire, in a sort of peer-to-peer tone, which of the buyers below this higher-up you ought to be talking to. You need their advice, especially if your product may fit into several different categories. I've had instances in which the higher-up person directed me to a lower-volume department in the store, because he or she felt that the buyer in that department was more open to new concepts than the buyer in the higher-volume areas.

Understand your target

The next thing that's immensely valuable is *to know everything you possibly can about your prospective customer and buyer.* This is a vital part of preparing for the sale, and it should be ongoing while you're zeroing in on the right person to talk to.

If it's a store, how do they display? Are there clerks who actually sell at the retail counter? How many competing items do they carry? What price points do they carry? What are their profit requirements, and how are they measured? What's their current financial condition? Are they having a good year? What's the long-term trajectory of the company? What kinds of customers do they cater to? Are they leaders or followers? Are they best known for value, price, fashion, or some combination? What special requirements do they have, in terms of things like labeling, shipping, packaging, display, advertising, markdowns, quality guarantees, credit terms to their customers, payment terms to you, billing requirements, late-shipment policies, and so on. What's this buyer's personality? What's he or she known for, in the trade?

How do you gather all this intelligence? Do your homework, of course! If it's a store, shop the store thoroughly. Talk to the sales clerks. Take notes. Write down everything that's already in the department that you'd like to sell, and write down what's *not* there that you could provide. If it's a public company, get their most recent annual report (from your broker, off their Web site, or from their investor-relations person). Search them on the Internet. Talk to other people who sell them. Talk to the receptionists in the company. (In my experience, a bright and underchallenged receptionist is almost always a gold mine of information.) Study their ads. Get their catalogues (if they publish them). Read about them and their fiercest competitors in trade publications. Visit trade shows, and use these occasions to meet people and ask a lot of questions.

One goal of all this work is to enable you to individualize your call and be able to speak to your prospective customer's specific needs. Nobody likes to feel that they're getting a "canned" presentation. Conversely, everybody likes to think that they're special enough to deserve special attention from you. And they *do* deserve that special attention!

John Korff says that it's crucial to learn about the people you are going to address: "You have to understand intuitively why someone else should want to do what you want them to do. If there's no logical reason why, it isn't gonna work. That's like firing a shotgun out a window and hoping a duck flies by."

Understand your own and your competitors' positions

By this I mean, use what you've learned about the prospect to think again about your own products and services. What customer problems that you've identified can your products solve? How do the sales histories of your products track with what this buyer needs?

Study all your competitors, big and small, and put together a list of the pros and cons of each as they stack up against your company's offerings. This will sharpen your presentation and prepare you for buyers' questions.

Plan, plan, plan

Which accounts are you concentrating on, and why, and when? How often will you call on them? What information will you present to

---

DEFINING A SALE

What's a "sale"? This is less obvious than it may sound. Many inexperienced people, in their anxiety to get an order and keep the wolf from the door, overlook the fact that some so-called sales are not really sales at all. Here are some terms and conditions to memorize and look out for, as you head out into the world:

Projections: These are only a buyer's predictions of the amount of goods that he will purchase over a specified period of time. Sometimes they are provided to you, as a supplier, so that you can make plans accordingly. And in fact, they can be very useful in helping you plan your ordering, shipping, and cash needs. But keep your optimism under control when a buyer shares her exciting projections with you. These are *not* orders, and the buyer is under no obligation on the basis of projections.

It is often very helpful to ascertain exactly how the buyer came to a particular set of projections. Was it based on an actual sales test for your item, on sales history of similar items, or from a look at the heavens followed by a coin toss? It's also helpful to get a bead on the in-

Continued on next page

tegrity of the buyer who is making these projections. Is this someone who only looks to protect himself or herself? Or is it someone who is working diligently to project and procure their company's needs?

Let's say you ask these kinds of questions—politely—and get acceptable answers. You may then agree to supply against these projections, *conditionally.* In other words, you should get a release date from the buyer, stating that you are free to release the goods to other buyers unless the order is confirmed by a specific date. Of course, it would be nice to have this in writing, but buyers probably won't go this far for you; you'll likely have to settle for putting it in a confirming memo following up on your conversation.

Estimates: These are only written chitchat—the softest of the soft. They are guesswork rather than commitments. Never light a victory cigar based on a buyer's estimate.

HFC: Three little letters—standing for "hold for confirmation"—that can create a lot of heartache for the inexperienced. If you receive a purchase order that has "HFC" somewhere on it, file it in your "strong prospect" folder. Many times, this "order" isn't worth the paper it's written on. It's really only a formalized projection, which means that you have to be just as careful as you would be about a projection. But remember that buyers generally expect you to have goods ready to ship on an HFC, even though those buyers are under no obligation to give you an order. Without good communications in both directions, this can lead to trouble. Somebody once told me that he felt that HFC stood for "hold for calamity."

Just to be even-handed: The good aspect of an HFC is that in the case of certain buyers, it locks the money into the budget for that specific order. Better that than nothing!

Guaranteed sale: This can be a high-risk approach for the seller, because it means that the buyer can return all goods not sold and demand full credit for those returned goods. In many cases, the buyer will refuse to pay for *any* goods, including goods that have been sold and are long gone, until a specified sales period is over and returns (if any) are determined.

That's the worst case. If you are a regular supplier, the buyer may pay you in full, or may make a partial payment and settle up later. But the real danger in a guaranteed sale is if you count on the income from the billing on that shipment. It by all means should *not* be lumped in with a final sale. If you are using a factor, that company will insist on the separation, and will decline to loan against this kind of sale.

I don't mean to imply that you should never sell on a guaranteed sale. Sometimes it's a good way to get a test order—in other words, a foot in the door with a major account. It can be an appropriate tactic if you are a new company and you need customers to get started, or if you're an existing company trying to break into a new market. It's also relevant in certain industries (like book publishing) where the margins are sufficient to accommodate the losses on returns. This simply means that if you go this route, you have to *understand the numbers* behind the sale.

Consignment sale: This is similar to a guaranteed sale, except that the vendor retains the legal title to the goods even though they are in the store. This legal standing can be very helpful to the supplier in the event that the purchaser goes bankrupt. Expensive jewelry, for example, is often sold "on consignment."

them in what sequence? My friend Alex Giampetro says that those who fail to plan are planning to fail. I believe it. Each sales call should be planned, *carefully*.

EFFECTIVE SELLING TECHNIQUES

The work described in the preceding paragraphs is all designed to prepare you for that moment when you finally walk into the right office, for your meeting with the right person. Now's the time to *sell*.

Everyone sells differently. There's no right or wrong. As you read the following material, you may find yourself disagreeing with me. That's fine. My only suggestion, if that happens, is that you figure out *why* you disagree with me, and why what you do instead works better for you. That way, you'll have a better understanding of your own strengths, and you can steer your sales meetings in good directions.

Be persistent

Keep trying. Bob Wolf, president of Help Other People Excel®
(HOPE®), says, "Never hear the word *no* from a buyer. *No* is *on* in
the mirror." Your job is to turn the buyer on to your product or
service.

And never take rejection personally. Buyers simply can't buy everything they're shown. Their rejection of your offer could be based on
one of any number of things. Keep probing to discover the right approach to this buyer. Never get angry. Now that you've got a good
contact at this company, you're going to keep coming back with new
pitches, and possibly with new products and services.

Be creative

For example, learn to adapt to voice mail. For most salespeople, voice
mail is just another barrier for buyers to hide behind. Ron Goldstein,
our Valdawn sales manager, got in the habit of leaving a nice, friendly,
ten-minute message on the machine of one particular prospect every
morning. In his friendliest voice, he'd sing the praises of our products
and ask for an appointment. After three weeks, the somewhat peeved
buyer agreed to an appointment. It turned out that, in addition to
wanting an empty voice mail box, he admired Goldstein's persistence
and nerve.

Be patient

This is a quality that many people—especially salespeople—seem to
lack. In many cases, it takes *time* to cultivate a relationship. Bob Wolf
was advised by his mentor to make at least one round of calls without
ever asking for an order. He was advised to introduce himself, hand
over his card, offer to help in any way he could, and leave. This takes
patience (and confidence). In my experience, patience pays off.

Set the table

Assume you've got your appointment with the right person. The best
thing you can do to get a good reception from this buyer is to make
sure that the table has already been set. If the person you're talking to
has already heard of your product—or even better, has already seen
your ad—you may be halfway home. Sell before you arrive, by sending a note confirming the time of your appointment. Be on time.

Keep in mind how much time you have, and pace your presentation accordingly.

Hold your head up

This is a mental-stance tip. Tom Powers, a retired sales executive, advises his people to be *proud* of their selling careers, and this is excellent advice. Keep it somewhere in your mind while you're in the act of selling. By selling, you're performing an absolutely vital task. No business can succeed without orders, and you're the person responsible for getting this order. And guess what? If you act embarrassed about the act of selling, you will probably fail at it. Of course you can't be arrogant or presumptuous. But hold it in your head that in a very real sense, you are doing this buyer a favor. You're bringing a great product or service to his attention. If he buys it, you'll *both* benefit.

Ask questions and listen to the answers

More of your time with the buyer should be spent in active listening than in talking. Let the buyer tell you her problems, and then tell her how you can solve those problems. Almost every buyer I've ever talked to gave me clues—conscious or unconscious—about how to sell to that company. By and large, people want to tell you their problems, because they're always on the lookout for answers to those problems. So if you can solve their problems, you'll sell them successfully.

Share the right information

If you've done all the preparation recommended above, you're now a virtual fountain of information: about the buyer's company and its industry, and about your company and its industry. Share a little of this industry knowledge with your buyer, and if she seems interested, share a little more. Then share as much as they want to hear, as long as it's not confidential information about another customer of yours. Believe it or not, you may have a better perspective on the buyer's industry than she does. And by sharing information, you establish yourself as smart and collegial.

Dick Waldinger, consultant in the ad specialty industry, tells me that his motto is: "Take an idea in; take an order out." Don't just spew facts at the buyer. If you think you're on solid ground, take a creative leap. Give buyers an idea about how they might make better profits or otherwise solve their problems.

Be memorable

Buyers are swamped. They are overwhelmed by all the salespeople trying to sell them. In this context, it's sometimes useful to do something
that makes you memorable in a particular buyer's eyes.

We're on dangerous ground here, but let me start with an extreme
example. Jock Miller was our sales manager at Reiss Games in the
1970s and 1980s. He once found himself in the middle of a sales pitch
to a Woolworth buyer who was obviously not paying any attention to
him—and this after Jock had spent months trying to get in the door.
Jock took a ten-dollar bill out of his pocket, put it in the buyer's ash-
tray (back when smoking was permitted inside buildings), and set it on
fire. Now he had the buyer's full attention. "See how fast that bill is
burning?" Jock asked. "That's how fast Woolworth is losing money by
not carrying our products in your stores." Corny? Yes. But memorable, and ultimately effective.

Another person who repped for us had a more subtle approach. He
got into the habit of bringing little gifts for the buyers' secretaries.
These were exclusively oddball fruits and vegetables—things like a
head of lettuce, an artichoke, or a bunch of radishes. He had a knack
for presenting these in an understated, funny way. The secretaries loved
him, looked forward to his next visit, and somehow always found time
for him on their bosses' calendars.

Don't try anything like this that you're not completely comfortable
with. If you miss by a little, you'll miss by a lot. You want to be memorable, but not notorious.

Pitch positively and succinctly

As you talk to your prospective buyer, keep in mind what makes a
buyer more or less inclined to buy something. Don't knock the competition, even when you're invited to. Instead, emphasize the strengths
of your product or service, explaining why it compares so favorably
with those of competitors. This may not sound different from "knocking the competition," but in important ways, it is. You are coming
across as positive, confident, and pleasant. This can only help. And no
matter where you are, remind yourself that *it's a small town*. This person across the desk may be related to the president of the company
you're carefully declining to knock.

"I have one rule in business," Jonathan Axelrod once told me. "I
never say anything negative about anybody else; I just explain why I

think I can get the job done. What they're interested in is who's going to make them the most money—that's all they care about. We never say anything negative about any of our competitors, and we're actually all pretty good friends."

Don't smile relentlessly, but look for opportunities to use humor. Don't worry if you're a horrible joke-teller. (By the way: you're probably not as bad as you think you are.) Jokes aren't necessary. When a natural opportunity arises, bring up something interesting and amusing that happened to you recently. Share it. Make yourself human to your prospect.

This advice notwithstanding, keep your overall presentation *short and simple.* This will help ensure that you won't chew up your prospect's time, and it will make it easier for that person to carry your message up the line correctly.

Be prepared to say, "I don't know"

It doesn't hurt to admit candidly that you don't know the answer to a question—assuming, of course, that it's not an obvious question that someone in your position ought to be able to answer easily. Just say, "I don't know, but I'll find out and get back to you."

It's interesting how, within reason, this kind of candor can work in your favor. When you admit that you don't know a particular answer, it can reinforce the credibility of all your other answers.

Make an attractive and comprehensive offer

You've already figured out what price you'll have to ask (see chapter 7). Make a proposal that builds on your best possible price, and that comprises all the pertinent details of how your two companies would do business together. These might include, for example, product materials and dimensions, country of origin, freight terms, payment terms, shipping points, delivery time, warranties, servicing, packing-to-master-carton weights, billing names, address, cube dimensions, phone and fax, and names to call in your office for backup support.

Another category of important information relates to marketing and follow-up: your marketing plan for the product, the advertising you plan to run, the ad co-op money that is available, training programs for this customer's employees, demos, displays offered, publicity, premiums, and so on. If your strategy calls for limited distribution—such as "no discounters" or exclusive territories—this should also be included in your proposal.

All of this should be committed to writing, in a simple and professional form that can be left behind, or sent after your meeting. Your goals here are: (1) to stress the major points in your proposal; (2) to avoid making a mistake (either to your disadvantage or the buyer's); and (3) to spare the buyer the burden of filling in blanks in your proposal. If he or she wants to ask a thousand questions to get to another level of detail, fine; just don't expect a buyer to put together the fundamentals of your proposal for you.

Before you leave the meeting, try and reach an understanding with the buyer about what the next step should be. When should you call? (Try to keep the initiative on your side of the negotiations. You *don't* want to hear those terrible words: "Don't call us; we'll call you.") Is

WHY THE BUYER BUYS

Those of us with great products would like to believe that purchasing is done on a rational basis. In other words, those products featuring the highest quality, the lowest price, the best service, the highest brand recognition, and so forth, will be purchased.

Guess what? That's not the way it is. There are many emotional factors that can do battle with the rational during the purchasing decision process. You need to be aware of these kinds of buttons, and either push them or try like crazy *not* to push them, as you make your pitch. Here are just a few of the things, good and bad, that can influence buyers. Note that I've taken care to present them in a more or less random order, to make the point that any of these influences might come to bear on a given sales situation—and you won't necessarily know about it!

- The buyer's boss told him/her what to do—generally, or specifically.
- The buyer personally likes the salesperson or the salesperson's company.
- The buyer has trust and confidence in the salesperson. (This can be either rational or irrational.)
- This salesperson is smart, experienced, shares knowledge, and provides informal mentoring.

- The follow-up provided by this salesperson or this company is excellent.
- The buyer thinks the salesperson (or his/her company) is well connected with top management in the buyer's organization.
- There's a personal connection between the buyer (or the buyer's boss) and the salesperson (e.g., school classmates, members of the same softball team, kids in the same third-grade class, a favorite watering hole in common).
- The buyer is offended by a competing salesperson. (Negatives might include bad personal grooming, arrogance, profanity, too old/too young, obesity, sexual innuendo, etc.)
- The buyer's customers want a particular product (or at least the buyer believes that they do). Someone out there is asking for it.
- The product has appeal, due to its quality, design, newness, price, the resale price it can command, brand recognition, collectibility, warranty, packaging, timeliness, promotional support, functionality, etc.
- The buyer is afraid that this product may prove to be "hot," and there's a chance that only the competition will have it.
- The buyer sees an opportunity for personal gain (i.e., payola).
- The services offered by the salesperson's company (e.g., technical support, stock balancing, returnability of product, sales training, servicing of stores, etc.) are superior.
- Previous products from this company sold well, and the vendor handled problems fairly and quickly.
- One vendor promises the most advertising dollars.
- One vendor's proposal includes a key ingredient (e.g., guaranteed sale, a guarantee of profit, payment for real estate, a buyout of a former vendor's old inventory, etc.).
- The previous buyer bought this product.

there anyone else in their company with whom you should make contact? Is there anyone else in *your* company this buyer would like more information from?

Ask for the order

Many salespeople get caught up in their own rhetoric and forget what they're there for: *to get the order!* Don't be shy about this. Buyers know what you're there for and expect you to ask.

Once you get the order, by the way, stop selling. Wrap up the conversation in the spirit of saving the buyer time—never your own time—say thanks more than once, and then leave. Again, the buyer should appreciate your judicious use of his/her time.

Be prepared to say no

Until you learn to walk away from a potential sale, you'll never reach your full sales potential. Buyers will push you with demands. (It's their job to figure out how much you'll give them.) It's your job to say no when the demands get to be too great. With experience, you'll learn to say no with humor and smoothness. Believe it or not, buyers will respect your resolve, and that resolve may help you get an order on more favorable terms in the future.

Leave good stuff behind you

Assuming that you said or have been told no, keep selling with the materials you leave behind you. Your primary leave-behind, of course, is your proposal. In addition, it's often smart to leave behind pictures of your products, with style numbers next to each. If you have a catalogue featuring lots of products, only a few of which are being offered to this specific buyer, it's probably better to cut out the pictures of the relevant products and paste them up on a separate sheet for this buyer. If the buyer wants a copy of the whole catalogue, then hand it over happily.

If you're seeing a buyer for the first time, you might want to leave behind a short (not more than one-page) history of your company. Use your understanding of the buyer's company to tailor your own history in a relevant way. If your target company prides itself on innovation, for example, point out how innovative *your* company has been over the years.

Follow up on your meeting

Maybe this is too obvious to commit to paper, but—I've been sold to by people who didn't take the obvious follow-up steps, so I'll just put in this place-holder here.

First, internal follow-up: Jot down notes on the meeting, as an after-action report. You'll need it the next time you deal with this buyer, and your colleagues should have some record of where key prospects stand.

Write a follow-up letter immediately, thanking the buyer for his/her time. If you got an order, make it clear how much you appreciate that order. If you didn't get an order but the buyer seems interested, reiterate your offer to provide more information whenever that would be helpful. Remind the buyer of your agreed-upon next step. If there is any new information that you can provide—new product features, an interesting development in another part of the country, whatever—now's the time to provide it.

I've found the fax to be a very good way to communicate. I personally like to write faxes in longhand (as long as it's not a formal proposal). This is particularly effective with management—it seems to encourage them to respond directly to you on your fax (if you leave room for a response!). Most bookstores sell collections of pre-printed humorous fax cover sheets applicable to almost every imaginable business subject. Yes, they're corny; but I've had great responses from overworked executives and buyers. They appreciate a laugh in the middle of a tough day, and very often, they respond.

Stay friends with your phone

Remember that your phone is your greatest ally. It puts you into the ear of the most important people in your professional life, efficiently and economically. In many cases, a phone call can stand in for an in-person contact.

Veteran salesperson Alan Grubow does a major part of his business on the phone. His buyers are well accustomed to hearing him say, "Get up close to the phone—I want to show you a new item."

Make something happen

We all have bad days—days when we doubt ourselves and wonder why things aren't going as planned. When that happens to you—and it will—don't hide in a corner. Pick up the phone and either sell on the phone or make an appointment to sell. Visit that trade show. Update your tickler file. *Take action,* even a small one!

SELLING AND SELLING AGAIN

The preceding section dealt mainly with getting in the door the first time and making an appropriate first impression. Sometimes that meeting results in an order, and sometimes it doesn't. But unless the fit was truly awful—unless you and the buyer agreed mutually that you could *never* do business together—you're now engaged in a continuing process.

This requires you to do lots of things:

Think "detail, detail, detail"

A good salesperson keeps a thousand balls in the air at once. He is constantly improvising, updating, and moving things forward. She is constantly dreaming up new opportunities—new ideas into old channels, old ideas into new channels, and so on.

The risk is that with all this activity, the salesperson will drop a stitch. Don't make this mistake! Serving an account is all in the details. The account whose stitch gets dropped will lose confidence in you. In my experience—including personal experience—salespeople screw up in the details rather than in the big picture. Pay attention to detail.

Build trust

This starts on Day One and continues forever. Once you create trust, it is your most important asset. People want to do business with people they trust (see chapter 1 for tips on building trust).

Don't B.S. people. In my informal survey of salespeople, designed to determine what helped them succeed, this came out number one by a mile. If you B.S. somebody, eventually you'll get caught, and this will destroy trust.

Keep your promises about everything, large and small. (This includes being on time for appointments.) Never overpromise. Your goal should be to promise a lot, and then deliver more than you promised.

Always be honest. This is easy to say, but sometimes hard to live. For example: "The package that contains our product has imperfections.

What should we do about it? Well"—we might rationalize—"the end consumer is just going to throw the packaging away, anyway. And maybe the buyer won't notice the imperfections. So let's not say anything, and hope we don't get caught."

Bad idea. Pete Danis, former CEO of Boise Cascade Office Products, told me that everyone is faced with a dozen decisions each day that test their trustworthiness. You have to pass each of these tests. Contrary to the advice of that best-seller, I'd say, "*Do* sweat the small stuff."

Never disclose confidential information

This is an extension of building trust. Never give a buyer sensitive information about another of your customers. Many will try to get this information out of you—information concerning sales, promotions, pricing, and so on. You may find yourself under pressure to disclose things just to demonstrate that you can be helpful, that you're on board, or whatever.

Resist this temptation—never do it! Politely decline, and point out that you'd never disclose similar information about *them* to some other company. This is one issue about which you can be absolutely, resolutely tough. The buyer may be frustrated, but ultimately, he or she will respect you for this stance. They *don't* want you talking about them!

Budget your time carefully

The old maxim has it that 80 percent of your business will come from between 10 and 20 percent of your accounts. Make sure you allocate enough time to these major accounts, and *never* take them for granted. Remember that your competition is probably not stupid or lazy. They know enough to hone in on this business.

By the way, if you're supposed to be selling, keep track of your time to make sure you're actually doing it. There are lots of distractions that will come your way, and all of them will cut into your selling time if you let them.

Treat assistant buyers with respect

In fact, treat everybody with the same respect that you show the buyer. Most important, this is the right thing to do. It's also good business. Assistant buyers eventually become buyers. When they do, they will remember with amazing clarity who treated them well before they got into the seat of power—and they'll make their purchasing decisions accordingly.

Treat small customers well

This is the flip side of taking care of big accounts. I can't tell you how often I've seen salespeople at trade shows talking to a prospective customer—presumably a small prospective account—and then abruptly dump that person when a bigger, higher-volume fish walked into the booth. Rude in the short term and bad business in the long term! Small customers can get to be big customers (or this individual can move over to a bigger company).

Stay positive

This is the same point that I made earlier, carried forward into your ongoing relationships. Nobody likes a whiner, so don't whine. Take responsibility for the mistakes made by you and your company, fix the problems that may have resulted, and then leave them behind. Be positive. When you're on the phone, get a smile onto your face whenever possible (smiles can be heard on the phone). Your enthusiasm, if genuine, will translate into goodwill on the part of the buyer, and eventually into orders.

Keep solving problems

For example, help your customer sell your product more effectively, or use it to better effect. Your problem-solving role doesn't stop with that order; in fact, it has only begun.

Get buyers out of their offices

They're too easily interrupted there. When they get away from the office, they can talk to you casually about their goals and problems—and, incidentally, tell you how to sell them. Lunches and dinners are good.

If appropriate, get the buyer to visit your office or your factory. This fixes you in their mind, presumably in a positive way, and puts you ahead of the competition that doesn't take this obvious step.

Personalize your business relationship

This is toy rep extraordinaire Ed Miller's prescription. Learn about your buyer's family. Meet and socialize with him/her. Become a friend. Find out his/her likes and dislikes. People prefer to buy from people they like, and find reasons not to buy from those with whom they're uncomfortable. Put yourself in the first category!

Remember that you're a team player

Let's assume that you turn out to be a very successful salesperson. A word of advice: Don't let it go to your head. We've already agreed that your work is critical to the success of the company, and that you're the company's front-line warrior. Well, great, but don't forget that there are many other people in the company, behind the scenes, who are contributing to your success.

You need to acknowledge that help. Take good care of the people who help make you look good. Thank them. This is a great investment both for you and the company. Think of yourself as a great quarterback. How great would you be without some equally great linemen doing all that blocking for you?

TIPS FOR DEALING WITH SALES REPRESENTATIVES

A *manufacturer's representative,* also known as a *sales representative, sales agent,* or simply a *rep,* is an independent business person who acts as the sales arm for one or more businesses, comprising one or more products or services. Reps are paid a commission for their sales efforts, rather than a salary. Some reps are permitted to take a *draw* (or advance) against expected commissions; others are not. The commission can vary greatly—from 2 percent to 20 percent—depending on such factors as:

- the selling price of the product or service
- the channel of distribution
- whether the item is advertised
- the extent of the rep's services
- the difficulty of the selling task
- the competitive environment of the product
- the industry tradition
- the power of the rep vs. that of the manufacturer
- the respective reputation of the parties
- the respective negotiating skills of the parties

- the manufacturer's margins on the product
- the potential volume of the product

Who becomes a rep?

In order to use reps effectively, it is probably important for you to understand why people become reps in the first place. Some do so out of the desire to be independent—to set their own hours, escape company rules and dress codes, and generally be the masters of their fates. Others like the fact that being a rep involves very low start-up costs, and also has no "ceilings" imposed on their potential income (other than by the limits of their own time, energy, and talent, of course).

Perhaps counterintuitively, some people see the rep's life as a relatively secure one. If you don't work for a corporation, the kinds of downsizings, mergers, and bankruptcies that worry many corporate employees hold no terrors for you.

And finally, some people become reps because they think their progress will be impeded in a corporate setting. Maybe they're members of a minority population, or women, or just free spirits. For whatever reason, reps in this category have decided that there are unfair hurdles in their way in the corporate context. Rather than trying to jump over them, they head in a different direction entirely. Think of reps as entrepreneurs—because that's what they are.

Why work with a rep?

There are two perspectives on this question: the manufacturer's, and the buyer's. From the manufacturer's point of view, reps bring in sales without the burden of a fixed salary or benefits. They give the manufacturer a relatively quick means of access to their customers. Many reps already have a relationship with the targeted buyer, and in some cases with other personnel in the target company. They have industry- and customer-specific knowledge that can be very valuable to the manufacturer. In many cases, they're well positioned to solve problems that arise with key accounts.

From the buyer's perspective, reps can fight the buyer's fight with the manufacturer for more favorable buying terms. Buyers in many cases feel they can trust the rep more than they can trust the manufacturer. Reps are easy to contact. They can keep the buyer aware of industry trends, including competitive shifts. And buyers turn over frequently, making reps valuable to the buying company as (1) an informal "training" resource for new buyers, and (2) an informal "institutional memory." Buyers also know that reps are more dependent on them than the manufacturer is. Because of this, they trust the rep more.

How to find and select a rep

First, ask yourself the fundamental questions: What are my objectives for the rep—To build volume? To maintain volume? To get access to top management? To help get bills paid on time? In servicing the accounts, how many and what kinds will they cover? What will their sales goals look like?

Next, think through the conditions under which the reps will work. Will they have to accept "house accounts" in their territories (accounts which you will control centrally)? What will the commission setup be, and what expenses (if any) will you pay? How long an agreement will you seek? What kinds of selling (e.g., demonstrations) will be involved? How much help and service are you willing to give your reps? Are there certain compatible lines you will want them to carry—and conversely, lines you *don't* want them to carry?

Based on the above, think through the resources, experience, and characteristics you want in a rep. Do they need a showroom? Do they need experience? (A key decision: Would you rather have a hungry young rep, or a more established rep with less time to give to your line? Both approaches have their merits.) Do they need to know above-buyer-level personnel in key targeted accounts? Are they detail-oriented?

How will you make your decision on whom to hire? Do you want more than one interview? Are references required, and if so, who will check them? (The two best places to check references are with buyers in the territory, and companies they currently represent and used to represent.)

When you've got these kinds of questions answered in your own mind, start trying to find the right person or people to fill the bill. As with reference checking, a good technique is to call buyers to whom you want to sell and ask them for recommendations. Alternatively, call a rep whom you trust and ask him or her. (Believe me: they all network, and the word will get around.) This has worked best for me over the years.

Check the appropriate media, and advertise in them. Reps looking for positions run ads in trade publications; you can scan those, and also place your own ("position offered"). Running an ad in a regular newspaper can also be a good idea. Call editors of industry magazines and ask them for recommendations. Visit trade shows and trade buildings. If you have a booth at a trade show, put up an ad there. Call up trade associations and ask if they maintain current listings.

And finally, find out if someone else has already done your work for you. Some industries produce books listing reps in all geographic areas. Many quality manufacturers, moreover, run trade ads listing the names and addresses of all their reps. Surely you can think of some way to use lists like these productively.

Reps' complaints about manufacturers

Reps don't lack for opinions about manufacturers. In my years of being a rep and dealing with reps, I often heard them talk about manufacturers. I present the following list to illustrate the range of problems that arise in the minds of reps, as they think about their relationships with manufacturers. If you can avoid these problems as a manufacturer, you're likely to have great representation in the field:

- They don't pay on time, or accurately.
- If I do too much business, they might replace me with in-house personnel, cut the commission, or shrink my territory.
- They don't communicate well:
    - They don't pass on enough product knowledge
    - I don't receive timely copies of invoices
    - When an item is a poor seller, I'm not told, and I stick my best customers with it
    - They don't tell me about new products
    - They don't share success stories from other territories
    - They don't send copies of ads from other territories
    - They don't keep me abreast of inventory status and out-of-stock items
- They give my customers better prices or terms than I am empowered to give.
- They don't listen to my input, and afford me no respect for my experience.
- They have a poor customer service department.
- They don't set realistic goals—or have *no* shared goals or expectations.

- They hire sales managers who don't understand the business.
- They don't ship on time (or ship incomplete).
- Product quality is poor.
- They don't innovate enough new products.
- Their new product introductions are always too late.
- They don't tell the truth, and break promises.
- They expect too much from the rep in terms of collecting bills.
- They talk to my buyers without keeping me in the loop.
- They have too many "house accounts" in my territory.
- They have poor follow-through and don't pay attention to detail.
- They don't understand the business.
- They hide problems.

Manufacturers' complaints about reps

To be even-handed, I should also present the kinds of gripes that man-ufacturers have about reps. Note that some of these complaints mirror the complaints in the preceding list. Again, if you can avoid this range of problems, you'll be in good shape:

- They carry too many lines.
- They don't sell my whole line; instead, they cherry-pick and sell the best-selling items only.
- They don't return my phone calls, faxes, or letters.
- They lack knowledge of my product line.
- They carry competitive lines.
- They are 98 percent in the buyers' camp and 2 percent in mine— and I write their checks!
- They don't stand up to the buyers when the buyers are wrong.
- They look to sell on price only.
- They spend too much time in their showroom.
- They give unauthorized deals to buyers and don't tell us.
- Their follow-through is awful.
- They don't give me feedback on their calls, or on our competition.
- They misrepresent the company.
- They don't always tell the truth.
- They don't train their sub-reps.
- Their sales are below my expectations.
- They keep pressing for higher commissions.
- We can't read their orders (which are often incomplete anyway).

Training the reps

Once you've gone through the arduous task of finding and retaining a good rep to work for you, don't make the mistake that many companies make. They mail their new reps some samples, catalogues, and price sheets, and wait for the orders to roll in.

Take this approach, and you're almost certain to be disappointed. And it won't be the rep's fault. Think about it: would you train any of your full-time people that casually?

What should you do instead? Depending on your budget, here are some ideas:

- **Have the rep visit your offices and/or factory.** There they can personally meet the people with whom they'll be dealing. This personal contact is important. You can show them your full line, fill them in on the history and traditions of the company, and share your vision with them.

  Meanwhile, you can also be stating clearly your expectations of them. You should pay careful attention to the issue of sales quotas. These should be worked out jointly, rather than imposed arbitrarily by you. (If your rep is as good as you hope, he/she knows more about some key things than you do.) Get him/her to buy into a shared number.

  If yours is a new company, your rep will expect you to pay for this trip. Perhaps you could arrange a deal whereby you share this expense, with their portion coming out of commissions.

- **Visit the rep.** If you can't afford to bring the rep to you, you should consider going to him/her. If your rep shares space with other people—e.g., shared office personnel or sub-reps—it may be beneficial for you to meet with all of these people. (Obviously, this doesn't apply to a rep working solo out of home.) You can learn about their resources while you're educating them about your company and its products.

  Ahead of this visit, ask the rep to set up sales calls for you to tag along on. These should include visits to some major existing accounts, and possibly some potential accounts. Making these calls will help you learn more about the rep's abilities and the strengths of his/her relationships with buyer. It will help you determine what kinds of information you need to supply to help sell your products. Meanwhile, you can be sharing your own thoughts about the best way to represent your company and its products.

You might try a variety of approaches on these calls. For example, at an early stop, you might present the product and company to the prospective client, and ask the rep to pick up the banner when it comes to talking specifically about benefits to this particular buyer. On subsequent calls, the rep might carry the whole load.

One fringe benefit of tagging along, by the way, is that this is one occasion on which your rep will talk only about *your* products. He or she certainly won't present multiple companies and their product lines if you're also in the room.

- **Work regional trade shows with your reps if they are exhibiting.** This will help you accomplish most of the ends described in the one-on-one calls above. It will also give you insights into your reps' other lines, how they allocate space to each, and how they deal with new and small customers.
- **Make time for socializing.** Whichever of the above techniques you employ, also try to spend some social time with your salespeople. If you're taking them out to dinner, invite their spouses to join you. Remember that you're seeking to build strong relationships with your salespeople.

And remember that these reps are, for the most part, strong-willed, skilled, entrepreneurial types themselves. You really *can't* order them around. Instead, you need to *persuade* them to give your products a fair share of their time—and if you're just starting out in a relationship with them, you're likely to be at the bottom of the priority list. So sell yourself to them, to their staffers (if any), and to their spouses.

The training of reps is a constant process. It doesn't stop after one visit, or after thirty visits. As you grow, one of the first major hires you should consider is a sales manager whose primary duty will be to work with and train the sales force. This will free you up to work on other important aspects of building your business. I strongly recommend, however, that you stay in touch with your sales force. Let your sales manager know why you're doing it, too: you're doing it to stay in contact with a rapidly changing marketplace.

Most of the preceding discussion also pertains if you decide to use full-time salespeople. One major difference, of course, is that you have more control over them, but again, if they're any good, simply issuing orders isn't going to do the trick. They still will need to be persuaded to make their best possible efforts to help you and your company succeed.

A tip for reps

Much of this chapter is devoted to helping entrepreneurs understand how the manufacturer-rep relationship works. I've made this a priority because I think that in many cases, reps can help entrepreneurs achieve perfection: low risk, high reward.

But I think I should include a reward here for any rep who's gotten this far into this chapter. What follows is an idea that took me many years to arrive at, and which turned out to be worth a lot of incremental profits to me.

First, let's reconstruct our starting point, which was a very traditional one: When we were reps, we sold goods for manufacturers who paid us a predetermined commission on the wholesale value of our sales. We worked on a national basis. Our approach was to look for one or two promising items, rather than extensive lines.

Given that focus, it was very common for us to come across "one-item manufacturers." In many cases, in fact, they came to *us,* and tried to persuade us to sell their product. The problem that many of these manufacturers had was that large retailers didn't want to buy from one-item companies. It was too expensive for the retailer to add a new vendor number; the freight factor could be high on single products; and the retailer's top management was always hammering on the buyers to cut down on the number of vendors.

After thinking about this for a while, we stumbled on the idea of having our own vendor number. This allowed us to put all of the single items in our line under this one number. Yes, the shipping points were all different, but the vendors' systems were accustomed to dealing with large companies that had multiple shipping points. And yes, by going this route, we became responsible for billing and collecting. So what we did was instead of working on a 10 percent commission, we marked the product up 35 percent. In return for the extra 25 percent, we took responsibility for billing the customer, carrying the credit, and performing some extra paperwork.

Manufacturers loved us, because suddenly they had a way to do substantial volume with one entity. We were an entity, moreover, that paid on time. They began treating us far better than when we were "only" commissioned reps. In fact, almost overnight, we went from being a lower life form to a higher one.

Buyers, too, loved us. They could now take advantage of one-item companies without making trouble with their own number crunchers. In fact, they got in the habit of referring good one-item prospects to us.

All in all, we loved this role as a "billing rep." We made much more money, and dramatically reduced the chances that we would have a good line taken away from us if we did "too good a job" and our commission checks got too big. In fact, because we were controlling the billing and not dealing in branded products, we could change the manufacturer without upsetting the buyer. Our only real risk was that a customer might go bankrupt and not pay, but we minimized our risk by selling this deal only to AAA-rated customers whom we knew well.

It was win–win–win, for all three parties involved.

The future of reps

As the preceding pages amply illustrate, the manufacturer/rep relationship is a complicated one, and frequently adversarial. But most of the time, in my experience, the relationship can be made beneficial to both parties, if both parties want to make it work. *Both parties need each other.*

I do perceive some outside-world trends that are today posing a threat to the traditional manufacturer/rep relationship. If you are contemplating signing on reps, you should be aware of these kinds of potential problems.

First of all, larger retailers are beginning to insist that all orders be placed electronically (EDI). Smaller reps and manufacturers either can't afford the equipment, resist it, or fail to realize the importance of adapting to new technologies. When a traditional rep service is eliminated, his or her job is less important and therefore less secure. Technology advances are generally working against the use of reps, unless a rep can embrace the technology that smaller manufacturers don't have.

Many large retailers are going to dominant manufacturers, giving them permanent real estate in their stores, and telling them to manage the space to produce a certain level of profits. When this happens, reps become less important. At the same time, many retailers are going to private labels on volume products, thereby increasing their margins. Again, the need for a rep is diminished.

Large retailers are consciously scrutinizing the amount of business they do with small companies, to prevent any of those companies from becoming too large a percentage of their business. At the same time, they are pressuring their buyers to deal with fewer resources and carry fewer sku's ("stock-keeping units," a common industry reference to every product offered for sale).

And not least important, given consolidations and economic dislocations, there are both fewer retailers and fewer manufacturers out there.

In light of these more or less ominous trends, it seems clear that manufacturers and reps have to get their act together and work more closely and honestly with each other. They have a shared challenge: to persuade the retailer that their team has something of value to offer to them. This is getting tougher—and you should be prepared to deal with it—but it's not impossible to do, and succeeding at it can be immensely valuable to your business.

SELLING WITHOUT A FIELD-BASED SALES FORCE OR REPS

Many companies acquire their sales without either salaried salespeople or reps. They choose this route because:

- it often has lower costs;
- it allows the company to control its sales message more effectively;
- it is more easily measured and assessed; or because
- it has faster cycle times (i.e., it allows for quicker strategic changes by the company, more rapid contact with the customer, and faster responses from the customer).

There are two primary techniques for "no-body" selling. They are *direct response advertising,* and *trade shows.*

Direct response advertising

The Direct Marketing Association (DMA), the leading association in this field, defines direct response advertising as "any direct communication to a consumer or business recipient that is designed to generate a response in the form of an order, a request for further information, and/or a visit to a store or other place of business, for purchase of a specific product or service." I am referring here to the first two of these three possible responses: an order, or a request for more information.

The media that are available for use are direct mail, billing stuffers (those things that come, for example, with your gasoline credit card statements), television, radio, magazines, the Internet, catalogues, and the phone (in the form of telemarketing).

Direct response advertising is a huge and growing sector. According to the DMA, total 1998 sales in this channel exceeded $1,371.5 billion. Between 1993 and 1998, this total has grown by an annual average of 8.8 percent, and is projected to increase by 8.4 percent annually between 1999 and 2004. Segments reflected in these figures include direct mail, telephone marketing, newspaper, magazine, television, radio, and other miscellaneous categories. (Note that these figures don't include the Internet, discussed below, which may ultimately be the leading direct response segment.) More than $162 billion in advertising dollars were spent in 1998 on direct response media.

Of course, direct response advertising figures can be a little misleading, because much of it is done in coordination with a sales force. My point here, though, is that you can use direct response advertising without a sales force, and still produce significant results. Look at Dell Computer, a company that has generated billions in sales without the use of *any* salespeople or reps having face-to-face dialogues with potential customers. Or take the example of the Oreck vacuum cleaner company, which has built and sustained a major business selling its product through direct response only. (To reinforce and assist their sales via direct response, Oreck refuses to sell their product to retail stores.)

If your product is right, and you find the right way to present it, direct response can be a gold mine, with much less risk than selling through retail. I believe this sector will grow dramatically in the coming years, as sales on the Internet continue to soar. Some Internet sales will cannibalize existing direct response channels, but more will come at the expense of retail. The best current example is Amazon.com, the Internet-based retailer. Barnes & Noble has been compelled to defend its existing retail network against incursions by Amazon, and has also jumped aggressively into Internet sales.

For more information on direct marketing, contact DMA at 1120 Avenue of the Americas, New York, NY 10036-6700 (212-768-7277). Fax 212-302-6714. E-mail http://www.the-dma.org

The Internet

Business owners above a certain age—unfortunately including me—didn't grow up with computers. Many of us dinosaurs tend to discount the potential of doing commerce on the Internet. But this skepticism extends to other business people as well, including successful mainstream or niche businesses who believe that:

- at worst, the Internet can't hurt them;
- the Internet isn't really applicable to their kind of business; or
- the Internet (and its very visible sidekick, the World Wide Web) are a passing or overhyped fad.

Sorry; I have to disagree. The numbers say that the Internet is a serious, established channel of distribution. Yes, it's still in its infancy, but it is clearly destined to be the fastest-growing channel for the foreseeable future. Here are the kinds of numbers I'm talking about:

- There are 20 million online shoppers in the United States with a projected 80 million by 2003. Worldwide, there were over 92 million Internet users in 1998, and the current expectation is that this number will swell to 320 million by the end of 2002.
- Holiday sales via the Internet in 1998 tripled to $5 billion, while per capita spending more than doubled. Online spending was projected to exceed $20 billion in 1999. Current projections for annual Internet-based spending in the early years of the twenty-first century range from $500 billion to $1.3 *trillion*.

More evidence? The investment community is certainly betting heavily on the future success of the Internet. Venture money continues to pour into ongoing and start-up Internet companies, whose stocks sell for astounding multiples (despite their lack of profits). And look at some of the current corporate valuations of Internet-oriented companies, which underscore the dramatic changes now under way. As of this writing, AOL is worth more than all of the following companies *combined:* Sears, General Motors, Toys "R" Us, Barnes & Noble, Mar-

riott, J. C. Penney, Disney, Caterpillar, and Union Pacific. Microsoft—
not strictly an "internet" company, but increasingly a player in that
arena—is worth more than AT&T, Procter & Gamble, and Coca-Cola
combined. Could anyone have imagined this dramatic turn of events,
even ten years ago?

The Net seems to lend itself to almost every imaginable product or
service, but some in particular are proving well suited to e-commerce.
These include:

- products with great selection that benefit from data-based "search-
  ability" (books, CDs, videos, toys)
- products that are information-rich (e.g., software and associated
  documentation)
- products that are sold largely through information (vitamins, phar-
  maceuticals)
- products that are "anonymity-attractive" (contraceptives, books
  with sensitive titles, etc.)
- products that traditionally have been sold by high-pressure salespeople (e.g., cars)

Were you surprised at that last category? I was. AutoNation, one of
the largest auto retailers, recently announced sales of $150 million in
1998 through its Web sites. It expects this figure to rise to $750 million
in 1999.

It seems to me that the Internet is particularly well suited for exploitation by small and entrepreneurial businesses. It doesn't require
enormous resources to get into or play the game. There is no real estate to buy, no factories to build, and (on an apples-to-apples basis)
fewer bodies to worry about. Your screen size is the same as General
Motors's, in the eyes of a Web user, which means that the playing field
is somewhat leveled. Yes, a huge company will still have advantages
over you. It can buy more expensive Web designers, and it can spend
tons of money advertising its site. One reason Amazon.com, the Web-
based retailer, hasn't made money is that it continues to invest heavily
in getting people to visit its site online.

But this is an exciting new medium and channel, and it is evolving
rapidly. One reason for this rapid evolution is that both established and
new talents are migrating to the Internet, because there's a general
agreement that it's changing the way we do business, and live our lives.

This cycle will feed on itself: the more good people that go into this field, the faster it will change and the more important it will become in our lives. The challenge for small business entrepreneurs, of course, is to figure out a way to benefit from the current window of opportunity.

As I see it, this is a field in which creativity and flexibility will be at least as important as brute financial strength. And when it comes to creativity and flexibility, your company should have it all over most Fortune 500 companies

Trade shows

Most industries sponsor annual trade shows, where buyers come to a central location to make contact with exhibiting vendors in a particular industry. These shows can be national or regional in orientation. Many small businesses focus on exhibiting and selling at these shows, rather than deploying a sales force to call on these same prospective customers.

Sometimes the product simply demands this kind of approach to the sales challenge. For example, some products are simply too big for salespeople to carry, or they perform tasks that can't be demonstrated easily in the buyer's office or the customer's home.

There are pros and cons to the trade show approach. You can put together certain kinds of razzle-dazzle at a show that are hard to duplicate one-on-one, and of course, you can put your best salesperson front-and-center at a trade show. At a show, you can control your message, and you're not depending on a rep (who probably has other lines he or she is promoting) to get your message across clearly.

On the other hand, there's a quality of communication that occurs in a one-on-one meeting that isn't duplicated at a trade show. Trade shows can be overwhelming: in a context where *everybody* is razzling and dazzling, your razzle-dazzle may get lost in the shuffle. And of course, you can't count on all of your prospective customers showing up at your booth, or even at the show. Buyers also have less time to give you at a show—and two of them may show up at the same time. If you're a newcomer to an industry, you may have to get on a waiting list to get space on the floor, or you may have to accept a poor location. (Using a well-established sales rep might solve this problem for you, because many of them control high-visibility floor space at trade shows.)

The upshot, obviously, is that you have to figure out the best solution for *your* product—and your budget, capabilities, and style. There's no one correct method or mix of methods. Try something. If it works, then try adding something (or, less likely, taking something away).

———

At the beginning of this chapter, I promised that I wouldn't give "a complete selling tutorial in this short chapter." The chapter got to be longer than I suspected, but it's still far from complete. I hope you can take useful tips away from it, and I'm sure you can add to it.

The next chapter carries the sales challenge to the following step: the reorder stage.

9

THE REORDER

Now that we've got that coveted initial order—the sale, as described
in chapter 8—perhaps the most challenging task that faces your company is to get a *repeat order*. This sounds simple enough, on the face of
it. If your company provides a service, a reorder will come if the customer is, first, completely satisfied with that service, and second, still
needs that service. If your company provides a product to a retailer, a
reorder will come if that product sells through to the end consumer,
and if the retailer feels that your product is in demand, and will stay in
demand. "Staying in demand" means not only that original demand
outstripped original supply, but that satisfaction with the product and
good word of mouth will create an ongoing demand.

But this all-important "second sale" is very often neglected by entrepreneurs. Ask an entrepreneur with a fairly new product or service
how sales are doing, and he or she is very likely to say, "Great!" And
this may, in fact, be true: that product may be flying off the shelves of
the warehouse, or all the hours of the people providing that service
may be sold out. The problem arises, however, when all of this great
sales volume consists of initial orders and doesn't include *re*orders.

Entrepreneurs are optimists. With a rush of initial orders comes a
certain kind of euphoria. "It's working," the entrepreneur is likely to
conclude, with justifiable excitement. "This product we've been slav-
ing over and lavishing time and money on all these months is a hit!"

And it's a short step from there to saying, "Let's pile up inventories so we'll be prepared to meet this soaring demand!"

Big mistake! I learned this the hard way in the late 1980s, when my company—working in partnership with a picture frame manufacturer—secured the license for picture frames from a number of major magazines, including *Time, Sports Illustrated, Golf, Cosmopolitan, Modern Bride, Bon Appetit, Life,* and *Playboy*. The idea was that the consumer would put a picture of their own in the frame, which had a clear acetate cover that replicated the magazine's cover. Your doting mate could put you on the cover of *Time* as "Man of the Year," or nominate you as "Golfer of the Year," "Chef of the Year," "Playmate of the Year," and so on.

We were able to work out deals with most of the magazines to get free ads promoting their respective frames, and directing the reader to a retailer who was carrying the product. (Low risk!) Buyers absolutely loved this product. The orders came pouring in. We and our manufacturing partner began to have visions of ourselves as a major, major frame company. Seduced by this dream and by the very positive reactions of the buyers, we cranked up production and waited for the anticipated avalanche of reorders.

What happened next? In a word, *nothing.* Despite our strong advertising, good retail displays, and distributors' enthusiasm, there was a deafening silence from the marketplace. Our customers—department stores, mass merchandisers, gift stores, catalogue houses, and home-shopping networks alike—all came back to us with exactly the same bad news: the consumer had *absolutely no interest* in this product any more. We wound up taking a bath on our heavy excess inventories, and giving away the profits we could have pocketed from our heavy initial orders.

The point of my sad story is that reorders are essential to sustain and grow a business. What can an entrepreneur with limited capital do to stimulate that all-important "second sale"?

Reorders, according to the textbooks, are one of the results of an activity called *marketing,* which the dictionary defines as "all business activity involved in the moving of goods from the producer to the consumer." This is the broadest possible definition, and it includes distribution and other getting-the-product-to-market kinds of activities. The word *marketing* is also applied to promotional activities like "marketing a celebrity," which in my mind further clouds its meaning.

So, I'll nominate an alternative term to serve as an umbrella for the activities described in this chapter: *sell-through.* As explained in the last chapter, when you focus your sales effort on the middleman, you are "selling in." But when you focus your sales efforts on the end user, you are selling through. You are creating the demand that will pull your product through the channels of distribution. First, I'll run through some of the techniques you can use to promote sell-through. Later in the chapter, I'll focus on three additional activities of critical importance to the reorder process: keeping the customer satisfied; managing your inventory; and controlling knockoffs.

GETTING SELL-THROUGH

There are all kinds of techniques available to stimulate demand for your product. They range from expensive to free and from complicated to simple. Some involve the use of outside help, and others can be wholly or mostly homegrown. Most companies use several of these techniques in combination, or in a sequence that makes sense from budgetary and other perspectives.

Word of mouth

This is the best and highest-quality advertising for a product or a brand. This is mainly how successful movies become successful—people tell other people about how much they liked a particular movie, and the word spreads. Think how quickly the news about a great movie gets around. Word of mouth, both good and bad, is powerful!

So, we can agree that good word of mouth is highly desirable, but we should also admit that it's extremely difficult to generate. For the most part, your product or service has to make its own friends. It has to fill a customer need and meet consumer expectations, be of high quality, need minimal maintenance, have a value price, be easy to use, come with instructions that are both thorough and easy to understand, have strong service and warranty support, or have some combination of these or other virtues.

Refer back to chapter 7 (products) for a refresher course on how to push your product up to this level of excellence. Meanwhile, keep in mind that *word of mouth usually takes a lot of time.* Movies benefit from unusually speedy word of mouth, in part because it doesn't take long (90 minutes, more or less) to consume and assess that product. If your product is a snowblower, by contrast, it may be quite a while before it gets tested under just the right conditions, before which there's no possibility of good word of mouth. If your product or service is trying to win market share in a highly competitive sector—toothpaste or laundry soap—it may take several word-of-mouth "hits" before a consumer will switch from an existing product to yours. Or someone may become convinced through word of mouth that your vacuum cleaner is absolutely the one to have, but she's going to wait until her old machine conks out before switching to your superior brand.

A good way to "jump-start" word of mouth is to provide samples of your product in advance of your launch to carefully selected opinion leaders. If you can get a movie star or famous athlete to use your product, it's likely to create a buzz around that product. Don't know any movie stars? Well, is there another kind of celebrity, or expert, to whom you *can* get access?

To summarize: make sure your product fosters good word of mouth, avoid bad word of mouth like the plague, concentrate on getting your initial orders so that your great product gets in front of the consumer—and also make sure that you've got the resources to hang in there until word of mouth saves the day.

And meanwhile, think of reinforcing your good word of mouth with some other techniques—described below—which can add momentum to your product.

Advertising

Anyone who has been paying attention in capitalist countries over the past few centuries will recognize this tactic: using ads to get consumers to buy your product. Effective advertising can make the difference between a product's life or death.

But figuring out *how* to advertise—where, when, and how extensively—is no simple task. The first and most important question to answer is, How much can you afford to spend? Companies with large advertising budgets can (and in most cases should) retain an advertising agency—a group of professionals who greatly assist them with media strategic and creative decisions. If you're in that situation, my only advice is the same as I offered in earlier chapters regarding the use of professionals: *Stay involved.* Understand the biases and incentives of the people you're working with, and make sure all decisions are made in your company's best interests.

But companies with bottomless ad budgets are uncommon, and don't need any help from me. In this context, I'd like to concentrate on the needs of the company with a limited advertising budget.

Cooperative advertising. Let's assume that you are selling to a retailer. In this case, an effective limited-budget strategy is to give "cooperative money," which is used to share the cost of an ad with that retailer. Often, this cooperative money takes the form of a percentage allowance on purchases. In other words, rather than paying 100 percent of what they owe you, the retailers pay (for example) only 95 percent, and that 5 percent difference (called the *allowance*) goes into a pot of money that is used to create and run ads that benefit both you and the retailer. These ads may appear in newspapers, in flyers that are inserted into newspapers, in catalogues, or in materials that are mailed directly to consumers.

This approach has many advantages. First, of course, it transforms your ad expense from fixed to variable—a basic tenet of low-risk, high-reward entrepreneurship. Second, it's a lot cheaper than paying for the ad by yourself—not only because costs are shared, but because a big retailer probably can purchase the ad space at a major discount because of their larger overall ad volume. Also, you get the credibility of that retailer's name, which is better known to the target consumer than is yours. Remember that the retailer most likely has been "training" people to look for its ads in a certain format and in a certain place, week after week. By joining forces with that retailer, you instantly get access to eyeballs that are paying attention and are predisposed.

Remember, too, that when a store decides to run an ad on a product, a number of related actions are usually triggered. The store buys more product, which is fine from your point of view. In addition, they are likely to conduct a sales meeting with store clerks to familiarize them with the product. They may give you more and better real estate in the store. What this all means is that even if the ad itself is not espe-cially effective, the *side benefits* of that ad are likely to push up sales. This is particularly true if your product is an impulse buy, or if you have the benefit of great packaging.

Except for cost, there's no reason not to carry the cooperative con-cept into other media, as well. If your retailer advertises on radio or TV, they may agree to include your product in those ads (and draw on the cooperative money to help pay for them). Rest assured that other large retailers will be reviewing these ads, and they may decide as a re-sult that it's time to start doing business with you.

One thing you should fight very hard for, in all these various kinds of cooperative ads, is to get your *company name* mentioned along with your product's name. This is a low-cost brand builder, which over the long run can work very well for you. It can help you transfer con-sumer loyalty from your older products to your newer products. It also gets store management in your partnering company familiar with your company name, which usually strengthens your bargaining position down the road. Anything you can do to raise your company's profile, both with consumers and with store management, is likely to have a whole range of beneficial effects.

Multiple retail listing advertisements. Another approach is to run your own newspaper ad in a given city or region, and list in that ad all the stores in that area which are carrying your product. Obviously, this is more expensive than a cooperative ad with one store, but it has the great advantage of spotlighting more retailers in your overall market-ing campaign. It lets consumers see all the places where they can shop for your product, and—hopefully—find one that's convenient to their home or office. And like the cooperative ad, it can also help foster a "stampede mentality" in the marketplace. Upper-level-stores man-agers come across an ad like this and look for their store's name on the list. When they don't find it, they may well cut it out and send it to the appropriate buyer with a pointed note attached: "Why aren't *we* buy-ing this item?"

Multiple retail listing ads can be particularly effective if you are sell-ing to large numbers of smaller stores. In many cases, these are compa-nies that don't do much advertising themselves, and that often feel their suppliers are working in cahoots with the big stores. When you pay to put their name in print—often in the company of their larger and better-financed competitors—you may be doing something pretty special for them. You may engender both loyalty and larger orders.

You will, of course, make an appointment with the right person at each of these stores and bring this ad to their attention. But you and your sales team can be proactive ahead of time, as well. As you make your sales calls, show the buyers the proposed layout of the upcoming ad, and tell them that you'd be happy to include their store's name in the ad at no cost—if they're prepared to place a minimum order for your product.

When you are preparing multiple retail listing ads, remember that this may be a good opportunity for you to get into magazine advertising. Most national magazines have regional *splits,* which allow you to list different retailers in different sections of the country in the same national ad. (And in many cases, you can also buy a strictly regional ad.) There are also city magazines in most of the major markets. Ads in these contexts can help you both with selling in (to retailers) and selling through (to consumers). Magazines have a longer shelf life than newspapers, which gives them an edge for some purposes.

Just to state the obvious one more time: In these ads, you control the "creative" (as the ad's copy and layout are informally referred to in the advertising business). So *make sure to get your company's name and logo into these ads,* as well as product details. Build awareness of and loyalty to your company, at the same time that you're pushing today's products.

Home-shopping companies

Selling your product to home-shopping companies like QVC, HSN, and CVN is a form of free advertising. Usually they show your product for at least five minutes on TV, at no cost to you. (Be prepared, however, to take back any unsold goods. This is less of a problem on reorders, obviously.) In addition to generating orders, you are receiving TV exposure, which can only help your sell-through in other areas. Getting an expert or celebrity to present your product will help you gain acceptance with home shoppers. There are also reps who specialize in these kinds of accounts.

Statement inserts

Another good technique is to put your money into what's called *statement inserts.* These are those little announcements that show up tucked into your monthly statement from your credit card, retailer, or gasoline-card sponsor. Yes, most people just throw them away most of the time; but a small number of people actually do buy things this way, and you don't need a big response to justify the cost of a statement insert.

Direct mailers will measure their responses by percentage pull (one-half-of-1 percent = 1 in 200) or in dollars per thousand (total retail dollar sales divided by the number of thousand inserts used). Either way, you need to know all your costs and your per unit profit, to determine your Breakdown Response.

The placement of these inserts varies by channel of distribution. In department stores, the process generally originates with the buyer. The store can prepare the insert, or they may use your art. It's relatively expensive to work in this channel, because department stores usually treat advertising as a profit center, and require you to pay for the full cost of the insert program. They usually don't allow you to raise the cost of the product to them to help offset your costs.

Most companies like J. C. Penney and Sears have separate departments and buyers to handle inserts. If you pay for the inserts, you can get more money for your product. Sometimes, you can pay nothing, but sell at a reduced cost (low risk!). The retailer usually holds most of the cards, however, since there are usually too many companies vying for limited insert space. As a result, some retailers are now asking for a guaranteed minimum profit to them for an enclosure. This can be risky. I'd advise you do this in small quantities, first time out.

Inserts with oil companies, banks, and other generators of monthly statements are placed through third parties termed *syndicators*. They can be reached by calling them directly, or through the specialty reps who service them. Syndicators either create the insert at their expense, or bill you for creative services. In many cases, they will ask you to drop-ship to consumers for them, particularly during the testing period. Prices vary considerably, depending on who's paying for what, your relationship to the syndicator, and the uniqueness of and demand for your product.

Per inquiry advertisements

Let's assume that you have *no* advertising budget. How do you get your name out there, among the consumers you hope will pull your product through the stores?

One answer is *per inquiry* (P.I.) ads. How does this work? In most cases, media outlets (newspapers, magazines, radio, TV, etc.) fail to sell all of their advertising space. Think of ad space as the equivalent of hotel rooms. If a hotel room sits empty, it's revenue potential that's gone forever. The same holds true for ad space. When that show's broadcast ends, or that newspaper or magazine hits the streets, the opportunity to sell space is over.

How do you take advantage of this? Easy. You prepare an ad with a coupon for direct response, and give it to (for example) a magazine. They run the ad at no advertising cost to you. In return, you give them a percentage of the sale—perhaps 50 percent. This is a P.I. deal, and in my experience, it's a true win-win. The magazine gets a chance to generate some income where they otherwise would have generated nothing. The manufacturer generates some immediate sales, and also gets a "free" ad that can help create sell-through at the retail level.

Be aware that the P.I. approach requires you, as the manufacturer, to have the capability of shipping individual customer orders. The magazine's only involvement is to run the ad; after that, all inventory and fulfillment responsibilities belong to you.

I used a magazine for my example because that's by far the most common medium in which P.I. ads show up. Newspapers and TV and radio outlets also accept P.I. ads, in some circumstances. In the case of electronic media, you will need to supply the completed ad in whatever format that station or network requests. Again, fulfillment is entirely your responsibility.

One word of advice: In most cases, you're better off not including your company name in the coupon. Some retailers with whom you're already working may feel, if they see your name in that coupon, that you're competing with them by drawing off some of their potential sales. I know that this kind of ad exposure can only help them—but it's not always an argument that they buy. So this is one case in which you want to be careful about a high company profile.

Public relations

In chapter 6, I talked about how public relations can be helpful in building your company. Obviously, publicity can be the crucial element in the sell-in and sell-through of your product. PR-generated publicity can be much less expensive and—under the right circumstances—far more powerful than advertising.

Where's the proof? It's all over the place. The Pet Rock—one of history's less indispensable products—began its astounding run with a blurb in *Newsweek*. Trivial Pursuit became the all-time best-selling game in a single year mainly because of publicity. The Tickle-Me-Elmo doll craze began when Rosie O'Donnell featured it on her TV show. And when Oprah anoints a book with her "book club" designation, author and publisher alike click their heels with delight.

There are no guarantees with PR, but—depending on how you do it—it's affordable, and even the smallest of businesses can play the game. The media are particularly susceptible to a herd mentality, and once one story appears on your company or product, others are likely to follow.

So, how do you get good publicity? As with advertising, there are many different approaches, which may work separately or in combination.

The PR firm

The traditional way to generate publicity is to hire a PR firm. PR firms specialize in getting appropriate media to pay attention to their clients, mainly by using media contacts whom they've cultivated over the years. They may also be skilled at staging events that get free media coverage, ranging from press conferences to personal appearances to attention-grabbing stunts. The result is generally "soft" news, but remember that the media are always hungry for material to fill pages or air time.

Engaging a PR firm can start as a limited commitment—say, sixty to ninety days in duration—which can be extended if it proves effective for you. If you go this route, try to find firms that have had experience with products like yours. Get the firm to tell you exactly who will be working on your account, and what that person or those people bring to the task.

Press releases and samples

Have no money for PR, or not sure it's the best way to spend your limited marketing resources? Try doing it yourself.

If you have an appropriate product, try sending samples accompanied by a note to key media people. Follow up your package with phone calls, letters, and more phone calls. Keep following up until something happens.

If you are selling your product to a major retailer in town, talk to their publicity people about contacting the media regarding your product. Realism pays off, in cases like this: the media are likely to be more responsive to companies (like large retailers) who buy lots of ad space from them. Give the retailer's publicists free samples of your product. With their permission, mail or hand-deliver publicity packages under their name.

Send product releases to major national media that you feel reach your targeted customers. Again, don't hesitate to send free samples (as well as pictures and succinct product descriptions) to these outlets, especially after you've figured out who the right contact person is (see below). Remember that this approach is likely to work *only if you take care of the details, especially follow-up.* When one of your target media outlets finally responds to your overtures, you have to be prepared to answer their questions or otherwise meet their needs quickly and thoroughly.

I like Mike Hsieh's approach to press management. He identifies an influential reporter who specializes in an area that corresponds to one of Mike's products. He then contacts that reporter on a regular basis, and focuses the conversation on an interesting piece of industry or market news—in other words, *not* on himself or his company. In this way, he becomes the expert on the industry, and the reporter tends to look to Mike whenever he or she needs to quote an authoritative voice. Mike tells me that this approach has worked very well for him.

Standard Rate and Data Service (SRDS) puts out monthly publications covering all the magazines and newspapers in the country. These summaries include circulation figures, rates, phone numbers, key editorial staffers (and in the case of magazines, the subjects covered by these staffers), and other vital bits of information. They can be reached at 847-375-5000 (phone), 847-375-5001 (fax), or www.srds.com. If you know someone who works at an ad agency, ask them to give you their last month's copy of the relevant SRDS publication.

Other directories include Leadership Directories's *News Media Yellow Book,* a quarterly publication which lists newspapers, television and radio stations, magazines and other periodicals, and news services, and gives information on each company's addresses and personnel. They are in New York and can be reached at 212-627-4140 (phone), 212-645-0931 (fax), or www.leadershipdirectories.com.

The *Editor and Publisher Year Book* is an annual directory covering newspapers in the United States and Canada, wire services, and syndicated columnists. They can be reached at 212-675-4380 (phone), 212-691-6939 (fax), or www.mediainfo.com.

I recommend that you make media outreach someone's explicit responsibility—whether yours or someone else's—to make sure that things don't fall between the cracks. Media people work under more or less intense deadline pressure, and very often go with the path of least resistance. If you're on that path, you're far more likely to get rewarded.

Demonstrations

Another very effective way to pull sales through the distribution channels is product demonstrations. If you make a food product, for example, you can hand out tastes or free samples to consumers in the store where your product is available. Stores are usually willing to go along with a demonstration, and even put it in a high-traffic area, because it creates excitement and makes their store stand out from the pack.

The downside of demonstrations is that they put you into the personnel business (high risk!). In almost all cases, you've got to provide the trained personnel to pull off a successful demonstration. For this reason, many companies limit their demonstrations to the product launch stage. A smaller number, though—usually with high margins and a history of successful demos—use demonstrations as an ongoing selling tool.

Part of the high cost of demonstrations can be recouped by giving the retailer smaller margins. Many stores will go along with this—in part for the excitement factor mentioned above, and in part because demos generate incremental sales at no risk or cost to them. (Retailers, too, think low risk/high reward.)

Sales training

For many products, particularly those with a heavy technical component, a trained sales force is crucial to success.

Everyone who sells for you—whether on-staff salespeople, reps, or people on the front lines selling direct to consumers—needs training. Training not only helps people understand the product and its consumer benefits, but also creates enthusiasm for your product and your company. This kind of excitement translates directly into sales.

If your products are sold at the retail level, it's usually a great idea to have a sales training meeting with the sales clerks who are staffing the counters where your products are sold. (This applies both to technical and to non-technical products.) Although this kind of meeting can be very difficult to get, it can also be very valuable in turning the sales clerks on to your product and company. Besides getting them more comfortable and knowledgeable about your product, it sets the stage for a relationship that can give you important feedback from them.

Videos on your company and products can be an effective training tool. In addition, many of your larger customers will have satellite hookups to their employees, which they use to transmit large volumes of information. Try to get in on one of these broadcasts to inform these employees about your company or product. If they won't let you go this route, try scripting a message for your buyer.

Packaging

In chapter 7, I encouraged you to help your product succeed by coming up with great packaging. I'm taking this opportunity to emphasize that effective packaging can make the difference at the reorder stage, as well as at the initial order stage.

Companies that make certain kinds of industrial or generic products can get away with thinking of their packaging as merely a protective receptacle. For those companies, the package is simply a cost item, and those costs need to be minimized as much as possible.

I'm always amazed, though, when I run across companies that carry this cost mentality into the retail and direct-marketing realms. Your package in the retail setting has to do a lot of hard work in a hurry. It has to explain the contents of the package, convey the product's benefits, answer the question of why buy this one rather than that one, and heighten awareness of the manufacturer's brand—all within a few nanoseconds in an often crowded and distracting environment.

Even in the direct response channels, where those distractions aren't present, your packaging has a lot to accomplish. The recipient of the shipment from your mail-order house attaches a higher perceived value to your product if it comes in an attractive package. That person thinks better of both your product and your company.

This is marketing. I'm arguing that if for a manageable incremental cost you can get your packaging to do some of your marketing for you, that's likely to be a good investment.

Web sites

Develop your own Web site, where your customers and potential customers can be educated about your company and the advantages that your product offers to them. Web sites are increasingly easy to author and mount, and they have a huge advantage over brochures and other paper-based products: updating is (almost) free. For this reason, and because of increasing technical literacy across the workforce, Web sites will become increasingly important. Investigate how you might retain a "webmaster" on a contracted-services basis, at least until your company gets big enough to build this function into an internal position.

Events and promotions

I've already mentioned events and promotions in the context of public relations firms. Done well, a promotional event can be an affordable and highly effective way of generating major sales of your product. I personally believe that money spent well in this arena gives you much more bang for your buck than traditional advertising. And because events call for more creativity than money, they are doubly suited for new and growing companies.

The best events and promotions are those that are designed specifically for your product or service. The tie-ins between the event and your product's benefits should be clear and memorable—not only to help sell the product, but also to discourage competitors from trying similar stunts. If possible, hook up with an appropriate partner who can bring a major contribution to the table. (This could be money, a brand name, or marketing savvy.) If you use third-party individuals or organizations to help stage the event, you should make sure that everyone gets sufficient benefit from the event to give it their all.

Let me give an example from my own experience. In 1976, our company—Reiss Games—developed and introduced a line of magic. We designed full-color packaging to contain a collection of tried-and-true magic tricks that could be learned in a very short time (15 minutes was our targeted maximum). We purposefully stayed away from tricks that required sleight-of-hand dexterity, and also from tricks that professional magicians used to make their livings.

To develop the line, I signed up for an evening course on magic, taught by the celebrated magician George Schindler. The course was geared to beginners like me, and it was a great deal of fun. Eventually, we signed on Schindler to help us develop the line, and for a period of about two months, our office was a fun factory. George would come and demonstrate tricks that met our easy-to-learn requirement. We'd select a trick, cost out and fabricate its components, and develop a suitable line of patter that our customers could use. (Magicians will tell you that "sleight of mouth" is an important piece of a successful trick.) All told, we prepared a line of twenty-four magic kits and introduced them to the marketplace.

One of our customers was J. C. Penney, which sold our line through their catalogue and retail stores. It was very successful both for us and for them, and as a result, we sat down with Penney to figure out a strategy for increasing sales of the magic kits.

Penney's buyer for the magic line was very bright and ambitious. He came up with the idea that we demonstrate the magic in his retail stores, which he projected would drive up sales dramatically. We suspected he was right, but (as noted above) demonstrations are personnel-intensive and therefore very expensive. We declined this opportunity to get poor.

But the Penney buyer loved our line, thought it had great upside potential, and kept after us. We knew we had to do something to satisfy this important customer, yet we couldn't figure out what we could do that would be both effective and affordable. Then I remembered one of the many conversations I had had with George Schindler.

Over lunch one day, Schindler had told me about the Society of American Magicians. This group had some 10,000 members at that time—mostly amateurs, who had to demonstrate a certain skill level to gain acceptance into the society. One of the society's missions (Schindler explained to me) was to perpetuate the art of magic. One way they did this was to declare a "National Magic Week" every October. The goal of National Magic Week was to commemorate the death of escape artist Harry Houdini and to perpetuate the art of magic. During National Magic Week, magicians around the country performed in hospitals, nursing homes, and a variety of other venues where they could get an audience.

I remembered this conversation well. I also thought about the magicians I knew, including Schindler. They came from all different walks of life, but almost without exception, they loved magic. They loved performing a good trick well. They craved the limelight—and in many cases, didn't get enough of it.

After thinking through the rough details of a plan, I asked Schindler to set up a meeting between me and the president of the Society of American Magicians. At that meeting, I said that we could help the society in its goal of promoting magic, and that we could put large numbers of magicians in front of appreciative crowds—in J. C. Penney stores. We couldn't pay these performers, but we could probably persuade Penney to run local ads featuring the event and the magician, including a promotional picture of the performer. The president was intrigued, and suggested that I broach the idea at the society's upcoming national convention.

I immediately accepted this invitation. I then called a quick meeting with my frustrated Penney buyer, and laid out my scheme. "I'm pretty sure I can get top magicians to perform in your stores at no charge," I told him, "if you can advertise the events and put the performer's name and picture in each ad." He said he was interested, but would have to go up the ladder to find the necessary ad dollars. Together, we went down the hall to Penney's head of public relations, who controlled a healthy discretionary budget. The PR head liked the idea—so much so that he suggested that he accompany me to the society's convention. I assume that the fact that this meant three days in Miami Beach during the winter had some bearing on his decision.

The day came, and I proposed my deal to the assembled magicians. I emphasized that there would be no pay involved—only good publicity and most likely a good crowd. I ended my pitch by saying that when the meeting was over, Penney's PR director and I would be at a desk in the lobby ready to sign up anybody who wanted to participate. We had no idea what kind of response we'd get. To our amazement, by the time we got to the lobby, we had scores of magicians standing in line, eager for the chance to sign up and perform.

Penney delivered on its part of the bargain magnificently. They produced an ad with a banner headline reading: "J. C. Penney and the Society of American Magicians Celebrate National Magic Week." Below the headline, the ad included the date and time of the demonstrations, and a picture of the local performing magician. For our part, we hired (on a contract basis) a PR specialist who worked out of her house in California to coordinate the effort.

In my view, this was a win-win-win: Penney got their demonstrations at no cost to them, sold tons of merchandise, and earned excellent publicity and goodwill through their affiliation with the magicians. The society got far more publicity than it had ever received before. Individual magicians got their names and pictures in their hometown paper, with the Penney "seal of approval" implicitly associated with them. We sold goods, and greatly enhanced our relationship with a key customer—at hardly any cost to us.

The lessons I took away from this and similar experiences include the following:

- **Everything is possible.**
- **Understand people's emotional buttons** (e.g., many magicians crave recognition more than money).
- **Don't be embarrassed to state your intentions clearly and bluntly.** In this case, we needed to get magicians to perform for us for no pay. Our frankness seemed to be appreciated.
- **Persistence can pay off, in both directions.** In this case, the persistence of the Penney buyer set the stage for a very successful promotion. In other cases, it's been my persistence that made the difference.
- **Think outside the box.** Yes, this is becoming a tiresome cliché, but it captures the essence of a great promotion: how can we do something so fresh and different that the customer and consumer will find us irresistible?

The offer

The type of offer that you make on your product—in other words, the way you propose to put your product on the market—can have a dramatic impact on its salability. Your offer can be a critical piece of your overall marketing effort.

There are many, many ways to sell a product. For example, you can offer a premium with each item bought. This is common in the case of department store–based perfume sales. Buy a vial of expensive perfume and get a "free" umbrella, travel bag, grooming kit, or whatever.

You can create an "on-pack" offer, whereby a premium is attached to the product. These are common in drugstores and supermarkets. In many cases, the free product is related in some way to the sold one. Free razor blades, for example, may get packed with a can of shaving cream. You can also offer multiple unit pricing, in which the purchase of two units earns the customer a 10 percent discount, three units earns 15 percent, and so on.

And of course, there's always the old stand-by: a sale. Many consumers only buy non-necessities when they go on sale. A SALE! sign next to your product gives those consumers permission to buy. This only works up to a certain point, after which it loses its impact.

In addition to these fairly standard approaches, an infinite number of specialized offers may be appropriate for use by your company. Think of the vast range of mailings that arrives at your home and your office. Last week, I received a clear plastic tube about eight inches long. In the tube was a car ignition key. The flyer that accompanied the tube told me that I should come into the such-and-such dealership and find out if my key fit one of four vehicles. If so, *I could drive it away.*

And how about those sweepstakes that are used to sell magazines? No one is required to subscribe to a magazine in order to register for the sweepstakes—but clearly enough people do, or these offers wouldn't continue to be made.

In all of these examples, you're trying to accomplish two things. First, you're trying *to get the consumer to act in a certain way.* And second, you're trying *to make it as easy as possible for the consumer to act in that way.* Great offers get both of these things done effectively and economically, and pave the way for the orders (and soon, the reorders) that we're looking for.

KEEPING THE CUSTOMER SATISFIED

Let's assume that (1) we've made our initial sale, and (2) we've done the necessary marketing job to move the product off the counter by helping your customer sell it to their customer. Your customer places that first reorder to restock the shelves. Are we done yet?

Not quite. Now we have to make sure we get our second reorder, our third reorder, and so on. Repeat business comes only partly from marketing; to a greater extent, it comes from keeping the customer satisfied. The customer or end user has to experience *a fulfillment of their expectations* with your product. This has several aspects. Even if your quality is acceptable, your advertising may have overpromised to an extent that your product is doomed to "underdeliver."

So the goal is to promise the right things, and then deliver. How do you accomplish this important task? Again, there are several techniques that you can employ in the combination that best suits your product. They include:

Giving them quality

In today's competitive world, quality can't be optional. Quality has to be built into your product or service. It's the price of entry, in most market sectors—you have to be skilled and add value, or you won't be in the game.

In the bad old days, a company could decide to cut back on quality to improve margins and hope to get away with it. Not today: consumers are far more educated than in the past, and in many cases have more options.

Quality is your best offense; it's also your best defense. Think of all the ways that poor quality in your product could cause harm, and then take whatever steps are needed to eliminate—or at least mitigate—those potential hazards. The United States is the most litigious society in the world, and if you give people a good reason to sue you, they almost certainly will.

Quality is a chain that is only as strong as its weakest link.

Providing useful instructions

I've mentioned this obligation in earlier chapters. *The instructions on the usage of and care for your product are extremely important.* This is especially true for products requiring assembly.

Maybe this is my own personal bugaboo. But is there anything more frustrating than buying a product that claims to be easy to assemble and turns out to be a nightmare? Have you ever spent late-night hours squinting at the small print on a cramped sheet, which features atrocious writing and low-quality (or no) images? If so, have you rushed out to buy a product from that company again?

You can pour love and money into making a great product, but if you don't give people the information they need to *use* that product, you are probably wasting your love and money.

Giving great service

The manufacturer's job continues well beyond producing and helping to sell the product. The manufacturer also has to help the consumer *use* the product successfully, which includes good assembly and setup instructions and also extends to routine maintenance, warranty-related service, and troubleshooting.

Put yourself in the shoes of your customer. They've experienced satisfaction with your product, but after a long period of time, the product conks out. It doesn't really matter at that point what they paid for the product. Both inexpensive and expensive products generate unhappiness at this point.

So, what do they do now? Do they pull out the operator's manual? If so, will that be a concise and thorough resource? If there isn't a manual, or if the problem isn't covered in the manual, is there a phone number for them to call? If there is a phone number, does that phone get answered promptly (either by a person or a machine) and does the customer get through to a qualified customer service representative within 30 seconds, five minutes, or never?

If a service call is needed, does the technician provide competent and courteous service, and otherwise serve as a good representative of the company? Does the representative show up on time? If the product is still under warranty, does the company move quickly to make good on its commitments?

The mistake that many companies make, as they answer one or more of these questions in the negative, is in thinking that they are only inconveniencing one customer. How important is a single customer in the bigger scheme of things?

My answer is that each customer is extremely important. Remember word of mouth, described above? If you don't make that individual happy, he or she is likely to spend a lot of time bad-mouthing your company over the next few days, weeks, months, or even years. If your reputation is your most precious and vulnerable commodity, shouldn't you take every possible measure to protect it?

Let me relate a story from the consumer's perspective, which I think illustrates just how vulnerable the provider of poor service is, and just how far some crazed consumers may go to get "justice" in response to bad service. In this case, the crazed consumer was me.

Two years ago, my wife and I decided to go to Colorado for a summer vacation. We had skied in the Rockies, loved the area, and always intended to visit there in the warm weather. Now we were about to realize this longstanding daydream.

Only one airline flew nonstop from Newark, New Jersey, to Colorado Springs: Western Pacific Airlines. I had never heard of them, but I'm always inclined to try new, upstart airlines. I had had good experience with Southwest, Kiwi, and Midway, among others, so why not try this latest entry? The outbound flight was fine, and our time in Colorado was wonderful. Then came the return flight.

We were scheduled to leave at 11:00 a.m. for a four-hour flight back to Newark. We left at noon and ended up at the Pittsburgh airport at 11:00 p.m. In those intervening ten hours, we heard endless on-board announcements about weather delays in the New York–New Jersey area, congestion problems in the Northeast corridor, and a total shutdown of Newark Airport. (Later we found out that at least some of these announcements weren't true.) While in Pittsburgh, we were boarded and unboarded several times without explanation.

Among our group of beleaguered passengers—who included three unaccompanied minors—tempers began wearing very thin. It was clear that our chances of getting out of Pittsburgh were minimal, at best. Experience told me that Western Pacific would have to put us up overnight in Pittsburgh, and fly us to Newark the next morning. I remember wondering what happened to the unaccompanied minors in cases like this.

Finally, our embarrassed captain told us what Western Pacific had decided to do. There would be no overnight stay in Pittsburgh. Instead, they were unloading the baggage off the plane, and several buses were on their way to convey us to Newark Airport—although they weren't sure exactly when the buses would reach us. We could look forward to an *eight-hour* bus ride to Newark.

This was not how Grace and I intended to end our vacation. I immediately booked us on a flight leaving the following morning—on another airline—and then found a local hotel room. We got a good night's sleep, and had an uneventful flight back the next day. Our total additional cost for the hotel and new tickets: $728.

Immediately upon our return to New Jersey, I wrote a letter to the president of Western Pacific, in which I recited the facts of our trip back from Colorado and asked for a refund of my $728. I waited a week, and then a month. No response.

Now, I'm really not the kind of guy who wastes a lot of his time writing cranky letters. On the other hand, when I *do* write one, I expect to get an answer. I obviously wasn't going to get one from Western Pacific. So I called my friend Ira Weinstein, who owned an advertising agency in Chicago, and told him to run a full-page ad in the local newspaper in Colorado Springs, where Western Pacific was headquartered. I asked him to reproduce my letter with a banner headline on top, reading: "Mr. Western Pacific President: Read your mail!" Weinstein placed the order for the ad, and told me that the cost was going to be $2,000.

Now an interesting thing happened. On that very same evening—after my ad was placed, but before it ran—I got a call at home from a senior manager at Western Pacific, apologizing to me for my experiences and my overlooked letter. The airline wanted, he said, to make good.

I asked him why he was calling me on this particular evening. After some hemming and hawing, he finally admitted that the newspaper had called him and tipped him off about my upcoming ad. What he was prepared to do, he said, was to refund me my $728 by overnight mail and give me a credit of $400 on a future Western Pacific flight. I accepted his offer, and told him I now saw no reason to run my ad. He sounded relieved.

What he didn't know was how much trouble he had spared his employer. I had fully intended to run my ad in Colorado Springs—and then to send a bill for $2,000 to Western Pacific. If they didn't pay me the $2,000 plus the original $728, I also intended to take out ads in all of the major cities that Western Pacific serviced, and send bills to Western Pacific for those ads, too. Believe me, I was prepared to advance *lots* of money to humble that airline.

Not long afterwards, Western Pacific went out of business. I wasn't surprised.

Now a story from the other end of the contented-customer spectrum. When we were in the watch business, we shipped all of our watches from Hong Kong. A large percentage of these watches went directly from our factory to our customers, which spared us the task of actually handling the product. Because watches are light and take up very little "cube," most of our shipments were air-freighted via Federal Express.

But there was a nagging problem with this otherwise flawless delivery system. When Federal Express delivered to our customers, the paperwork from Customs was attached to the shipment. Invariably, that paperwork spelled out the price we had paid to the Chinese factory for the watches. Not good! Our customers, and especially our *direct* customers, shouldn't have our costs sitting right next to their costs, just inviting a calculation of our markup.

We called FedEx and asked that they remove the Customs paperwork before they delivered these packages. We were told that this simply wasn't possible, for obscure logistical reasons. Well, I've always admired FedEx and its founder, Fred Smith, so I immediately wrote him a letter on the subject. In so many words, I told him that I couldn't comprehend how they could handle millions of packages almost flawlessly every day—to the extent of being able to tell me exactly where a given package was at any point in time—and still not be able to remove a single sheet of paper from a shipment.

Here comes the contrast with Western Pacific: Within a week, I received a phone call from a FedEx vice president based in Hong Kong. He told me that he, too, was perplexed at their inability to solve my problem, but that he was determined to do so. Shortly thereafter, I received a delegation of four FedEx employees—including a vice president—at my office in New Jersey. We discussed my problem and their systems, and soon hit upon an easy way for them to remove the offending paper.

My company was relatively tiny. On the face of it, we didn't warrant the kind of overwhelming attention that FedEx gave us. I'm sure, though, that in the process of solving *my* problem, FedEx was also figuring out a way to make itself far more attractive to small businesses all over the world. Smart? I'd say so.

This level of excellence can (and should) be achieved by businesses of any scale, in any industry. My friends Michelle and Herb Rosenfeld own a quality art gallery in New York. When a customer buys a painting from them—usually expensive—the Rosenfelds have specially trained people deliver the work to the buyer's home and install it where the buyer specifies.

These delivery people range from petite to burly, but in all cases, they show up at the buyer's home wearing white gloves and surgical booties over their shoes. This has a *huge* impact on customers who are subjected to this treatment. You can be sure stories about white gloves and surgical booties are told and retold around dinner tables in great neighborhoods.

And incidentally, I *never* stop talking about what a great company FedEx is, or how good the Rosenfelds are at what they do. Remember word of mouth, with which I opened this chapter? This is how great word of mouth happens.

MANAGING YOUR INVENTORY

For those who sell products, one of the key challenges in responding to a flow of reorders is keeping a large enough inventory on hand—but not too large. The constant dilemma you face is that you know your customer is grading you on your ability to ship reorders, but you also know that too much carryover inventory can wipe away all your hard-earned profits and wreck your cash flow. Important, right? So inventory shouldn't be solely the concern of a purchasing agent; it deserves continuing attention from your sales manager, your vice president of sales, and/or you.

Purchasing agents, accountants, and other people involved in pushing papers around tend to be historians. By that I mean that they often do their jobs based on an analysis of past shipments. This is important information, of course, but it's far from adequate when it comes to projecting future needs. It's your salespeople who have the best insight into likely future activity, and far too often, it's their input that's ignored.

Yes, there's a potential downside to building the sales force's perspective into projections. Salespeople tend to err on the high side when they make projections. They don't want to frustrate their buyers—and lose their commissions—because an item is out of stock. But I'll bet that you can identify some very responsible people in your sales force who can make a valuable contribution to your inventory management process.

I've already recounted the story of our ill-fated picture frames. When they died, we were left with tons of them (almost literally) on our hands. When you get in this situation, your profits get wiped out and your cash flow suffers terribly. Getting "overinventoried" is an ongoing peril in fashion-oriented, trendy, or seasonal businesses. As a rule, I say that it's better to run out of something than to get stuck with mountains on unmovable goods. I'd also recommend finding a way to quickly and consistently sell off your excess inventories and recoup at least some of your costs.

Inventory management is getting to be an ever bigger challenge, as retailers attempt to shift this burden more and more onto the shoulders of the manufacturer. Manufacturers need to manage their relationships with key retailers, thereby minimizing unfair pressures. At the same time, they have to reduce their production cycle times in order to reduce their distribution lead times. The quicker you can make your product and get it to your retailer, the lower your risk is of inventory surpluses.

Another current trend that increases the importance of inventory management is retailers' increasing tendency to demand the right to return unsold goods. If too many goods come back unexpectedly, it will wreak havoc with your planning, profits, and cash flow. As with all such developments, manufacturers have to find creative ways to cope. For example: You might develop new markets for these returns. You might charge handling fees for returns. You might sell stores on the idea of taking markdown money from you instead of sending back goods.

If you are a sub-S corporation that's growing rapidly, surplus inventories can represent a double whammy. As profits flow through to the individual shareholders, so do the tax obligations. If your company is generating good profits, you'll have to pay taxes. The Feds won't be interested in your explanation that the money to pay all those taxes is tied up in the inventory you need for future profits.

CONTROLLING KNOCKOFFS

Let's recap: Now you're rolling. You're producing a quality product at a good profit, you're collecting satisfied customers, and you're getting wave after wave of reorders. What happens next?

In lots of cases, what happens next is that you get "knocked off." Not in the Cosa Nostra sense of the phrase, but in the sense of someone stealing your idea or copying your product. This is an ancient problem—probably as old as the first coin—and it's one that I think is likely to intensify in the future. Because new or fast-changing entrepreneurial companies often have the best new products and ideas, large companies keep a close eye on them. And when the large companies see something they like, they tell their existing suppliers to copy it. In other cases, the large companies go ahead and knock off the hot new product on their own.

Many small businesses feel like they're powerless to respond to knockoffs. They have limited resources, and the offenders—if they can be identified—may be far from home, and hidden behind many corporate veils.

In the following section, I'll offer a number of concrete ideas on how to prevent knockoffs in the first place, and how to respond to them when they do occur. I don't plan to delve deeply into the legal details of this battle, except to offer an extract from the U.S. Patent and Trademark Office (Exhibit Z) that defines *copyrights, patents,* and *trademarks.* These are three different kinds of legal protections that are available to you. They have different costs and advantages. If your product lends itself to copyright and patent protection, and if you think the product has more than a minimal life span, you should seriously consider going for some kind of government protection.

Protecting your ideas

Developing an idea for a new product (or a new company) can be an exhilarating experience. This euphoria can be rapidly deflated, though, when you are advised that your great idea can't be protected. And

Exhibit Z

What is a Patent?

A patent for an invention is a grant of a property right by the Government to the inventor (or his or her heirs or assigns), acting through the Patent and Trademark Office. The term of the patent shall be 20 years from the date on which the application for the patent was filed in the United States or, if the application contains a specific reference to an earlier filed application under 35 U.S.C. 120, 121 or 365(c), from the date the earliest such application was filed, subject to the payment of maintenance fees. The right conferred by the patent grant extends only throughout the United States and its territories and possessions.

The right conferred by the patent grant is, in the language of the statute and of the grant itself, "the right to exclude others from making, using, offering for sale, or selling" the invention in the United States or "importing" the invention into the United States. What is granted is not the right to make, use, offer for sale, sell or import, but the right to exclude others from making, using, offering for sale, selling or importing the invention. Most of the statements in the preceding paragraphs will be explained in greater detail in later sections.

Some persons occasionally confuse patents, copyrights, and trademarks. Although there may be some resemblance in the rights of these three kinds of intellectual property, they are different and serve different purposes.

Copyrights

A copyright protects the writings of an author against copying. Literary, dramatic, musical and artistic works are included within the protection of the copyright law, which in some instances also confers performing and recording rights. The copyright protects the form of expression rather than to the subject matter of the writing. A description of a machine could be copyrighted as a writing, but this would only prevent others from copying the description; it would not prevent others from writing a description of their own or from making and using the machine. Copyrights are registered in the Copyright Office in the Library of Congress. Information concerning copyrights may be obtained from the Register of Copyrights, Library of Congress, Washington, D.C. 20559. (Telephone 202-707-3000)

Trademarks/Servicemarks

A trademark or servicemark relates to any word, name, symbol or device which is used in trade with goods or services to indicate the source or origin of the goods or services and to distinguish them from the goods or services of others. Trademark rights may be used to prevent others from using a confusingly similar mark but not to prevent others from making the same goods or from selling them under a non-confusing mark. Similar rights may be acquired in marks used in the sale or advertising of services (service marks). Trademarks and service marks which are used in interstate or foreign commerce may be registered in the Patent and Trademark Office. The procedure relating to the registration of trademarks and some general information concerning trademarks is given in a separate pamphlet entitled Basic Facts About Trademarks.

unfortunately, this is generally the case, especially when it comes to copyrights.

There are lots of gray areas here, and I'm far from an expert on the subtleties of intellectual property law. If you plan to act on an idea that I present in this chapter, think carefully about whether you need some legal help. (As you'll see, the answer is sometimes yes, sometimes maybe, and sometimes no.) Meanwhile, I suggest you keep two somewhat contradictory rules of thumb in mind: *Do everything you can to secure all protections available to you;* and *don't count on the law to adequately protect your idea or product.*

This second rule of thumb can be tough to accept. I've known too many people who develop a new product but who—through fear and paranoia about being knocked off—never come to market, or even share their idea beyond a few trusted confidantes. My feeling is, I'd rather come out with my product and risk the knockoff than keep it in my closet. I wouldn't take much comfort in telling my grandchildren about the great idea that I protected against all exploitation—including exploitation by me!

For those of you who want to take the risk and forge ahead, here are some ideas about how to protect yourself and fight this battle.

Prior to sharing your idea, ask the person you're showing it to to sign a non-disclosure. Many companies won't sign such a form, either because they don't want to help you create the kind of paper trail you're interested in creating, or because they're legitimately concerned that doing so would limit their options. Maybe they're already working on something like this, and signing your form would put that work at risk. But many *will* sign such a form, because they're hungry for good ideas and new products. A signed non-disclosure form in your back pocket isn't bulletproof, but it constitutes pretty good protection.

A parallel approach is to copyright your work. This is most appropriate for computer programs, artwork, songs, various kinds of writing, and so on. Copyrights are cheap and easy to obtain. Just get the form from the U.S. Patent and Trademark Office (at the Copyright Office, Library of Congress, 101 Independence Avenue S.E., Washington, DC, 20559-6000 (24-hour form-ordering phone no: 202-707-9100; main information no: 202-707-5959; Web address: http://lcweb.loc.gov/copyright/); fill out the application; and send it back with $20. Within about two months you'll be issued a copyright. U.S. copyrights are recognized by more than 100 countries around the world, and they can greatly aid you in stopping infringers and collecting money.

At one time, it was legally required to put the c-in-the-circle copyright notice (©) on your product to let people know that the product was protected. Even though this is no longer required, I still recommend that you do so. Why not let potential offenders know that you worry about this kind of stuff? It's far better to ward off potential violators than to fight them later. By giving them notice, you undermine the "innocence defense"—in other words, that they simply didn't know about your copyright.

A third recommendation: Retain a lawyer to help you with trademark and patent registrations. Yes, I know I tend to recommend minimizing legal fees whenever possible, but this is different. In contrast to copyrighting, trademarking (although not expensive) has many subtleties, and patenting is both complicated *and* expensive.

When cash is tight in a small company—as it usually is—you may feel that you have to defer trademarking your brand or company name. This is a safe gamble within the United States, but it is not safe in the international arena. If you think you may someday want to enter international markets using your brand or company name, don't delay! If you don't trademark your name, someone else can. Recently, I read a story about somebody in Canada trademarking the name of one of the largest retailers in the United States. When that retailer finally got around to entering the Canadian market, they had to pay a hefty sum to get the right to use their own name up north.

By the way, since you're already an Internet-savvy company, or plan to be in the near future, take the time to register an appropriate Internet domain name as soon as possible. (Call your Internet service provider for the latest information on domain registration.) Trust me—you'll kick yourself if you wait too long and somebody else registers your name on the Internet. The point is well illustrated by the story of the AltaVista search engine—one of the more popular tools for navigating the World Wide Web. Digital wrote the software that made AltaVista possible, but when that company went to register the AltaVista name, it discovered that a small California-based company already had it. Digital reluctantly registered the "Altavista.digital.com" domain name, which it used for several years. When Compaq purchased Digital in 1998, it decided to fix this longstanding domain-name problem—and wound up paying millions to the tiny California-based Altavista to get the necessary rights. (Alta-Vista has since been sold again.)

Back to general ideas for protecting your ideas: When bringing your product or concepts to potential partners, investors, customers, and so on, *write up minutes of all your meetings.* Also, send confirmation and follow-up letters to all parties involved in your meetings. Keep notes of your phone calls—dates, times, subjects discussed, people involved, etc. In other words, build the kind of paper trail you'll wish you had if and when things go wrong. Then, when the time comes, make some casual references to your good record keeping. In my experience, the people who are eyeing you will get the idea, and they'll be that much more likely to behave themselves.

Another kind of preventive medicine: Do some homework on the kinds of people to whom you're bringing your concepts and products. A little digging here can go a long way. See if they've been involved in other lawsuits. Talk to people they've done business with.

By and large, I like to bring my products and concepts to larger companies, and particularly public ones. This is especially true in cases where I plan to let someone else produce and market the product while I collect royalties. Yes, going to a big public company can be like going into the den of a *really* big lion, and they can bring huge resources to bear on any kind of legal action. On the other hand, these companies are much more vulnerable to public pressure (a topic we'll discuss again later). A related advantage of dealing with large companies is that they usually have more competent counsel. In my experience, it's always better to deal with smarter people. They understand their best interests. The smart corporate lawyer will recognize when you "have the goods" on the corporation and will settle quickly, whereas a smaller company may not recognize the weakness of its case, or may let emotions enter into its calculations.

Another good idea is to try to get an audience as high up in the company as possible. The underassistant vice president for product development is, in most cases, far more likely to knock you off than the CEO. The CEO is already sitting on top of the world, after all; why risk all those perks just to steal something from you? And by the same token, the higher up in the chain of command you can get, the more likely you are to get a quick and decisive response—and, at least in my experience, a positive response.

One point that I'll try to make very clear in this discussion of knockoffs is that perception is reality. You have to create a certain kind of aura around yourself and around your company which will discourage knockoffs. You want to look aggressive. Very aggressive, in fact. And you want to look just a little bit crazy about your eagerness to pursue thieves of your intellectual property.

There are lots of little ways to reinforce this aura. When sending out samples of your product, put a tag on each item that declares that this is an item that is copyrighted. Give the item a number, and ask for its return when the buyer is through with it. Request that your sample *not* be put in the buyer's showroom if other vendors have access to that showroom. (This is surprisingly common.) The reason for these measures is that it's the buyers, in many cases, who instigate the knockoff. They take your product and send it overseas to their buying office— or simply give it to another favored manufacturer—to price out and knock off. Tagging is a not-so-subtle message that you're not a wimp when it comes to pursuing violators of your rights.

You want to give the buyer *pause,* before he or she goes that route. In your presentation to buyers, let them know you will be very aggressive in pursuing violators. (There are lots of polite ways to say this "in code.") You'll find that for the most part, legitimate buyers welcome an aggressive defense on your part against knockoffs. They aren't happy when they actively promote your product in their stores, and then knockoffs (usually of poorer quality) start to appear at competing stores at significantly lower prices.

You can also spread the word in the industry that you retain a very tough law firm on a contingency basis. You can run trade ads that proclaim that a particular item you make is copyrighted or patented, and that you will pursue violators aggressively. But make sure that all of these preventive activities are backed up by *action,* and make sure that your action gets adequate publicity. People watching this display will take the path of least resistance, and go knock somebody else off.

A few words about lawyers: One way to manage lawyers is to inform them clearly at the outset of a particular knockoff episode of the costs you're willing to incur in pursuit of this violating company. Above all, don't be intimidated by lawyers. Yes, you can discuss their fees, and you can dicker with them. Try to get a commitment from them to a cap on overall costs. Ask if they're willing to work on a contingency (which means they'll receive a percentage of whatever you win, either in court or by means of a settlement) instead of on a fee basis.

This is good for you—because your legal costs go from being fixed to variable—and it can be very good for your lawyer. If you recovered big damages in your intellectual property case, your contingency-based lawyer would do very well indeed. The problem is that while it's fairly common for lawyers to work on a contingency basis in liability cases, this is much rarer when it comes to intellectual property cases. I've had discussions about this with law school professors, and I still don't understand why more lawyers don't pick up fairly easy money working in this specialty on a contingency basis. When an attorney is just starting out, is hungry for business, and hasn't yet strapped on a lot of overhead, I think that she should be open to the idea of a contingency relationship.

Don't worry too much about retaining a lawyer who is young, as long as you're convinced that he is competent. Copyright infringements are usually very simple to document and take to trial, so a recent law school grad can probably handle your case. If they suspect they can't, they'll probably tell you so.

In many cases, legal costs can be staged. This will minimize your legal costs, which (in addition to getting damages and dissuading future counterfeiters) is one of your goals. For example, you might begin simply by sending the offending company a legal-sounding threatening letter on the attorney's letterhead. The next step would be to file a lawsuit, which is still a relatively inexpensive move. Keep in mind, however, that once you file a lawsuit, you are committing yourself to certain kinds of activities, and in certain circumstances, you may not be able to pull out easily.

The next level of intervention is *discovery,* by which you compel your legal adversary to disclose all relevant documents and other materials in their possession. In many cases, discovery will reveal the sales volume of the copied product, the profits the company made on those sales, and who bought the products. This kind of information can be very valuable in determining how far you should proceed in your legal actions. It can also give you the legal ammunition you need to compel the offending company to settle, and avoid additional legal costs.

A second piece of the discovery process is the deposing of the principal parties to the knockoff. *Depositions* are simply questions answered under oath. This is a more expensive step, but it can provide you with additional information that may prompt an early settlement.

The last and most costly legal weapon is *to go to trial*. I always look for a settlement, and usually as early in the process as possible. But think your options through carefully, in consultation with your attorney. There are times when a trial is needed—both to protect your rights and to mandate the payment of damages.

Fighting back

In the first two years of my watch company's existence, we averaged two settlements a year, and collected nice sums of money in the process. We created original artwork for the faces of our watches, which we always copyrighted. (Remember: there's no legal fee involved—just a twenty-dollar check to the U.S. government.) Most knockoff people are lazy. The ones involved in these cases certainly seemed to be. They just took a picture of our best-selling designs and copied them exactly. They could easily have gotten away with creating new art that would have been similar enough to knock us off successfully without infringing on our copyright. But being lazy, or greedy, or both, they didn't.

We did have to hire a lawyer to file the actions. However, this initial filing was not very expensive. As noted above, it's not until you actually go to court that you start racking up huge legal bills. We never had to go to court, because the infringements in these cases were so obvious. I can easily imagine the discussions that went on in the offices of our adversaries. "Hey, guys," their lawyers say, shaking their heads and frowning, "they've got you dead to rights. You're gonna get killed in court. We'd better start looking for a settlement."

It's also possible that someone else at that table replied, "Yeah, well, maybe we were wrong and we got caught, but these guys probably don't have the money to see this kind of legal battle through. Let's hang tough."

Assuming you *do* wind up in court, the judge is either going to rule in your favor or against you. If the judgment comes out in your favor, you are entitled to all the profits made by the party that knocked you off—and perhaps also to the profits of those to whom it sold.

Some common sense has to be exercised in the extent to which you pursue an infringer. If the volume of knockoffs is small, and if the company that's knocking you off appears to have little in terms of net worth, you probably are best served by just sending them a letter in scary legalese and telling them to cease their illegal behavior immediately. On the other hand, if the offending company is big and appears to have deep pockets, I'd say you should go after them. Most big companies can't stand adverse publicity, and the "Goliath clobbers David" story is one that the press loves to jump on. Go after them, and look for a nice big settlement.

I'm always amazed how certain companies continuously knock off products, time after time, and yet never get punished for it in the marketplace. Believe it or not, these companies allocate money for legal defenses in the same way that "legitimate" companies allocate money for R&D and advertising. They're betting that they can steal your ideas with impunity because you will be too thinly capitalized to fight them. Sadly, they're often right.

But don't complain to me if you get ripped off by one of these buccaneering companies. I blame them for the offense, but not for getting the opportunity to do it again and again. That's *your* fault, not theirs. If people keep seeking out these companies—like lambs walking into the lion's den—well, I'm not going to fault the lion. Figure out who you're proposing to do business with, and act accordingly. Don't do business with pirates. To rephrase the old saying: "Copy me once, shame on you; copy me twice, shame on me."

For the same reasons, when a large company infringes on my rights, I don't hesitate to contact the CEO and tell him/her what's going on. They'll tell you they had no idea that this sort of thing was going on, and that assertion is probably true. In the wake of this embarrassment, the CEO is likely to come down very hard on the offenders within (or supplying) the organization.

This is a good opportunity to turn the tables to your advantage. Tell the CEO that rather than suing his company—at least for the time being—you'd like to *sell* to his company. Ask for a meeting as soon as possible, stating that you would prefer not to take legal action, but that you will of course vigorously protect your rights.

I've also found it helpful to contact members of the board of directors, or at least to copy them on my correspondence with the CEO, if the CEO doesn't respond within a reasonable time period. If the CEO is already on thin ice for other, entirely unrelated problems, you may find one or more directors want to seize upon your David vs. Goliath story as yet another opportunity to pile on the shaky chief executive.

In these kinds of correspondence, I very deliberately portray myself as someone who is very aggressive—even though I'm a relatively small fish—and will go on the attack if not appeased *quickly*. Those of you who travel a lot have probably seen airport ticket counter agents, and hotel desk clerks, cave in when some angry traveler starts really lighting into them. Nobody wants a fight, especially when they know that it was their screwup that created the problem in the first place. Companies behave in exactly the same way. I let them know I'm ready to fight.

If your intellectual property right (patent, copyright, or trademark) has been violated, if you have limited funds, and if the infringer is a large company, *publicity* can be your single most effective weapon. Let's say you've taken the initial steps outlined above—letters to the CEO and the board, and so on—and you've gotten nowhere. This is the time to hire your lawyer and file your action. (This isn't particularly expensive.) The lawyer does his or her thing, and you wait. If the company *still* doesn't respond favorably, here's where you start to publicize your action.

Let me underscore that: What you're setting out to do here is to publicize *your* position—not the shortcomings or excesses of the other side. Don't seek out the media and start talking about how evil your adversary is. (This may possibly set you up to be sued by the company for defamation, and at that point, we're *really* talking legal bills.) Talk all this through with your attorney. What's smart to say and what's not so smart to say?

Once you've got these signals straight, then the sky's the limit. Send a press release about your lawsuit to the relevant trade publications. If the Buzz Sawmill Company stole your new log-peeling device, send a notice of your suit to *Pulp and Paper* magazine and similar special interest journals. Not all will be interested, especially if Buzz Sawmill is a big advertiser—but some will be. Contact business publications: local, regional, and national. Local publications that have high visibility in the offending corporation's home town can be particularly effective. Contact local TV and radio stations and tell them your story. But once again, don't undervalue those trade publications! Believe it or not, a damaging piece in a trade journal—which reaches an important and targeted audience—can be more effective than a spot on the evening news, and it's *much* easier to get.

In media relations, definitely play up big vs. small. Normally, a reporter whom you've interested in the story will attempt to contact both parties to come up with a balanced report. Assume that the other side—the Big Guys—will have little or nothing to say to reporters beyond what you see them saying on TV: "Our policy is never to comment publicly on pending litigation," or whatever. So it's likely that your side is the one that will be heard. Let it be heard, but stick carefully to the facts that are outlined in your action. Avoid name-calling.

Talk about *your* company—how good your products are, how hard you work at being innovative, and so on. Craft your public persona with your ultimate goal in mind. If you want to do business with the offending company, then try to come across as a reasonable person to do business with. If you want to scare them, don't hesitate to look just a little bit crazy—like the kind of guy who might spend $50,000 to win a $10,000 settlement.

The net result of these media plays is that they can jump-start a settlement process, especially if you come across as somebody the public might decide to get behind. The management of the infringing company will get nervous quickly, especially if your hangdog (or chipper, or slightly deranged) face starts showing up in a variety of media outlets. If they know they're wrong, and if they conclude that you are the kind of character who's going to fight this through to the bitter end in the morning paper and on the evening news, they'll soon start thinking about how to meet you halfway.

Another war story from my own experience: During our second year in the watch business, we submitted a design for one of our watches to a major retailer. Now, mind you, this design was *copyrighted* in a very obvious and thoroughgoing way. The retailer didn't take the watch, which wasn't unusual. But imagine our surprise when, six months later, their Christmas catalogue came out with an *exact copy* of it in it—right down to the finest details, including, of all things, our company's name right there on the watch face! Most design pirates are smart enough to take off the name of the company they're knocking off; these guys weren't. This was what some would call a *dumb* knockoff.

We were amazed. We figured we'd caught them with both hands in the cookie jar, up to the elbows. We filed an action immediately. To our surprise, they started playing hardball with us. They told the watch company that had made the watch for them—a major watch company, as it turned out—to contact us about a settlement. But the settlement offer was insultingly low. We held out for more.

Then we started our publicity campaign. We contacted *Crain's Business Weekly,* a highly respected publication, and told them our story.

The story showed up on page 2, complete with a picture of their absolutely identical watch. Immediately upon publication, we were contacted by the offender and offered a settlement that was reasonable.

We accepted the settlement happily, but we knew that in a sense, we were hurting ourselves in the long run. We still wanted to do business with that retailer, sneaky as they were. They represented a huge chunk of a metropolitan retail market, and we wanted in (on reasonable business terms, of course). It was many years before their buyers would return our calls. On the other hand, any retailer or manufacturer that followed this story in the papers and on TV would have thought twice about knocking us off, and we protected a property that had some commercial value at that time.

Two years later, a knockoff of one of our copyrighted watches appeared in a chain of jewelry and watch stores that was a customer of ours. Our New York–based intellectual properties lawyer, Dan Ebenstein, wrote a magnificent letter to their in-house attorney. Dan's letter (which I've included as Appendix 2 at the back of the book) advised the company of their infraction, and also of our determination to stop them from (1) selling any more of this particular knockoff; and (2) selling copies of any of our other products. At the same time, Dan's letter clearly stated that we were prepared to work these problems out amicably with them and avoid legal action if possible.

The retailer got the letter, thought about the options, and then asked their buyer to call our sales manager, Ron Goldstein, whose previous calls hadn't been returned. Ron went to visit with them, and worked out a much larger program with them than we had ever had before. They pulled the knockoffs from their stores, and never sold copies of our products again. We paid our own legal fees, which weren't that high, and wound up with a valuable account. They also had newfound respect for us as business people. We were subsequently told as much by a departing buyer, who also added that we were the only company that ever challenged them, out of all the companies that had complained to them about knockoffs over the years.

The bottom line? I'd say that if you can avoid a trial, keep your costs down, and maybe even grow your business, you should do so. Court proceedings will chew up astonishing amounts of your time and your company's resources. And courts are a dreary place to spend your time. Far better to be outside, doing business. Remember your goal: "Sell—not sue!"

Another good remedy for knockoffs is to bring third parties into the act. If a manufacturer is selling a knockoff of your product to, say, a major retailer, get in touch with the retailer and inform them that the product they're selling is a clear violation of your intellectual property rights. Be sure to consult an attorney for the appropriate wording of this communication, to protect yourself from incurring any liabilities of your own. If the retailer thinks your assertions have any merit at all, they are likely to stop selling the product as a precaution. Inventories will begin to back up at the offending manufacturer's warehouse, and they'll have an increasing incentive to settle with you.

Here's an ally you may not have thought of in your efforts to stop international knockoffs: the U.S. Customs Service. This can often be the cheapest and most decisive way to frustrate design pirates. When you get evidence that someone is importing knockoffs of your products into the United States, contact Customs, inform them of your relevant copyrights or trademarks, and ask them to keep an eye out for infringers. It helps to know the identity of the infringing company, but it's not a prerequisite in order for Customs to act.

Once you obtain a copyright or trademark and you suspect that it will be knocked off, record it with the Washington Customs office immediately. When the knockoff occurs, contact the Restricted Merchandise office in the port(s) of entry where you suspect the goods are entering the country. (There are 190 such ports.) As a reinforcement tactic, you can visit that office (or those offices) in person to show them your product.

Assuming that you've made your case, Customs will seize incoming shipments of the copied product. This will really put the screws to the offending importer, because they very likely have paid for the goods with a letter of credit, and now have no way to recover their costs. There's no way for you to recover through Customs any damages you've already suffered as a result of the knockoff, but this is just about the quickest, cheapest, and most satisfying way to slam the door on companies that are stealing from you.

Customs officials are very cooperative in these kinds of efforts. My guess is that in addition to wanting to do the right thing—and helping a U.S.-based business fight off knockoffs falls into that category—they welcome the good publicity they get when they seize counterfeit and illegal merchandise. After all, most of us only have contact with Customs when they're taxing goods we're bringing back from trips overseas. Here's a case where their vigilance makes us appreciate them!

One more government agency deserves mention: the U.S. Department of Commerce. I'm always amazed that more U.S. business people don't take advantage of this great resource, which provides its services free of charge—unless you count the individual and corporate taxes you pay, of course.

If you know the country where the knockoff is being produced, provide that information to the Commerce Department's office in that country. They're there in that country to help U.S. businesses succeed there. Obviously, they don't have any authority in (say) India to stop Indian companies from knocking you off. But they *can* be a very effective stand-in for you in that faraway place. For example, they can get plenty of background on the offending company. They can help you better understand the intellectual property laws of India (or wherever). In some cases, they can recommend an effective course of action, and even play a key role themselves in making that plan work.

I've found the Commerce personnel in Japan and Hong Kong to be exceptionally competent people. The Hong Kong branch was very eager to help me in one recent case. They wrote an intimidating letter on official U.S. government letterhead to a factory that was making knockoffs of one of my products, and the problem ceased almost overnight. In some cases, this is because the offender is worried about getting the U.S. government on its back. It sometimes happens that the local authorities will raid a pirate as a result of pressure from the U.S. government. More often, the U.S. government can help you hook up with a real smart local lawyer, who can take your case to court and (if it's a good case in the right country) win it for you.

Keep in mind that in many cases, the offending company is completely unaware that they're producing an illegal product. All it takes is a letter, on the right letterhead, to get them rushing out of the business.

Sometimes you'll find that a knockoff is in a gray area. This is particularly true for some kinds of more or less commoditized manufactured goods. One American manufacturer I worked with was convinced that an Asian competitor was reverse-engineering his fractional horsepower motors, copying their fundamentals, and then altering them just enough to get away with it. The U.S. manufacturer countered by introducing a completely useless internal element. Within weeks, the same useless element showed up in motors that were being imported from

Asia. When confronted with the evidence, the Asian knockoff artists backed off.

Be prepared to knock off your own product. There are times when you need to be objective, and take as much emotion out of your thought processes as possible. There are many, many clever people out there who have built their businesses around copying successful ideas. You're not immune. They can change the artwork just enough. They can make slight alterations to dodge your patent. What should your reaction be when it turns out that your creation—your baby, of sorts— on which you've received some legal protection, turns out to be copyable?

In many cases, the answer is to knock yourself off. You are in the best position, after all, to know why something you're selling is succeeding. Which particular features are making the difference? I plan in advance for the day when I will make a product that is similar to my own, but will sell for a lower price. (See chapter 7.) Then I simply sit on that idea until the first knockoff shows up—or when the sales of the original item start to drop off at the end of that product's natural life. You also may want to offer a knockoff to certain large accounts or channels of distribution, where a lower price can generate new high volume. Remember: The higher your profit margins, the greater the chance that your product will be knocked off. Sometimes, the way to beat the knockoff crowd is to preempt them.

Another effective strategy is to get to market first, fast, and with power. Much of the time, you know in your bones that being copied is inevitable, and you won't be able to protect yourself against it. So being first and best may be all you need. This is a favorite ploy for Keith Mirchandani, president of Tristar Products, a TV direct response firm. By advertising heavily and quickly on a tested item, he feels that he can be first to build a brand for that product, and that retailers prefer to carry the item that was introduced first, and is known as the "original."

One last strategy, which I refer to as "fighting fire with fire." I usually go into a knockoff battle with a determination to be pleasant and tough, all at once. But sometimes you know enough about your opponent to make the "pleasant" part difficult. When I was in the toy business—a highly competitive industry—we tended to come up with between twenty and thirty new games a year. There was one medium-sized competitor who always copied a couple of our best-sellers, without fail. He also copied other companies, and was accomplished at making just enough changes to get away with his antics.

One day I ran into him on the street. I was extremely frustrated with the state of things at that time, and he had a lot to do with my frustration. I stopped him, looked him in the eye, and said something like the following: "Listen, Joe. If you *ever* copy one of my games again, here's what I'm going to do. I'm going to copy your two best-selling items"—I named them—"and then I'm going to offer them to your five top accounts"—which I also named—"at cost. And I'm going to keep doing it to you, every year, until I decide that you've learned your lesson."

To my knowledge, he never knocked me off again.

Take solace in the knowledge that sometimes knockoffs of your product expand the size of the market for your item or category. Although you may now have competitors who are getting a piece of the pie, the pie has grown, and your own volume (despite those pirates) has soared. This isn't all bad.

Pleasant when possible, tough always: that's the rule for heading off and responding to knockoffs. (My personal style is to start with a soft approach, even with some humor thrown in, and then to escalate.) As I said at the outset, this problem won't go away. Indeed, it's likely to get worse, due to larger structural changes in business. Your job is to reduce the chances that you'll get knocked off in the first place, and then make it costly when somebody is bold enough to try it. This is one of the best ways to reduce the risks of short product cycles, and to maximize the profits that a good product—one you've sweated hard to bring to market—can deliver to you.

So now we've got your company in great shape, we've put your product on a solid footing, we're keeping your customer satisfied, we're managing your inventory, we're controlling knockoffs, and we've got orders and reorders pouring in.

I was a little bit tempted to end this book here, but I decided there was one more chapter I really had to walk you through. This last chapter describes what I'll call the "reassessment" phase.

The fact that you get to ask a question like "What's next?" means that you've already achieved some success. You have options. You have the luxury of figuring out what's best for you, and what's best for your company, over the long run.

10

REASSESSMENT: WHAT'S NEXT?

It's easy to make an analogy between your company and one of your children (real or imaginary). This thing is of your making, right? You brought it into the world, you poured yourself into it and nurtured it, you took pride in its success, and so on.

But there are some problems with the company/child analogy. For example, your child doesn't usually increase your net worth. (In my experience, that calculation runs in the other direction!) And more seriously, as a parent, you rarely sit down and reassess your relationship with your child. What I want to argue in this final chapter is that this is exactly what's required between you and your company. Unconditional love, from you to your company, isn't necessarily a great thing forever.

I advised you, early on, to ask yourself some basic questions about yourself. Why do you want to become an entrepreneur, anyway? What will constitute "success"? How do you think about risk and reward?

Now it's time to ask and answer another round of questions. Many are as tough as the first round. They include:

- Is my company a success, failure, or work-in-progress?
- Can my company in its present form, and with its present products or services, sustain itself over the long run?

- Have my own passions, values, goals, and energies changed?
- If there is a "next level" for my company, what does it take to get there? Does the company have what it takes? Do I have what it takes? If the company can get there, do I want to go there with it?
- Do I want to put my hard-earned savings at risk in order to help the company go to the next level? Can my company get there *without* that kind of financial commitment from me?
- Do I have the balance I want in my life? How has attending to my business affected my family, and our mutual relationships?
- Am I happy?
- Are there any dreams or goals I want to pursue—either through the business or apart from it? What realistic options are out there for me?
- What do I want for my business after I'm gone (however "gone" happens)?
- What do I want for my coworkers?

Let's look at some of these questions. You'll soon find that I have no answers that apply equally well to everyone—and you may decide that I haven't even asked the right questions for your unique situation. My challenge back to you, in that case, is to come up with the right half-dozen questions that will prompt a productive reassessment.

I'm also assuming that you're reading these pages *before* you're at the reassessment stage. In fact, you should ask these questions before you start your company. File your answers away in some safe place. Then, when the reassessment phase starts—often many years later—answer these questions again, and compare your new answers with your old answers.

DEFINING SUCCESS

The dictionary defines "success" as "a favorable outcome or result— the gaining of wealth, fame, rank, etc.—coming about, taking place, or turning out to be as was hoped for."

That's a pretty clever definition. By invoking the idea of *your* hopes, the dictionary effectively says, "It's up to *you* to define it." Fine with me: I think "success" in your business *should* be defined by you. Letting other people define success makes it more likely that you won't attain it. Both in your professional life and personal life, "keeping up with the Joneses" tends to be difficult, unsatisfying, and transient. And what if the Joneses are trying to keep up with you?

Too narrow a definition of success is also likely to lead to trouble. If accumulating lots of money is success, then how much is enough? And what if somebody else accumulates more? If success is a happy marriage and well-adjusted kids, is that something that's substantially separate from a certain amount of material success? Or is there at least a threshold of affluence that's a necessary underpinning for that marriage and those kids?

For me, defining business success is easier than defining personal success. If my business has survived its early years, is earning a profit by selling a good product (or service), and is doing right by its various stakeholders, that's good enough for me. As for personal success, that's a moving target, and no one size fits all. One thing is for certain: When you're sorting through all the complex options that add up to your possible futures, you don't want to be bogged down by other people's definitions of success.

So far in this chapter, for argument's sake, I've been pretending that your business life and your personal life are separate things. This is almost never the case. No matter how good you are at compartmentalizing, there are sure to be overlaps—probably more than you want to admit. So while it's important to arrive at useful definitions of success for the several aspects of your life, it's also important to think through how they overlap.

One reason is that you might one day choose to separate them.

FIVE OPTIONS

Let's assume you have a small company that's "successful," according to your definition of that condition. You probably are already focused on all the things that have to be done, *urgently,* to make sure that success continues into the future. But "more of the same," led by you, is only one of your many options at this stage.

1. Keeping the company as is—or shrinking it

"Grow or die" has been a common prescription for business over at least the last century. Maybe there's some profound economic rationale for this—like economies of scale—or maybe it's just the corporate equivalent of "keeping up with the Joneses." In either case, I don't take it as gospel truth.

Barter entrepreneur Peter Benassi told me, "I can make much more money in a much smaller arena. I mean, I could shrink the company and make more money with the few clients that I have. Having a big company isn't always the answer."

What's so bad about staying the same size indefinitely? Maybe you enjoy things just the way they are. Your company is small enough to allow you to stay "hands-on," spend time selling, and follow up with customers. It's throwing off enough in the way of profits to provide you and others in the company with a very satisfactory standard of living.

All of these good things can be disrupted if you grow the company substantially larger. You will have to hire more people, delegate more, spend more time on people problems, and become less involved with customers. Your risks will almost certainly go up. The previous success of the business has allowed you to build up your own net worth; now you may feel compelled to risk that security by reinvesting in the company.

There are certainly downsides to staying the same size, which are exaggerated if you go so far as to shrink the business. For example, you may find it harder to hire and keep good employees if it looks like there are few opportunities for promotion. If you deal with licensed products, you stand a good chance of losing your license, given that most licensors want growth. If you cut back on new product introductions, aggressive competitors are likely to target your customer base. Perhaps most dangerous of all, a stand-pat mind-set may inhibit your company's creativity and flexibility. Creativity and flexibility are qualities that you'll need *more,* not less, of if you shift gears to a new smaller model.

In my experience, holding fast or shrinking are most likely to succeed when you have (1) a more or less unique product, (2) a distinctive marketplace niche, and (3) strong established relationships. One great advantage of being small is that you don't make it onto the radar screens of big companies, and they fail to come after your markets. Smaller is sometimes better.

2. Growing the company

Let's assume that your product or service has ben well received, your reorders are consistently good, you have steady growth and good profits, and—based on this track record—you want to grow the company. In most (but not all) cases, cash is the key determinant of your growth options. I'm sure that some would argue that *people*, rather than cash, are the most important determinant. In my experience, though, you won't have the good people over the long run if you don't have the cash.

In general, there are two kinds of growth that you can shoot for, based on which financial strategy you adopt. The first is growth that can be financed through internal cash flow. In choosing this option, you may be choosing slow growth, because most companies don't throw off enough cash to meet all of their operating needs *and* invest heavily in the future.

The second is growth based on something other than cash flow— either debt or equity. Let's look briefly at both of these.

Debt is money borrowed from a bank or other institution. In most cases, someone will have to sign personally for the debt, which may be limited to an amount equal to that signatory's assets. I never had much trouble signing bank notes back when I was young and foot-loose. I didn't have much to lose, I had plenty of time left in life to re-cover from a dumb financial move—and the bank wasn't willing to loan me very much, in any case. As I got older and accumulated some assets, though, two things happened. The banks got interested in lend-ing me more money against those assets, and I got more protective of those assets.

This is a very personal issue, about which you'll have to make up your own mind (maybe more than once). One good measure is: Will taking on this debt and putting my savings at risk make it harder for me to sleep at night? If so, then maybe it's not the right course of action.

When you sell *equity*, you give up some percentage of ownership in the company. Many entrepreneurs I dealt with are hung up on keep-ing at least 51 percent of the company in their own hands—even if that limits their companies' growth. They evidently believe that it's better to have complete control over a smaller company than a minor-ity stake in a larger company. I don't necessarily buy that, although each case has to be considered on its own merits. I know plenty of company founders who are only minority shareholders who benefited enormously from sharing ownership in the company, and still rule with an iron fist. No one is suggesting that Bill Gates is irrelevant just because he owns less than half the company.

Again, this is intensely personal. If and when you face this issue, try to separate out the emotional components, acknowledge them as real and important, and then act as much as possible based on rationality.

One way to sell equity is to team up with a venture capital firm. We first encountered venture capital companies in chapter 5, when I was writing about finding the money to get your company started. Well, here they come again—this time as a vehicle for pushing your company to the next stage of growth, and eventually helping you cash out by going public or selling.

Let's suppose that you decide to sell equity to a traditional venture capital or "private equity" firm. They will probably want to have control of the company, or at least have the ability to take it over if the company doesn't meet its projections. In other words, understand the trade-offs involved in dealing with a venture capital firm. You can get the financing you need—and in many cases, access to invaluable expertise—but there's always the chance that you'll lose the company if it fails to perform. Less drastically, under the watchful eyes of the VCs, you may also lose some of your flexibility and daring, and these are handy characteristics to have when change is needed.

Venture firms comes in all sizes, shapes, and specialties. Their help tends to come in two forms: cash and expertise. Both can be very expensive—and may be worth every penny. This is an arena in which there's all kinds of room for negotiation and comparison shopping. What's the most appropriate kind of partner for you?

Some venture firms will lend you money for, say, five years at a high interest rate, take a small stock option, and stay out of your way entirely. Others will play an active role on your board—which some entrepreneurs have a hard time getting used to. Still others are active operational partners, in some cases adding real value. One example is L. F. International, a San Francisco venture company that is a division of the Hong Kong–based trading company Li & Fung. L. F. International looks to take a minority position in its investments, and concentrates on companies producing consumer products that are made overseas. The venture company calls upon its parent, Li & Fung, to add value by doing all the overseas trading for the portfolio company.

Again, the point is to understand who you're dealing with, what they expect from you, what they expect to contribute, and what happens when things don't go according to plan.

After you decide on a financing strategy, here are some of the most important questions you'll have to answer about growing the company:

How will you fit in? As the size of the company changes, your role must also change. You'll probably spend less time with your customers and more time dealing with investors and their representatives (unless you self-finance). To the extent that you've been inclined to act intuitively in the past, this may have to give way to more methodical approaches. Your planning horizon will inevitably lengthen. You will attend more meetings. You will spend more time fighting the insidious effects of office politics. You won't have close personal relationships with all of your employees.

Dennis Boyer of Brothers Gourmet Coffee found that the fun went out of it when his company got larger. "That's why I left," he recalls. "I don't like board meetings, committees, and the seemingly inevitable creep of the political process. I don't like the time wasted prepping for Wall Street. And I don't like spending a large portion of my day looking at spreadsheets. You can blame me for not personally having or wanting to have these particular skill sets. But that's where it was."

Change in a company is neither good nor bad, inherently. It's just *different.* How will you fit in? Will you like it? Will you have the necessary skills, or the patience to learn them? There's a lot of evidence out there—in the form of other entrepreneurs' experiences—that suggests you *won't* thrive in the context of a larger company. But you may be the happy exception. With size, the entrepreneur tends to have to become more of a manager than a builder. Can you handle that? Or can you sidestep the issue by bringing in some great people to help you manage things?

Where will the people come from? Obviously, as the company changes, you'll need people with new kinds of skills. Finding good people with new skills is not always the entrepreneur's forte. An even greater challenge is dealing with your current employees, who have worked long and hard to bring the company to where it is today. As the company grows, their roles will change, and they will be forced to adapt in all kinds of ways—some subtle, some not so subtle. Many of them will be unable to handle these changes.

In some cases, retraining helps. But at some point, you're likely to be in the position of having to fire people who can't keep up with the changes. This can be an agonizing process. If you're like most people, you'll avoid and delay this as long as possible. But without exception, all of the people I've talked to who shepherded their company from small to large say *they waited too long to make key personnel changes, and wound up regretting it.*

So try to get tough. "I don't have trouble firing people," Peter Benassi told me. "I just did it a month ago. I fired a six-figure person who wasn't doing anything wrong but wasn't doing anything right, either. 'The party's over,' I said. I pull the trigger very quickly. Remember: I worked for two sets of entrepreneurs. I've tried to make the best of both of those experiences and also learn from their mistakes. One of their mistakes was the hangers-on. That's why we go through our list all the time—to see who we should have and who we shouldn't have. I don't want to have a company of four hundred people when three hunded of them are useless. And that can happen!"

You may have the option of keeping some longer-tenured employees in different jobs while protecting their current salary levels. This can be expensive, but it's usually an affordable tactic. It's humane, and sends a good message to the rest of the team that your company has a heart. In some cases, it's very helpful to have some senior people around who are a strong link to the company's past, and who understand its development. But be aware of how much this is costing you, and be prepared to revisit this decision.

Intermediaries, too, must be assessed. Gourmet soup expert Jerry Shafir once told me, "As we grow, we find that people who were middlemen for us start to lose their value. We need to deal directly with sources. So we outgrow them, and they tend to understand. We tell them up front: It doesn't make sense for us to buy 10,000 pounds a week through you when we could just buy it direct."

What new systems and procedures will be needed? With growth necessarily come new systems and procedures. You can't keep the whole thing in your head any longer; you have to get more systematic—and you have to find effective ways to share your evolving game plan and vision. You will have to formalize more aspects of the business, and create more rules. You'll need a vacation schedule for employees, sick leave rules, health plans, pension programs—whatever you didn't get into place as a small company will have to be put in place now. Your compensation system will need to be understandable, and perceived as fair by most or all employees. Your personnel review policies will have to be formalized.

Department heads will set up new reporting rules (and possibly departmental compensation schemes) that will need central monitoring, support, and possibly revision. Be aware that the wrong moves by a department head can have large repercussions. You don't want the new regulations that resulted from your vice president of sales' good intentions to lead to a mass exodus of your top sales producers. Believe me, this sort of stuff happens in big companies.

How can the company stay flexible and opportunistic? This is perhaps the biggest challenge of all. Big companies usually act like big companies. All too often, they promote and otherwise reward people who don't make mistakes. But very often, the people who don't make mistakes are also the people who don't try new things.

Maybe my own biases are peeking through around the edges here. (Big companies, in my experience, rarely pursue low-risk, high-reward strategies.) But let me finish up big company strategies before moving on to other approaches.

3. Going public

Your company most likely began as a small operation that you controlled completely. Perhaps you retained all the shares in the company, or perhaps you've at some point let coworkers, family members, or private investors share in the ownership. In any case, your company is still privately held. The alternative is to be publicly held—that is, to permit your stock to be bought and sold by members of the public. If the offering is successful, it will raise substantial sums of money and also protect your personal savings.

In almost all cases, companies going public hire an investment banking company to manage the process. This is costly. The banker will generally take 7 percent of the proceeds on the first round. (If you raise $100 million through a stock sale, in other words, the investment bank takes home $7 million—a good day's pay.) On smaller offerings, of $10 million or less, the fees are likely to go above 7 percent.

There's no guarantee that an initial public offering, or IPO, will go well. This is determined by the perceived quality of the offering—that is, your company—and also by the general mood of the markets. There are good "seasons" for IPOs, and also bad ones. Your sector (e.g., technology) may fall out of favor, entirely apart from your own company's merits. If your bankers can't sell your shares, they will probably come back to you and suggest that you lower your asking price. If you do and they *still* can't move the stock, they are likely to drop the project.

A new development on the horizon bears mentioning here. There is an emerging breed of specialist who takes companies public by selling shares on the Internet. This appears to be much cheaper than the traditional investment banking route—costing 4 or 5 percent of the overall take, rather than 7 percent. It's possible that by appealing directly to individual investors rather than intermediaries, these specialists will be less vulnerable to the moods of Wall Street.

Going public has its attractions. Aside from raising money, it permits you to pass on your equity to family members in a relatively "liquid" form. (Before you go public, there's no ready market for your shares, which makes them relatively "illiquid.") You get the opportunity to cash in some or all of your shares, although you may have to wait a while to do so. Your company gets access to new kinds of management incentives, like stock options, and this helps the company succeed.

But going public also carries with it some real potential for frustration. You probably didn't go into business, all those years ago, hoping you could spend a lot of your waking hours with Wall Street analysts. After you go public—assuming you stay in a leadership position with the company—you're likely to spend a lot of time defending your stock price. This can be intensely frustrating, especially if, first, it's outside-world trends that hurt your stock price; and second, you're convinced that week-to-week fluctuations in your stock price shouldn't determine the actions of the company.

You also will have to learn to treat your shareholders differently (especially if they include institutional investors with large blocks of stock). Your board is likely to get feistier, since that's now their legal obligation. You can lose your job if you don't perform. You may have to give up some of the "perks" that you've taken for granted, all these years, and this could mean a change in your lifestyle. You'll definitely give up a lot of privacy, in part because as a public company you're required to disclose much more financial data.

Have you ever published your salary before? Get ready. And in addition to having your salary broadcast far and wide, you'll be giving your competitors a clear view of your company's margins and profits.

This could cause problems with your major customers, who may push for lower margins. If you're enjoying *really* great margins, making them public may invite new competitors into the field.

Before raising public money, be sure you know exactly what you're going to do with the money that gets raised. If the money isn't spent wisely, your shareholders will surely hold you accountable for those bad decisions.

I don't want to end this section on an unnecessarily sour note. Going public isn't for everybody, but it *is* for some people. Do you feel that your company needs more visibility and credibility—that you're the best-kept secret in your industry? Going public may give you that visibility and credibility, and win you new customers. And of course, going public may be the best way to pay yourself back for the many years of hard work you've put into your company. It's your call.

4. Selling the company

This is sometimes the toughest choice for the entrepreneur, because it feels so much like selling a child. Even when the case for selling seems clear and compelling, it's not always easy to tell how you're going to feel *after* the sale—and this is something that you wish you could take into consideration *before* the sale.

Again, this is personal turf. My recommendation is that you talk to people whom you respect who have been through the sale of their company. Ask them how they see the pros and cons, after the fact. Ask them if they'd do the same thing again. And to balance out the picture, see if you can find some people who contemplated a sale, and decided against it. How are *they* feeling about life?

I've sold companies at two different times in my career. If I had it to do all over again, I wouldn't have sold the first time. I have no such second thoughts about the sale of my watch company several years ago, even though I knew I wasn't getting the best price and terms for that enterprise. Why? Because life is short, and I wasn't having enough fun and needed some new challenges.

Here are some words of advice about selling out, based on my experience and the experiences of others I've talked with:

- Don't count on the word of the buyer that you'll continue to run the company with little or no interference. This simply isn't a realistic expectation. It's *their* money, and therefore, it's got to be their final call. If their sales and profit goals are not met, you should expect to be asked to leave. Remember that if the company grows dramatically after you sell, you may not have the skills needed to contribute in a leadership role—and the new roles of leadership may not be satisfying to you.

- In the same vein, if you stick around, expect to be faced with situations where you'll be told what to do by someone who isn't as smart as you. Could you handle taking instructions from a newly minted MBA who's still wet behind the ears? Could you handle watching that person chart a new course for the company? Two things may make these unpleasant tasks easier: (1) if you got a great payout from the sale (and your money isn't tied up in the future success of the company); and (2) if you're used to being flexible and making mental adjustments under duress.

- If your sale price for your company includes non-cash components like notes for future payments, you should mentally prepare yourself for possible default on these components. Who knows what the future will bring for this company? I knew a guy who sold his motor-parts company in Ohio, moved to Florida, bought a yacht—and during the next energy crisis was forced to sell the yacht and move back to Ohio to help out. So much of his payout was in the form of notes that he couldn't afford to let his company go under. Ask yourself: Is the cash component alone enough to make me feel good about this deal? If so, then going ahead may be the right choice.

- If you sell to a public company and receive stock in part or in full payment, then you need to determine the future viability of the company. Beyond viability, is this a stock that is subject to dramatic fluctuations in value? If so, you should try to get a guarantee on a "floor" for the stock price. If you have a holding period before you can sell your stock—and this is common—then there is a risk that the stock may fall in value before you can sell.

This happened to me when we sold our rep company to a company on the American Stock Exchange. When the dust settled, we had sold a good profit-earning company for a pittance. This is a lesson that is etched in my memory. Don't try it yourself.

It's a good idea to consult a tax expert if you will take stock as part of the sale. Between the changing federal, state, and securities laws, you may have to pay taxes on the stock you receive. Obviously, it's far better to pay only when you sell—and a tax expert may be able to structure this kind of favorable outcome for you. If not, you can negotiate a cash stipend payable to you at the time of sale, in order to cover any taxes that may be immediately due upon receipt of the stock.

- If you sell your company, one of your major concerns may be for the loyal and hardworking employees who helped you build it. Once again, the new owners are likely to give you assurances that these employees can stay on with the company under its new ownership. And once again, these may be empty promises. If sales or profit projections aren't reached, everything is on the table.

    You can protect employees to some extent by getting them employment contracts, negotiating healthy severance packages for them, or by sharing some of your sale money with them. And in situations where the acquirers need your expertise on a continuing basis, you may have the required leverage to protect these people.

- In evaluating an offer to buy your company, you need to determine the after-tax dollars you will receive. This most likely means that you will have to bring in a tax expert to give you advice, since this can get very complicated. There are many options to consider. If you sell for all stock, for example, this can be considered a "pooling of interests," and in that circumstance there is no tax liability on the value of the stock. (You pay taxes when you sell the stock.) If you sell for cash, on the other hand, the amount of profit you make (cash in excess of your investment and/or reinvested profits if you are a sub-S corporation) usually gets taxed at the federal level at a capital gains rate of 20 percent. State taxes vary. Finally, if you sell for a combination of stock and cash, you'll need good advice on how the transaction is likely to be taxed. (The IRS may view the transaction as a merger rather than a sale.)

    What you're trying to do is pay the minimum tax within the bounds of law, which in turn affects how many dollars you will net on the sale. The offer price is important, of course, but it's not the only important factor. Get the best possible tax advice before you settle on a final deal structure.

5. Closing the company

Sometimes reassessment leads you to a painful conclusion: that your company is not a winning proposition. Maybe it's only breaking even. Or maybe it's only viable because you're still putting in 70-hour weeks, at a stage of life when you should be in a position to cut back. Or worse, maybe you're still sinking your own money into the operation, which either means that you're eroding your personal savings or taking on new debt.

Is it time to throw in the towel?

For most entrepreneurs, it's tough to say yes to this question. Most are fighters. They don't want to give up. They know of too many cases in which an entrepreneur persisted against long odds and finally achieved a big payoff. Maybe you've got an example of such a case which you cite for inspiration. Mine is Jerry Shafir, who poured himself into Kettle Cuisine for eight years before the company made a dime. Today, the business is in its second decade and it's a dynamic and growing concern. (He was featured in a front-page *Wall Street Journal* story in April 1999.)

So tenacity can pay off. But what if Jerry had gone nine years without a profit? A decade? At some point, it's best to give up, and live to fight another day.

When this happens, be prepared to deal with the psychology of failure. This can be devastating to an individual whose entire identity has been wrapped up in his or her business. When the business disappears, it may feel to the entrepreneur that he or she has disappeared, too.

Two observations: First, not all "failures" are forever. Lots of companies (for example, Toys "R" Us) came back from bankruptcy. And second, most of the veteran entrepreneurs I interviewed said that their most important growth experiences—the experiences that taught them the most, and gave them the greatest motivation to succeed— were their business failures.

This is a case where you need to see the glass as half full rather than half empty. First of all, you've already made a wise decision. Horseless carriages were sweeping the nation, and *no matter what you did,* your buggy whip business was doomed to go under. You read the handwriting on the wall, pulled the plug, and got out with your head up. And what are you now? You're still the kind of person who is energetic and talented enough to grow something from nothing. And now you know a whole lot more about how to make a business succeed. True, your business didn't survive, but you had a priceless learning experience.

If you decide to close, try to do so with class and dignity. If you can pay off all your debts, do it. If you can't, call each company or person to whom you owe money, *personally* explain what happened, and tell them what (if anything) you're going to be able to do to settle accounts. Yes, these are going to be uncomfortable calls, but they are likely to pay big dividends for you in the future, when you start up in business again. People will remember that you didn't run away from them, but made your best effort in a tough situation.

If you're deeply in debt and see no other options, you may feel compelled to declare bankruptcy. For me, this would be the absolute last option. I read about people who seem to think nothing of going bankrupt and then continuing on in the same business after wiping out (or reducing) their debt. To these people, bankruptcy is simply a form of financing that they build into their business plans—the ones they *don't* show to the bank—while still drawing their salaries and enjoying all their perks. To me, this is just a legal form of stealing. It's the opposite of class and dignity. The bankruptcy laws should be amended to prevent this kind of abuse.

If you do have to declare bankruptcy and you are able to continue on with the same business, do everything in your power to make it up to the people who lost money with you. It's a small world, and it's getting smaller all the time. Great vendors and great customers are hard to find. Make the necessary sacrifices to be able to keep working with these great people.

THE CHECKLIST

Lots of options, right? At one end of the spectrum, you've got the option of growing a winner, or figuring out a way to let someone else grow it while you enjoy the fruits of your labor. At the other end, you've got the option of shutting down a loser. And in between are all the less clearcut options, where you're more likely to be making trade-offs and—yes—taking some risks. How do you decide what to do?

Once again, there's no formula. The answer lies in your own goals, beliefs, aspirations, family circumstances, and phase of life. But if you can take the following steps honestly and thoroughly, you'll be better prepared to make the right choice:

Go back to the basics
Follow Ben Franklin's example: for each option, put down in writing the pros and cons as you see them. (Be honest and thorough.) It's

amazing how this discipline sharpens your thinking and clarifies your choices. You're not necessarily going to go with the longer list, either; you'll go with the more compelling list.

Talk it out

Sit down with people who know you well and ask them what they'd recommend. Begin with family members, and then branch outward to include your accountant, your lawyer, and any other professionals whom you respect. If you have directors whose advice you value, talk with them. Finally, try to have discussions of your options with entrepreneurs who have been through some of these options before you, and—ideally—who also have been in the position of acquiring businesses. (They'll see both sides of the choices.) Listen to them. Make a new list of pros and cons. How has your list changed?

Price it out

Determine as closely as possible the price you can get if you sell. Then determine what you can get, and what you'll have to give up, if you use a venture capitalist. Then decide if you feel that the values offered today are acceptable, or whether they're not high enough in light of likely appreciation in the near future. Remember: There's no reason to go through this if you're not going to be honest with yourself.

Assess your finances

Figure out how much wealth you have personally accumulated. (It's interesting how many entrepreneurs fail to focus on this. Maybe we're not motivated solely by moneymaking after all!) Then figure out how much of that wealth you are willing to risk in going forward. Pete Danis, who as the CEO of Boise Cascade Office Products bought many entrepreneurial companies, says that most of the entrepreneurs who sold to him had made just this calculation, and had decided not to roll the dice again on the wealth they had already accumulated. This is a perfectly valid choice. But you'll have fewer second thoughts, after taking this route, if you were perfectly clear in advance as to why you were taking it.

Assess yourself

How have you yourself changed since you started running the business? Is your passion still there? Has your industry changed in ways that make the business less fun for you? Do you need new challenges? Do you feel like you've achieved balance in your life? How is your health?

Do you feel obligated to build the business for your children to take over? (Do they *want* to take it over?) Can you share power with your children, and will it be fun working with and mentoring them? Or will it be better all around if you make a clean break and let them take care of the business?

Is retirement something you're ready for? Have you really thought through what you'll do with yourself all day?

I'll take the liberty of putting my finger on the scales here, one last time. One thing I honestly believe is that it is very healthy, energizing, and renewing to start a new career somewhere in midlife. Try that idea on for size. You did it at least once before, when you first jumped into the entrepreneurial frying pan. Is it time to jump again?

If so, in which direction?

———

So, we're back where we started: with self-assessment, and understanding what you want and need to get out of life. In my mind, knowing what you're all about is the best way to achieve the things that will make you successful—and happy.

APPENDICES

CREATING AND READING A 12-MONTH OPERATING CASH FLOW STATEMENT

The following tables are intended to serve as examples and extension of the cash flow section in chapter 2. I strongly recommend that you read the relevant material in that chapter first, and then come back to these exhibits.

ASSUMPTIONS

average receivables	30 days
selling terms	net: 20 days
cost of goods sold	55%
average sales commission	7% (including non–commission sales)
sales commission	payable month after sale
purchases	paid in 15 days
royalties	6% (takes into account non–royalty sales; due month after sale)
bad debts/returns	3%
warehouse expense	6% payable month after shipping (net 30 days)
advertising/sales promotion	4% of projected yearly sales, spent in last 5 months of year
wages	$180,000/year ($60,000 for owner/ entrepreneur and balance for 4 employees

PROJECTED MONTHLY SALES

December (previous year)	$120,000[1]
January	60,000
February	45,000
March	40,000
April	40,000
May	35,000
June	35,000
July	30,000
August	50,000
September	80,000
October	120,000
November	250,000
December	135,000
PROJECTED YEAR	$920,000

[1] *Dec. of previous year is not included in total for projected year. It is stated because it's needed for cash flow. It becomes January's accounts receivable.*

MONTHLY CASH FLOW STATEMENT

	JAN	FEB	MARCH	APRIL	MAY
Accounts receivable collections	116,400	58,200	43,650	38,800	38,800
Other income	——	——	——	——	——
Total cash receipts	116,400	58,200	43,650	38,800	38,800
Cash paid out					
Purchases/materials	64,020	32,010	24,750	22,000	22,000
Sales commissions	8,400	4,200	3,150	2,800	2,800
Royalties	7,200	3,600	2,700	2,400	2,400
Warehouse	7,200	3,600	2,700	2,400	2,400
Advertising/sales promotion	—	—	—	—	—
Rent	3,500	3,500	3,500	3,500	3,500
Wages/officer salaries	15,000	15,000	15,000	15,000	15,000
Leases	2,000	2,000	2,000	2,000	2,000
Accounting/legal	700	700	700	700	700
Telephone	400	400	400	400	400
Office supplies	150	150	150	150	150
Interest	—	—	—	—	—
Insurance	800	800	800	800	800
Travel and entertainment	600	600	600	600	600
Purchases/fixed assets	—	—	—	4,500	—
Miscellaneous	500	500	500	500	500
Total cash paid out	110,470	67,060	56,950	57,750	53,000
Monthly cash surplus (deficit)	5,930	(8,860)	(13,300)	(18,950)	(14,200)
Beginning cash balance	27,000	32,930	24,070	10,770	(8,180)
Cumulative cash balance	32,930	24,070	10,770	(8,180)	(22,380)

JUNE	JULY	AUG	SEPT	OCT	NOV	DEC	JAN
33,950	33,950	29,100	48,500	77,600	116,400	242,500	130,950
—	—	—	—	10,000	10,000	10,000	—
33,950	33,950	29,100	48,500	87,600	126,400	252,500	130,950
19,250	19,250	16,500	27,500	44,000	66,000	137,500	74,250
2,450	2,450	2,100	3,500	5,600	8,400	17,500	9,450
2,100	2,100	1,800	3,000	4,800	7,200	15,000	8,100
2,100	2,100	1,800	3,000	4,800	7,200	15,000	8,100
—	—	7,360	7,360	7,360	7,360	7,360	—
3,500	3,500	3,500	3,500	3,500	3,500	3,500	3,500
15,000	15,000	15,000	15,000	15,000	15,000	15,000	15,000
2,000	2,000	2,000	2,000	2,000	2,000	2,000	2,000
700	700	700	700	700	700	700	700
400	400	400	400	400	400	400	400
150	150	150	150	150	150	150	150
—	—	—	—	—	—	—	—
800	800	800	800	800	800	800	800
600	600	600	600	600	600	600	600
—	—	—	—	—	—	—	—
500	500	500	500	500	500	500	500
49,550	49,550	53,210	68,010	90,210	119,810	216,010	123,550
(15,600)	(15,600)	(24,110)	(19,500)	(2,610)	6,590	36,490	7,400
(22,380)	(37,980)	(53,580)	(77,690)	(97,190)	(99,800)	(93,210)	(56,720)
(37,980)	(53,580)	(77,690)	(97,190)	(99,800)	(93,210)	(56,720)	(49,320)

COMMENTS ABOUT THIS
CASH FLOW STATEMENT

The statement clearly indicates that this company needs more cash, and also when it needs that extra cash (in April). Finally, it shows that the company will lose money for the year. What it doesn't show, and what you should understand, is that most of the time things don't go as well as projected, and your company is likely to need even more money than you predicted.

It's clear that some decisions have to be made at this company. One response would be to accept the loss for this year and hope things improve next year. (This assumes that the company's managers can get the cash needed to get through the year.) More proactively, the company's leaders could change assumptions, strategies, overheads, etc., to respond to the problem indicated by the projection.

Let's look at some specifics.

The yearly breakeven for this company, based on all costs in this statement, is $1,359,473. Here is how this figure was arrived at:

Variable expenses	*percentage*
Cost of goods sold	55%
Sales commission	7
Royalties	6
Warehouse	6
Bad debts	3
Advertising	4
Total variable	81
Gross profit margin	19

Fixed costs monthly = $23,650 (rent, $3,500; wages, $15,000; lease, $2,000; accounting/legal, $700; phone, $400; office supplies, $150; insurance, $800; T&E, $600; miscellaneous, $500)

Yearly fixed costs = $283,800 ($23,650 × 12)
However, there was $30,000 in other income for October, November, and December, and there was a onetime asset purchase in April for

$4,500. This leaves an additional net income of $25,500, which reduces the yearly fixed cost to $258,300.

The break-even figure is obtained by dividing the yearly fixed cost ($258,300) by the gross profit margin (19%), in this instance, of $1,359,473.

What else can we learn from looking at this example?

- The company's peak cash shortage of $99,800 is reached in October.
- By January, the peak need is reduced by $50,000, to $49,320.
- So the cash flow statement clearly tells the "numbers story" for the year.

How can that story be improved? Here are five possible approaches:

1. The company could meet its additional $100,000 peak need by borrowing it, or by securing additional capital. The company would be able to pay back $50,000 of the $100,000 by January, so perhaps a short-term loan of $50,000 and additional capital of $50,000 is the way to go. If the company borrows the money, of course, it will have to add the interest payments into the cash flow calculations. This will slightly alter the break-even and peak-needs calculations. (There is a line in the statement for these expenditures.)
2. Additional sales of $526,315 would mean that the company would not need the $100,000. Of course, the company would have to decide how realistic this extra sales figure would be to achieve, and whether this would require any additional fixed expense.
3. The company could increase its profit margin of 19% to reduce its additional cash needs. This could be done (for example) by lowering the cost of goods through better purchasing, or by cutting the variable costs. When cutting these costs, of course, the company has to decide whether such cuts might adversely affect sales projections.

   If the company increased its gross margin by 5%—that is, up to 24%—its breakeven would be reduced to $1,076,250, and it would need to raise $46,000 less ($920,000 × .05). You could also raise prices to increase profit margins, but usually this isn't feasible.

4. The company could cut back on fixed expenses. Maybe it could let one or two people go, using temps when absolutely necessary, and also nibble away at other cost items.
5. The company could use a combination of all of the above.

My point is that this cash flow statement clearly articulates a need to *act*. It tells the manager how much action is needed, and it suggests areas in which actions might be taken.

Finally, remember that this is an ever-changing document. You will need to update it, and analyze it, constantly.

Appendix 2

ATTORNEY LETTER
RE KNOCKOFFS

In chapter 9, I devoted a lot of space to the difficult issue of "knock-offs"—when a competitor deliberately sets out to copy one of your products.

A letter from your attorney to the offending manufacturer or retailer can be effective, and can sometimes eliminate the need for more costly legal action. My attorney, Dan Ebenstein, gave me permission to reprint a masterful letter that he wrote to a division of F. W. Wool-worth, which was then purchasing and selling a watch astonishingly like one my company was making.

Dan's letter prompted an immediate retreat on the part of After-thoughts. The letter is included here in its entirety.

AMSTER, ROTHSTEIN & EBENSTEIN

COUNSELORS AT LAW

PATENTS · TRADEMARKS · COPYRIGHTS

90 PARK AVENUE

NEW YORK, NEW YORK 10016

(212) 697-5995

MORTON AMSTER
JESSE ROTHSTEIN
DANIEL S. EBENSTEIN
PHILIP H. GOTTFRIED
MICHAEL J. BERGER
NEIL M. ZIPKIN
ANTHONY F. LO CICERO
JOEL E. LUTZKER
KAREN ARTZ ASH
KENNETH P. GEORGE

DANIEL H. CALDER

NEAL L. ROSENBERG
LEONARD S. SORGI
ABRAHAM KASDAN
IRA E. SILFIN
BARBARA KOLSUN
LAURIE J. GENTILE
CINDY M. ZELSON
DOLORES A. MORO
PATRICIA A. PASQUALINI
JAMES TRAMONTANA
CHESTER ROTHSTEIN
KENNETH K. CHO
ANNE VACHON DOUGHERTY**
ALAN FEDERBUSH
NEIL S. GOLDSTEIN
DAVID H. KAGAN
RUTH E. LAZAR
SHERYL D. JASSEN
GARY H. MONKA
STACEY HALLERMAN
DENISE A. LINDENAUER

INTERNATIONAL DEPARTMENT
DAVID R. BROWN*

CABLE ADDRESS
AMROTHPAT

TWX NUMBER
710-581-4766

FACSIMILE NOS.
212-286-0054
212-286-0082

*NON-LAWYER
**NOT ADMITTED
IN NEW YORK

July 18, 1994

1172688646

VIA FEDERAL EXPRESS

Afterthoughts Boutiques
Division of F.W. Woolworth Company
233 Broadway, 19th Floor
New York, NY 10279

Attn: Mr. David Pfau
       Executive Vice President

Dear Mr. Pfau:

We are copyright counsel to Valdawn, Inc. and its
related company R&R Recreation Products, Inc., both of
Englewood Cliffs, New Jersey. As you may be aware, our
client designs and sells a line of unique and distinctive
wrist watches and has been a vendor to Afterthoughts for
several years.

Among many watch styles which our client has sold
to Afterthoughts is a watch identified by our client as Style
No. 3033, "Clown With Juggling Balls" and a photocopy of our
client's Clown With Juggling Balls Watch is enclosed herewith
for identification. This watch design, as all our client's
distinctive designs, is fully protected by the Copyright Laws

278

of the United States and we enclose herewith a copy of our client's Copyright Registration VA 465,835 of August 5, 1991, covering the Clown With Juggling Balls watch.

Within the past several days, our client has learned that Afterthoughts has begun purchasing and selling exact copies of our client's copyrighted watch designs. Specifically, our client recently purchased, at an Afterthoughts Boutique, a watch which is virtually identical to our client's Clown With Juggling Balls Watch, except that our client's Valdawn and R&R names have been replaced with the Afterthoughts name. While our client purchased only a sample of the Clown With Juggling Balls knockoff, information from your retail store indicates that Afterthoughts has purchased and is in the process of offering exact copies of other copyrighted Valdawn watch designs which our client has previously sold to your company.

Your purchase and sale of watches copied directly from our client's copyrighted watches is a clear infringement of our client's copyrights and is causing our client immediate irreparable harm and damage. Based on our review of the watches provided to us by our client, it is clear that our client is entitled to an immediate Temporary Restraining Order and Preliminary Injunction enjoining further sale or other disposition of your infringing Clown With Juggling Balls watch and other watches copied from our client's designs. At the same time, our client has heretofore viewed Afterthoughts as a valued customer and was, frankly, shocked that Afterthoughts would be selling blatant knockoffs of Valdawn's designs.

Accordingly, our client has asked us to write to you directly and request an immediate meeting with your senior management and counsel to review this situation and try to prevent it from escalating into a legal conflict. If you are willing to set up such a meeting of this sort without delay, please have your counsel contact me directly or you may contact Bob Reiss, who is President of Valdawn, at 201-871-1616.

Please understand that while our client has valued its relationship with Afterthoughts, it cannot and will not tolerate duplication of its designs or the ongoing sale of knockoffs of its products. Accordingly, unless a prompt meeting can be arranged at which this situation can be resolved on an amicable basis, our client will have no choice but to take immediate legal action to enjoin further sale of infringing products and seek appropriate damages.

Afterthoughts Boutiques   -3-   July 18, 1994

I await an immediate reply from you or your counsel.

Very truly yours,

AMSTER, ROTHSTEIN & EBENSTEIN

Daniel Ebenstein

DE/vd
Encls.
7044D

1172688672
cc: Gary Bahler, Esq.
    Legal Department (w/encls. - via Federal Express)
   Mr. Bob Reiss (w/encls. - via Federal Express)
       1172688661

Appendix 3:

THE R&R CASE:

The case that follows has been taught at the Harvard Business School and the Columbia Business School for the past ten years. I know this for a fact because I've attended almost all of these case discussions.

I'm told that the case also has been taught at more than fifty other business schools around the United States, at the undergraduate, graduate, and executive-program levels. I have personally spoken to classes discussing R&R at schools like Miami University of Ohio, Monmouth University, Fairleigh Dickinson University, the University of Wisconsin, Northwestern University, Florida Atlantic University, George Washington, and UCLA.

At Harvard and many other schools, this case is used to open the first session of courses focused on entrepreneurship. It seems to appeal to both faculty and students—most likely not because the central protagonist is so appealing, but because unlike many business situations, R&R is very *manageable*. After all, there were only two R&R people directly involved: me and my secretary. Everyone else involved in the venture was brought in on a project basis.

Another reason why the R&R case appeals to students of entrepreneurship and their teachers is that it encompasses almost every aspect of starting a business, and within a very short time frame. The entrepreneurial experience is "telescoped" into only a few months.

There are other reasons why the case may be interesting both to students and teachers. One is that, unlike many Harvard Business School cases, this one includes the ending. (You learn how it came out.) Another is that the ending is more or less a happy one. Although I've heard lots of debate about whether everybody involved with the project did as well as they should have, most people who analyze and discuss the case wind up agreeing that all the protagonists were better off for having participated in the deal. This is not always true—in Harvard Business School cases or in real life!

And finally, I have reproduced this case in its entirety, and devoted space to an analysis of the lessons it contains, because I think it's a good, real-life demonstration of the low-risk, high-reward principles I've tried to lay out in this book. I hope you find some ideas—and more important, some attitudes and outlooks—that you can successfully adapt to your own special business context.

I'd like to thank the Harvard Business School and Professor Howard Stevenson for giving me permission to reprint the case in this context.

Harvard Business School Case 386-019. Reprinted by permission of Harvard Business School.

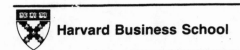

Harvard Business School

9-386-019
Rev. 11/87

R&R

During the summer of 1983, Bob Reiss observed with interest the success in the Canadian market of a new board game called "Trivial Pursuit." His years of experience selling games in the U.S. had taught him a rough rule of thumb: the sales of a game in the U.S. tended to be approximately ten times those of sales in Canada. Since "Trivial Pursuit" had sold 100,000 copies north of the border, Reiss thought that trivia games might soon boom in the U.S., and that this might represent a profitable opportunity for him.

Reiss' Background

After his graduation from Harvard Business School in 1956, Reiss began working for a company that made stationery products. His main responsibility was to build a personalized pencil division, and he suggested that he be paid a low salary and a high sales commission. He was able to gain an excellent understanding of that market, and by 1959 could start on his own as an independent manufacturer's representative in the same industry. His direct contact with stores that sold stationery products revealed that many of them were beginning to sell adult games. He decided to specialize in those products.

In 1973, Reiss sold his representative business to a small American Stock Exchange company in the needlecraft business in exchange for shares. He then set up a game manufacturing division and ran it for that company, building sales to $12,000,000 in three years.

Reiss decided to go into business for himself again in 1979 and left the company. He incorporated under the name of R&R and worked with the help of a secretary from a rented office in New York; Reiss promised himself that he would keep overhead very low, even in good years, and never own or be responsible for a factory. In addition to being a traditional manufacturer's representative, he did some consulting for toy manufacturers, using his extensive knowledge of the market.

This case was prepared by Research Assistant Jose-Carlos Jarillo Mossi, under the supervision of Professor Howard H. Stevenson, as the basis for class discussion rather than to illustrate either effective or ineffective handling of an administrative situation.

The Toy and Game Industry

One of the main characteristics of the toy industry was that products generally had very short life cycles, frequently of no more than two years. "Fads" extended to whole categories of items: one class of toys would sell well for a couple of years and then fade away. Products that were part of categories tended to ride with the fate of that category, regardless to some extent of their intrinsic merit. Many new products were introduced every year, which made the fight for shelf space aggressive.

Promotional plans for a new product were a key factor in buy or no-buy decisions of the major retailers. At the same time, fewer and fewer retailers were dominating more of the market every year. The largest one, Toys 'R' Us, for example, had 14% of the entire market in 1984. The success of a product was often based on less than a dozen retailers.

A few large manufacturers were also becoming dominant in the industry, because they could afford the expensive TV promotional campaigns that retailers demanded of the products they purchased. Billing terms to retailers were extremely generous compared to other industries, thus increasing the need for financial strength. Financing terms ran from a low of 90 days to 9 to 12 months. In general, major retailers were reluctant to buy from new vendors with narrow product lines unless they felt that the volume potential was enormous. On the other hand, the large manufacturers tended to require a long lead time for introducing new products, typically on the order of 18 to 24 months.

The industry was also highly seasonal. Most final sales to the public were made in the four weeks prior to Christmas. Retailers decided what to carry for the Christmas season during the preceding January through March. There was a growing tendency among them, however, not to accept delivery until the goods were needed, in effect using the manufacturer as their warehouse.

The Trivia Game Opportunity

"Trivial Pursuit" was developed in Canada, and introduced there in 1980. Its 1983 sales were exceptionally strong, especially for a product that had been promoted primarily via word of mouth. The game was introduced in the U.S. at the Toy Fair in February, 1983 by Selchow & Righter, makers of "Scrabble," under license from Horn & Abbot in Canada. Earlier, the game had been turned down by Parker Bros. and Bradley, the two largest game manufacturers in the United States.

"Trivial Pursuit" in the U.S. had a $19.00 wholesale price, with a retail price varying from $29.95 to $39.95, about 200% to 300% more expensive than comparable board games. Selchow was not known as a strong marketer and had no TV advertising or public relations budget for the game. The initial reaction at the Toy Fair in February had been poor. Yet, by August the game had started moving at retail.

Reiss thought that if the success of "Trivial Pursuit" in Canada spilled over to the U.S., the large game companies would eventually produce and market their own similar products. This would generate popular interest in trivia games in general and constitute a window of opportunity for him. The only trivia game in the market as of September 1983 was "Trivial Pursuit." Two small firms had announced their entries and were taking orders for the next season. Bob Reiss decided to design and market his own trivia game.

Developing the Concept

Reiss' first task was to find an interesting theme, one that would appeal to as broad an audience as possible. On one hand, he wanted to capitalize on the new "trivia" category that "Trivial Pursuit" would create; on the other, he wanted to be different, and therefore could not use a topic already covered by that game, such as movies or sports. Further, his game would have its own rules, yet be playable on the "Trivial Pursuit" board.

As was his custom, Reiss discussed these ideas with some of his closest friends in the manufacturer's representative business. Over the years, he had found them a source of good ides. One of the reps suggested television as a topic. Reiss saw immediately that this had great potential: not only did it have a broad appeal (the average American family watches over seven hours of TV per day), it offered a great PR opportunity. A strong PR campaign would be needed since Reiss knew clearly that he was not going to be able to even approach the advertising budgets of the large manufacturers, which would probably surpass $1 million just for their own trivia games.

Because licensing was common in the toy industry and was a way to obtain both an easily recognizable name and a partner who could help promote the product, Reiss realized he could add strength and interest to his project if he could team up with the publishers of TV Guide. This magazine had the highest diffusion in the U.S., approaching 18 million copies sold each week. It reached more homes than any other publication and could be called a household name.

On October 17, 1983, Reiss sent a letter, printed below, to Mr. Eric Larson, publisher of T.V. Guide.

Mr. Eric Larson, Publisher   October 17, 1983
T.V. GUIDE
P.O. Box 500
Radnor, PA 19088

Dear Mr. Larson:

I am a consultant in the game industry and former owner of a game
company.

Briefly, I would like to talk to you about creating a game and
marketing plan for a 'T.V. GUIDE TRIVIA GAME'.

In 1984, trivia games will be a major classification of the Toy
Industry. I'm enclosing copy of a forthcoming ad that will
introduce a game based upon the 60 years of Time Magazine. I am
the marketer of this game and have received a tremendous response
to the game, both in orders and future publicity.

This project can benefit both of us, and I would like to explore
the opportunities.

                                        Sincerely,

                                        Robert S. Reiss

     In a follow-up phone conversation, Mr. Bill Deitch, assistant to
the publisher of the magazine, asked Reiss for some detailed explanation on
the idea. Reiss sent the following proposal:

Mr. Bill Deitch   November 14, 1983
T.V. GUIDE
P.O. Box 500
Radnor, PA 19088

Dear Mr. Deitch:

In response to our phone conversation, I will attempt to briefly
outline a proposal to do a TV Trivia Game by TV Guide.

WHY A TV GAME? It is a natural follow up to the emerging craze
of Trivia Games that is sweeping the country. This category
should be one of the 'Hot' categories in the Toy/Game industry in
1984. This type of game got its start in Canada three years ago
with the introduction of Trivial Pursuit. It continues to be the
rage in Canada and was licensed in the U.S. this year. It is
currently the top selling non-electronic game. It retails from
$24.95 to $39.95 and is projected to sell 1,000,000 units. It is

not TV promoted. The 'Time Game', with 8,000 questions covering six general subject areas, only began to ship two weeks ago and had an unprecedented initial trade buy, particularly with no finished sample available for prior inspection.

WILL TV GUIDE BE JUST ANOTHER TRIVIA GAME? No. The next step is to do specialty subjects. Trivial Pursuit has just done a Motion Picture Game with excellent success. Our research tells us that a TV oriented game would have the broadest national appeal.

THE MARKETS - This type of game has wide appeal in that it is non-sexual and is of interest to adults and children. We feel we can place it in over 10,000 retail outlets ranging from upscale retailers like Bloomingdale's and Macy's to mass merchants like Toys 'R' Us, Sears, Penney, K-Mart, Target, etc. There is also a good mail-order market. The market is particularly receptive to good playing, social interactive games at this time. Video games are in a state of decline as their novelty has worn off. (To say nothing about profits).

WHO WILL DEVELOP THE GAME? Alan Charles, a professional game developer who did the 'Time Game', is free at this moment to do work on the project. He has satisfied the strict standards 'Time' has set for putting its name on a product and mine for play value and product graphics in a highly competitive market... No easy task.

WHO WILL PRODUCE & MARKET THE GAME? There are two options for producing the game.

1.   Give it to an established game company who would assume all financial risk as well as production and distribution responsibilities. Under this set-up, TV Guide would get a royalty on all goods sold.

2.   TV Guide assume all financial responsibilities to game. Production and shipping would be handled by a contract manufacturer. Bob Reiss would be responsible for hiring and supervising a national sales force to sell the game. This is not an unusual option, and I do have experience in this. All sales are on a commission basis. This way, TV Guide gets the major share of the profits.

       Attached exhibit explores some rough profit numbers for TV Guide, via both options.

POSITIONING OF GAME - We see the game as non-competitive to Trivial Pursuit and Time Magazine. It can be developed to retail at $14.95, as opposed to $39.95 for Trivial Pursuit and $29.95 for Time. (Mass merchants generally discount from these list prices). The TV Game should be able to be played by owners of both games as well as on its own. The name 'TV Guide' is important to the credibility of the product. Sales of licensed products have been growing at geometric rates in the last decade.

Consumers are more comfortable buying a product with a good name behind it.

PROMOTION OF GAME - Pricing of the product will have an ad allowance built into it. This will allow the retailers to advertise in their own catalog, tabloids and/or newspaper ads. An important part of promotion should be ads in TV Guide. Ads can be handled two ways: one, with mail order coupon and profits accruing to TV Guide; the other, with listing of retailers carrying the item, as you have so many regional splits, the listing could be rather extensive. Financially, you would probably opt for the first option on a royalty arrangement and the second if you owned the product.

This product lends itself perfectly to an extensive public relations program. This is an excellent product for radio stations to promote. This should be pursued vigorously.

BENEFITS TO TV GUIDE

... Profits from royalties or manufacturing
... Extensive publicity through wide distribution on U.S. retail counter, including the prestigious retailers as well as the volume ones. This is the unique type of product that can bridge this gap.
... Good premium for your clients. Can be excellent premium for TV Stations. Can be used as a circulation builder. In projecting profits, I have not included premiums. The numbers can be big, but they are difficult to count on.

TIMING To effectively do business in 1984, all contracts must be done and a prototype developed for the American Toy Fair, which takes place in early February, 1984. Shipments need not be made until late spring.

WHO IS BOB REISS? He is a graduate of Columbia College and Harvard Business School who started his own national rep firm in 1959, specializing in adult games, when it became a distinct category in 1968. He sold his company in 1973 to an American Stock Exchange Company. He remained there for five years and built Reiss Games to a dominant position in the adult-game field. For the last three years, he has been consulting in the game/toy industry and recently acted as broker in the sale of one of his clients, Pente Games, to Parker Bros.

I am enclosing some articles that have a bearing on the subject matter. I think what is needed, as soon as possible, is a face-to-face meeting, where we can discuss in greater detail all aspects of this proposal as well as responsibilities for all parties.

Sincerely,

Robert S. Reiss

RSR/ck
encl.

APPENDIX 3

ROUGH PROFIT POTENTIALS TO TV GUIDE

ASSUMPTIONS

1. Average wholesale cost of $7.15 after all allowances. (This would allow Department Stores and Mail Order to sell at $15.00 Discounters would sell at $9.95 to $11.95).

2. Cost to manufacture, $3.00 each.

3. Royalty rate of 10% - (Range is 6% to 10%, depending on licensor support and name. Assuming 10%, based on fact you would run No Cost ads in TV Guide).

4. Mail order retail in TV Guide is $14.95, and you would pay $4.00 for goods. Postage and Handling would be a wash with small fee charged to customer.

OPTION I - ROYALTY BASIS

Projected Retail Sales - 500,000 units.
    *Royalty to TV Guide of $357,500

Mail Order Sales - 34,000 units (.002 pull on 17,000,000 circulation). Based on full-page ad with coupon. It is extremely difficult to project mail order sales without testing-- too many variables. However, this is a product that is ideal for your audience.
    * Profit to TV Guide of $372,300

OPTION II - YOU OWN GOODS

Costs: (Rough Estimate)

Manufacture	$3.00
Royalties to inventor	.36
Fulfillment	.30
Sales Costs	1.43
Amortization of start-up costs	.10
TOTAL COST	$5.19
Profit per unit	$1.96

Profit on 500,000 units = $980,000.00
(Does not include cost of money.)

Another phone conversation followed in which TV Guide showed a clear interest in pursuing the subject. Reiss answered with a new letter on December 12, 1983, that outlined clearly the steps that had to be followed by both parties should they want to go ahead with the venture. Reiss had to send still another letter with a long list of personal references that TV Guide could contact. TV Guide finally opted to be a licensor, not a manufacturer. They would give Bob Reiss a contract for him to manufacture the game or farm it out to an established manufacturer, provided he stayed involved with the project. TV Guide would receive a royalty that would escalate with volume. Royalties were normally paid quarterly, over shipments; Reiss, however, proposed to pay over money collected, which TV Guide accepted. As part of the final deal, TV Guide would insert, at no cost, five ads in the magazine worth $85,000 each. These would be "cooperative ads"; that is, the name of the stores selling the game in the area of each edition would also be displayed. Reiss thought that including the name of the stores at no cost to them would be a good sales argument and would help insure a wide placement of the product.

Developing the TV Guide Trivia Game

The actual game was designed by a professional inventor, whom Reiss knew, in exchange for a royalty of 5%--decreasing to 3% with volume--per game sold. No up-front monies were paid or royalties guaranteed. Although the inventor delivered the package design in just a few weeks, the questions to be asked were not yet formulated, and Reiss realized he could not do this alone. TV Guide's management insisted that their employees should develop them. Reiss would pay per question for each of the 6,000 questions he needed; employees could moonlight on nights and weekends. Reiss felt it was important to put questions and answers in books rather than cards, like "Trivial Pursuit." The cost would be considerably lower, and the most serious bottleneck in manufacturing-- collating the cards--would be eliminated. The game also lent itself well to this approach, as the question books imitated the appearance of TV Guide magazine (Exhibit 1). Overall, the presentation of the game tried to capitalize on the well-known TV Guide name (Exhibit 2).

Initially, Reiss had not wanted to include a board with the game; he wanted people to use "Trivial Pursuit's" board and had made sure that the rules of the new game would take this into account. However, TV Guide wanted a complete game of its own, not just supplementary questions to be played on someone else's game. Another advantage of including a board, Reiss realized, was that a higher price could be charged.

Since TV Guide had opted for being merely a licensor, it was Reiss' responsibility to set up all the operations needed to take the game to market in time for the 1984 season, and there were only two months left until the February Toy Fair, where the game had to be introduced.

His first consideration was financial. He estimated that the fixed cost of developing the product would be between $30,000 and $50,000, but some $300,000 would be needed to finance the first production run. Those funds would be needed until the initial payments from sales arrived a few months later.

Reiss seriously considered raising the required money from the strongest among his manufacturer's representatives in the toy business, thinking they would push hard to sell the game to every account. Eventually, he decided against this approach: not only would it not contribute that much to the venture, reps could be motivated to sell in other ways.   Perhaps more important, Reiss feared the prospect of perhaps 20 partners who "would be every day on the phone asking how things are going."

Another option that passed through his mind, which he dismissed promptly, was venture capital.   He realized that he would have to give up too much and, even worse, that venture capitalists would not understand this kind of deal--one that had very attractive short-term profits but few long-term prospects.

Trivia, Inc.

With the agreement with TV Guide in hand, Reiss called Sam Kaplan--a long-time friend who lived in Chicago.   Kaplan, 65 years old, had a sizeable personal net worth, yet kept working at his small but successful advertising agency (25 employees) "for the fun of it," as he liked to say. Reiss thought that teaming up could be an important help, and Kaplan was indeed enthusiastic about the idea.

Reiss proposed to establish a company, Trivia Inc., that would develop the project.   The equity would be split evenly among the two partners.   Kaplan, besides lending his line of credit to purchase supplies for the initial run, would use his office to handle day-to-day details. (In fact, Trivia Inc. ended up having only one full-time employee.)   Also, because of his vast knowledge of printing and his contacts, Kaplan could secure press time and paper supplies on short notice, and he would supervise the product's manufacturing.   This was especially important, since the special paper stock on which the game was printed was then in short supply, and long lead times were generally needed to obtain it. Kaplan would also produce all the ads and the catalog sheets.   Reiss would take responsibility for sales and marketing of the product and would pay all reps and coordinate the publicity and the relations with TV Guide.   An important part of the agreement was that R&R (Reiss' company) would have the exclusive rights to market the game and would receive a commission of 20% of the wholesale price from which it would pay the commissions to the reps.

Production, Shipping and Billing

From the beginning, Reiss' intention was not to be a manufacturer.   Through Kaplan's connections, they found not only good suppliers for the question books, the board and the boxes, they even got lower costs than expected.   But, they still had to tackle the problem of assembly and shipping.   Kaplan was a long-time consultant to Swiss Colony, a manufacturer of cheese based in Madison, Wisconsin.   This company specialized in mail sales and had developed a strong capability to process mail orders.   As a result, Swiss Colony's management had decided several years earlier to offer that fulfillment capability to other companies. They took the orders, shipped the product, and billed to the retailer.

In the deal ultimately reached, Trivia Inc. would have the components sent by the different suppliers to Madison on a "just in time" basis, and Swiss Colony would put the boards, dice, and questions in the boxes, package and ship them. Swiss Colony would charge $.25 per box, including billing for the games, and would send complete daily information on sales to Trivia Inc. Trivia Inc. would pay $2,500 for a customized computer program. With all these measures, Reiss and Kaplan were able to lower their estimated costs by 30% and attained the flexibility they wanted. The final cost of manufacturing, assembling and shipping was about $3.10, not including the royalties paid to the inventor and to TV Guide.

A final point was financing the accounts receivable, once the sales started rolling in, and collecting the debts. Reiss was somewhat afraid that the bills of some of the smaller stores carrying the game would be very difficult to collect, since R&R did not have the resources to follow-up closely on its collections; moreover, Trivia Inc. needed the leverage of a factor in order to collect from the larger retailers on time. He and Kaplan decided to use Heller Factoring to check credit, guarantee payment, collect the money, and pay Trivia Inc., all for a fee of 1% over sales. Trivia Inc. would not need any financing for operations: after 45 days of shipping, Trivia Inc. would always be in a positive cash-flow. Thanks to Heller and Swiss Colony, Trivia Inc. had practically no administrative work left to itself.

Selling the Game

Selling was the most important issue for Reiss. He knew that placing the goods in the stores and selling them to the public (selling through) were two distinct, many times unrelated, problems. In any case, however, he thought that the game needed to be priced below "Trivial Pursuit" to make up for both their lack of a complete national advertising campaign that major manufacturers would launch, and their lack of the kind of brand recognition that "Trivial Pursuit" was achieving. Accordingly, the wholesale price was set at $12.50, with a retail list price of $25.

Reiss distinguished carefully between two different channels: the mass merchandisers and the department/gift stores. An important part of the overall strategy was to sell quickly to upscale retailers who would establish a full retail mark-up (50%). These were mainly department stores, such as Bloomingdale's or Marshall Fields, and mail order gift catalogs and specialty gift stores. This, it was hoped, would help sell mass merchandisers and give them a price from which to discount. Such a two-tiered approach was not common in the industry. On long-life products, many times only the full-margin retailers got the product the first year. But Reiss felt that this could not be done with his product, because it could well be only a one-year product. Mass merchandisers, however, had to be reached, since they accounted for at least 75% of the market. (Exhibit 3 shows some of the stores Reiss thought had to be reached.)

Two different sets of reps were employed for the two different channels; on average, they received a 7% commission on sales. Reiss' personal knowledge of buyers for the major chains proved invaluable. He was able to obtain quick access to the important decision-makers at the major chains. They also followed, when possible, the distribution pattern of TV Guide magazine. It was soon apparent that the statistics on demographics reached by TV Guide, which Reiss made sure all buyers saw

(Exhibit 4), had a major impact. As Reiss said, "It appeared that every outlet's customers read TV Guide." The cooperative ads in the magazine, with the possibility of including the store's name, were also a powerful attraction for different buyers, as Reiss had expected: the name of their stores would be displayed in far more homes that it would with a conventional advertising campaign in national magazines. The stores would not be charged to have their name in the ads, but minimum purchase orders would be requested. Many large customers, such as K-Mart and Sears, placed large orders before the product was even finished. (Exhibit 5 shows a cover letter that was sent to supermarket buyers.)

Promotion

In order to promote the game to the public, Trivia Inc. had a four-part plan, beginning with the five ads in TV Guide. (Exhibit 6) The first ad broke in mid-September, 1984, and was strictly for upscale retailers, with $25.00 as the price of the game. TV Guide had eight regional issues, and different stores were listed in each area with a total of about 120, including Bloomingdale's, Marshall Fields, Jordan Marsh and J.C. Penney. They all had to place minimum orders. The second ad, shown on October 6th, was just for Sears. The third, on November 10th, was devoted to mass merchandisers and did not include a retail price. The fourth, two weeks later, listed four of the most important toy chains: Toys 'R' Us, Child World, Lionel Leisure and Kay Bee. The appeal to the public, then, was not just the ad: Reiss knew that showing well-known upscale stores carrying the game initially was the best way to obtain instant credibility for the product. Finally, K-Mart, the largest U.S. Chain, gave Trivia Inc. an opening order to all their 2,100 stores, even before the game went into production, in exchange for the exclusivity in the fifth ad to be run in TV Guide on December 8, 1984. In that ad, K-Mart offered a three-day sale at $16.97.

The second part of the plan also tried to give credibility to the game. Trivia Inc. offered the department stores a 5% ad allowance (a 5% discount from wholesale price) if they put the product in newspaper ads, tabloids or catalogs. For similar reasons, Reiss wanted to have the game placed in mail order gift catalogs. Their sales in the toy-game business were only moderate, but catalogs gave a lot of product exposure because of their large circulation figures.

The final part of the plan was to obtain free media publicity. The publisher of TV Guide magazine wrote a letter to be sent to the producers of such shows as "Good Morning, America," "CBS Morning News," "The Tonight Show," and to 25 top TV personalities, together with a sample of the game. Through TV Guide's P.R. agency and the joint efforts of TV Guide and Trivia Inc., many newspapers, radio and TV stations were reached. In all, more than 900 press kits were sent to media organizations. As a result, the game was mentioned on many talk shows (TV and radio), and news of it was published in many newspapers (Exhibit 7). The cost of this campaign was split between Trivia Inc. and TV Guide.

The Results

By October 1983, Selchow, manufacturer of "Trivial Pursuit," started falling behind trying to meet the demand. By Christmas, when sales exploded, there was no hope of keeping up--and one of the most serious manufacturing problems was the bottleneck of collating the cards. By the February, 1984 Toy Fair, most of the major manufacturers offered triva games, which was projected to be the hottest category for the year.

R&R sold 580,000 units of the TV Guide game in 1984 at the full wholesale price of $12.50. There were few reorders after mid-October, as the market became saturated with trivia games (over 80 varieties) and "Trivial Pursuit" flooded the market. By Christmas 1984, all trivia games became heavily discounted; many retailers ran sales on "Trivial Pursuit" at $14.95, having paid $19.00.

Bad debts for Trivia Inc. were about $30,000 on approximately $7,000,000 billings, with hope of recovering $15,000. Losses from final inventory disposal (it was decided to close-out the game) were less than $100,000.

TV Guide was extremely pleased with the royalty collected from the venture. Kaplan, through his 50% ownership in Trivia Inc., made over $1,000,000 net. The total cost of designing and launching the product had been $50,000.

Commenting on the whole deal, Reiss said:

I think the critical aspects of success in being a contract manufacturer are to take care of your suppliers and to take care of your sales representatives. We want our suppliers to charge us full mark-up, so that we are a good customer to them, and we try hard to give them enough lead time to deliver. We pay on time always, no matter what happens. In exchange, we demand perfect work from them. They understand and like this relationship. We need their cooperation, because we are completely dependent on them.

The other aspect is how to deal with your customers, which for us are the manufacturer's representatives and the buyers of major chains. The manufacturer's reps are used to the fact that, when sales really do pick up in any product and they can make a lot of money, many manufacturers try to "shave" their commissions, perhaps feeling that they are making too much money. I never do that: I am happy if they make millions, and they know it. I also pay on time always. With this, I have developed a loyal and experienced work force and have no fixed or up-front sales cost.

All of these factors allowed us to move quickly. My contacts enabled me to print and manufacture the game for the same cost as a big company. But, a Parker Bros. or Milton Bradley would have incurred fixed costs of roughly $250,000 just for design and development and would then have committed to an advertising and promotion budget of at least $1 million.

The Future

According to Reiss, the big question at the end of 1984 was, "Do we add on a new version of the TV Guide game, do a new trivia game, or go onto something new in spite of the great market penetration and success of our game?"

He had been doing some planning for a new game to be called "WHOOZIT?" and, instead of questions, it would show photographs of famous people that the players would have to recognize. He had a preliminary royalty deal with Bettman Archives, who had the exclusive marketing rights to all the photographs of the news service UPI, in addition to their own extensive archives. But, he was unsure about what the best follow-up for the success of 1984 could be.

The market, however, did not seem to be in the best condition. The 1984 Christmas season had ended with large unsold inventories of "Trivial Pursuit" and other trivia games. Some major companies, like Parker Bros., Lakeside, and Ideal, had closed out their games at low prices, further flooding the market. Many buyers were saying that trivia games, as a category, were over, although they seemed to accept Selchow's estimate of 7,000,000 units of "Trivial Pursuit" sold in 1985. That figure was well below the 20,000,000 units sold in 1984 but was still an exceptionally high figure compared with other board games. Selchow had also announced a plan to spend $5,000,000 to promote the game in 1985. Some upscale retailers, however, had announced their intention to abandon "Trivial Pursuit" and other trivia games, mostly because of the heavy discounting.

Reiss thought that one of the reasons why the public seemed to have lost interest in trivia games is that they were hard to play; too often, none of the players knew the answers. In retrospect, he thought that the TV Guide game had had the same problem. But, that would be different with "WHOOZIT?." He was thinking of making easier questions and giving several chances to each player and really expected the new game to be enjoyable.

In addition to improving the intrinsic playability of the game, Reiss wanted to have more flexibility selling it. He planned to offer three different price points; one of the versions having only the questions so it could be played on the "Trivial Pursuit" board. In spite of all these improvements, however, he was not sure whether he should try to replicate the success obtained with the TV Guide game and wondered what his best strategy for a follow-up could be.

- 14 -

Exhibit 1: Box of the Game

STYLE NO. 048

TV GUIDE'S TV GAME

Copyright 1984 Triangle Publications, Inc.

OVER 6000 TV TRIVIA QUESTIONS

- Drama • Sports • Comedy • News
- Soaps • Kid's • Specials • Movies
- Talk Shows • Quiz Shows and More!

Nothing mirrors our life and times like the electronic eye of television. For over 30 years, TV GUIDE has been writing the book on television every week. The TV GAME is both a nostalgic trip through the days of Lucy and Uncle Miltie, and an exciting journey through today's video environment...its people, its programs, and the world we all experience.

TRIVIA
INCORPORATED
230 Fifth Avenue, Suite 1104
New York, NY 10001   1 212-686-6003

296

Exhibit 2: Book with the questions

Exhibit 3: Stores to be reached

Sears	879
Penney	450.
Federated	451
Dayton Hudson	1149
R.H Macy	96
Allied Stores	596
Carter Hawley Hale	268
Associated Dry Goods	332
Mercantile	79
K mart	2174
Woolworth	N/A
Wal-Mart	751
T.G.&Y.	754
Zayre	848
Bradlees	132
Murphy	386
Rose's	195
Kay Bee	500
Spencer Gifts	450
Hook's Drug	120
Toys'R'Us	200

Bob Reiss thought that some 5,000 independent stores would be suitable targets, too.

386-019

Exhibit 4: Data on TV Guide's audience

February 3, 1984

Mr. Robert Reiss
President
R & R
230 Fifth Avenue
New York, New York 10001

Dear Bob:

I had our Research Department pull together some statistics about TV Guide that should be useful in discussing the audience dimensions of our magazine with major department stores and mass merchandisers.

First off, TV Guide's circulation averages over 17,000,000 copies each week.

Included in TV Guide's average issue audience are:

1. 37,838,000 adult readers age 18 and over.

2. 8,829,000 teenage readers 12 - 17.

3. 46,667,000 total readers age 12 and over.

4. 19,273,000 readers age 18 - 34.

5. 28,085,000 readers 18 - 49.

6. 10,312,000 adult readers in homes with one or more children 10 - 17 years of age.

7. 16,334,000 adult readers in homes with $25,000+ household income.

8. 11,815,000 adult readers with one or more years of college.

9. 4,344,000 adult readers who bought games or toys for children 12 - 17 in the past year.

10. 3,688,000 adult readers who bought games or toys for adults 18+ in the past year.

Exhibit 5: Letter to Supermarket buyers

TRIVIA
INCORPORATED
Exclusive Marketing Agent
R & R
230 Fifth Avenue, New York, NY 10001
1-212-686-6003 Telex 238131-RR UR

June 29, 1984

Mr. Lamar Williams
General Mdse. Buyer
JITNEY JUNGLE STORES of AMERICA
P.O. Box 3409
453 N. Mill St.
Jackson, MI 39207

Dear Mr. Williams:

Once every decade a product comes along that is just right!

We think we have that product for you. It has two key elements:

1- It is licensed by TV GUIDE. I'm sure we don't have to tell
    you about the sales strength of TV GUIDE with its 17,000,000+
    weekly circulation, 46,000,000 readers, etc.. If your super-
    market is typical, TV GUIDE is one of your best sellers and has
    earned its exalted position next to the cash registers.

2- The Trivia Game explosion has taken America by storm and
    duplicated its Canadian heritage, where Trivia games have
    reigned for four years.

We have put these two elements together and with TV GUIDE'S help,
developed a TV GUIDE Trivia Game with over 6,000 questions and
answers. The enclosed catalog sheet gives full description and
pricing. All our sales are final. We will advertise the game in
5 full page color ads in TV GUIDE this fall and will reach your
customers.

We feel this game is ideally suited to be sold in your stores.
We would be happy to send you a sample and/or answer any
questions you may have.

We look forward to the opportunity of working with you.

Sincerely,

Robert S. Reiss

RSR/ck
encl.

Exhibit 6: Ads in TV Guide magazine

Party Fun For Everyone... 2 to 20 Players!

Over 6,000 TV Trivia Questions

TV GUIDE'S **TV GAME**

The Exciting New TV Trivia Game YOU Play at Home!

· Drama · Sports · Comedy · News
· Soaps · Kid's · Specials · Movies
· Talk Shows · Quiz Shows and More!

Nothing mirrors our life and times like the electronic eye of television. For over 30 years, TV GUIDE has been writing the book on television every week. The TV GAME is both a nostalgic trip through the days of Lucy and Uncle Miltie, and an exciting journey through today's video environment . its people, its programs, and the world we all experience.

The TV GAME will provide endless hours of fun for you, your family, and your friends

TV Guide's TV Game At These Fine Stores

Sears Available at Most Larger Sears Stores and Sears 1984 Christmas Catalog.

Copyright © 1984 Triangle Publications, Inc. Manufactured in USA by Trivia, Inc., Chicago, IL 60602

Party Fun For Everyone... 2 to 20 Players!

Over 6,000 TV Trivia Questions

TV GUIDE'S **TV GAME**

The Exciting New TV Trivia Game YOU Play at Home!

· Drama · Sports · Comedy · News
· Soaps · Kid's · Specials · Movies
· Talk Shows · Quiz Shows and More!

Nothing mirrors our life and times like the electronic eye of television. For over 30 years, TV GUIDE has been writing the book on television every week. The TV GAME is both a nostalgic trip through the days of Lucy and Uncle Miltie, and an exciting journey through today's video environment . its people, its programs, and the world we all experience.

The TV GAME will provide endless hours of fun for you, your family, and your friends

TV Guide's TV Game At These Fine Stores

Store Name Goes Here	Store Name Goes Here	Store Name Goes Here
Store Name Goes Here	Store Name Goes Here	Store Name Goes Here
Store Name Goes Here	Store Name Goes Here	Store Name Goes Here
Store Name Goes Here	Store Name Goes Here	Store Name Goes Here
Store Name Goes Here	Store Name Goes Here	Store Name Goes Here
Store Name Goes Here	Store Name Goes Here	Store Name Goes Here

Copyright © 1984 Triangle Publications, Inc. Manufactured in USA by Trivia, Inc., Chicago, IL 60602

Exhibit 7: Press releases on the game

The Indianapolis Star
INDIANAPOLIS, IND.
D. 225,148 SUN. 370,356

BURRELLE'S

The trivia edge

Walter Cronkite, reportedly a trivia
game enthusiast, will have an edge if he
plays *TV Guide's TV Game*, due in
stores in June. The former *CBS Evening
News* anchorman figures in more than
a dozen of the 6,000 plus TV trivia questions in the new game.

MAY 26 1984

DAILY ● NEWS

NEW YORK'S PICTURE NEWSPAPER®

★★★★ 30¢ | Tuesday, June 12, 1984 | Mostly sunny. Less humid. 85-90. Details p. 2

4 STAR FINAL

TV, too, gets into the trivia act

By BRUCE CHADWICK

SO YOU KNOW who was the
only vice president to resign.
So what? Okay, you know who
threw the ball that Babe Ruth hit into
the seats for his 60th home run. Big
deal. And you know the name of the
drummer in Glen Miller's band. Who
cares?

Think you're so smart at trivia?
All right, in addition to Matt Dillon,
who was the only other character
seen during the entire run of "Gunsmoke"? What business did John Wal-
ton and his father run in "The Waltons"? In the early days of "All in the
Family," what was the name of the
company where Archie Bunker
worked?

Gotcha, didn't we? Well, to find
out all the answers, see below, and
also see "TV Guide's TV Game," the
latest in the avalanche of trivia
games that are flooding stores.

What's different about this one,
though, is that it is limited to
television.

It's a board game with cards and
dice. You land on squares that have
questions in seven categories: drama,
sports, comedy, news, kids, movies
and other TV (questions are divided
into three levels of difficulty and
many are aimed at today's youngsters
and yes, there is a Mr. T question).
Whoever gets the most right answers
wins. The game is designed for individual or team play.

"Trivia games are hot because peo-

Milburn Stone

Mary Tyler Moore

ple are tired of video games and
computer games in which the player
is isolated," said Bob Reese, head of
Trivia Inc. and the game's founder.
"People want to play games with
other people and match wits with
talking faces, not TV screens. That,
plus the yen for nostalgia, is making
all trivia games, not just ours, big
sellers."

Reese wanted to get into trivia
games when Trivial Pursuit became a
best seller last fall. He needed something different and turned to
television.

"Everyone watches television, so

everyone will be interested in playing and, in fact, everyone will do
reasonably well at this game," he
said.

Reese turned to TV Guide because
the magazine specializes in television
coverage and has an extensive research department and library.

Researchers at TV Guide, led by
Teresa Hagen, compiled a list of over
6,000 questions from over 20,000 submitted by writers there. Each ques-
tion/answer had to have two written
sources. Those that did not were
dropped.

"It was harder than you'd think,"

said .Hagen. "We needed a good balance of questions, easy to very difficult, and wanted a game that everyone, regardless of age, had a decent
chance of winning."

The real research problems came
in early television history.

"We had a very difficult time finding out firsts—the first comedy
show, soap opera, president on TV,
baseball game on TV—because early
records were destroyed or sketchy."

They uncovered some unusual
facts about television. As an example,
the "Armed Forces Hour," an early
'50's musical variety show, was only a
half hour long. Dr. Ed Diethrich,
owner of the USFL Arizona Wrang-
lers, once performed open-heart
surgery on live TV. Mary Tyler
Moore's first major TV show was not
"The Dick Van Dyke Show," but
"Richard Diamond, Private
Detective."

Hagen thinks the game is more
than trivia. "We found that in playing
it, we'd slide into conversations about
what our own lives were like in
relation to TV, like who our own
heroes were, and our attitudes about
things 20 years ago," she said. "We
hope the game triggers conversations
about life as well as TV."

*The other continuing character on
"Gunsmoke" was Doc Adams, played
by Milburn Stone; the Waltons ran a
lumber mill and Archie Bunker
worked at Prendergast Tool and Die
Co.*

PERSONAL OBSERVATIONS ON THE R&R CASE

When I've attended class discussions of this case, I've often been surprised by the questions that get asked—and some of the ones that *don't* get asked. Sometimes these discussions get to the heart of the experience; other times, they never really touch the core of that experience or get to the key lessons I learned as I lived through it.

To help the reader get the most out of the R&R case—which I hope has some broader applicability to small businesses in general—I have added four related sections here:

- some questions and answers (questions that get asked a lot in class, and my answers to them)
- a break-even analysis
- key success factors
- the decision on "WHOOZIT?"

Questions and answers

Q: *Beforehand, did you know anyone at* TV Guide, *or was the letter to them a "cold-call" letter?*

A: It was a cold-call letter, and it proved to be the beginning of my successful effort to land the contract. I readily admit that the odds against getting an answer, and then an appointment, were high. But you can't start by assuming you'll fail; you have to assume success.

My wife, Grace, provides a great example of this. When she started a new business five years ago, she wanted to do taped interviews with celebrated women who could serve as role models to teenage girls. It seemed unlikely that she could get these women, all of whom were already overworked, to contribute their time—and Grace didn't have a list of ready-made contacts. Nevertheless, she secured interviews with more than 60 famous women, including Sandra Day O'Connor, Diane Sawyer, Chris Evert, Beverly Sills, Kay Bailey Hutchison, Sherry Lansing, Rosa Parks, Carol Moseley Braun, Alexis Herman, Johnnetta Cole, and many others. She assumed success, and then made it happen.

Q: *Were you afraid that* TV Guide *would take your idea for a TV trivia game and bring it to someone else?*

A: Not really, but it's a fair question. I answer it by turning it around: What was my alternative? I believe you have to take some (managed) risks and expose your ideas to the people who can help you execute them. Yes, you can take a great idea to your deathbed—but so what?

In addition, in this case, we had severe time constraints within which to execute, or the opportunity would disappear. It was "share or lose." We had also identified *TV Guide* as the only partner we wanted; we weren't going to go off to another magazine if *TV Guide* turned us down. Also, there are lots of precautions you can take to protect your idea from being stolen (see the knockoffs section in chapter 9).

And finally, these people came across as very ethical individuals, working for an ethical company. It didn't feel like a context in which ideas get stolen.

Q: *Why did* TV Guide *do this deal?*
A: Probably for many reasons, including brand exposure, additional profits, and very little in the way of risk or cost. In my opinion, two factors were paramount in their decision. One was the potential positive perception created in the advertising community when *TV Guide* came out with ads listing upscale retailers like Bloomingdale's, Marshall Field, Lord & Taylor, Macy's, and so on. *TV Guide's* chief source of income was advertising, and many advertisers thought that *TV Guide* had a lower-income audience. The fact that our game would be associated with upscale stores could alter that impression.

And from an entirely different corner of the ballpark: this project looked like it might be fun—as indeed it was. Fun is an overlooked element in too many business equations. Life in upper management can be, well, *boring.* Presidents of companies are human beings with families. They go home and play games with their kids. Wouldn't most executives like to arrive at home one night with a game that their own company had helped produce and that had their company's name on it? People like relief from the norm, especially if there are profits and fun involved. And by the way: wouldn't most of them know a lot of the answers to the questions?

I'm told that Walter Annenberg derived some personal satisfaction from the success of our game. I'll admit that I was surprised when I received periodic phone calls from the publisher's office saying they were calling on behalf of Mr. Annenberg, who had called in from overseas and wanted to know how game sales were going.

Q: *Why did* TV Guide *give it to a small and relatively unknown company like R&R?*
A: We were lucky, we were experienced, we asked, and we presented the right profile to them. They were entrepreneurial themselves, and understood how we operated. During a quick due diligence check, they called 13 references and liked what they heard.

Q: *Would you have proceeded with the game if* TV Guide *hadn't given you the license?*
A: Probably not. We needed their credibility to get orders quickly. We knew it was only a matter of time before all the major game companies introduced their own trivia games, and no major retail buyer was going to deny counter space to Parker Bros., Bradley, or Mattel. We had to beat them to the marketplace. To accomplish our quick placement strategy, we needed a major brand partner. When it came to television, there was only one candidate: *TV Guide.*

Q: *Why did you take on Sam Kaplan as a partner, and give him 50 percent of Trivia, Inc.'s profits?*
A: Whenever you go looking for an investor, try to find one with other assets. Sam fit that description. He had his own advertising agency, so he could make significant contributions to the creation of the game and all of its graphic components. He had access to a paper supply in a year of paper shortages. He had a great marketing mind, and was an expert in direct response advertising. He was very efficient and a strong taskmaster, had terrific people working for him, and had a strong credit rating.

Most important of all, he was a friend whom I could trust implicitly. (After all, he was going to handle the money!) By taking over all the operational details of the company, he was able to free me up to concentrate on selling. Remember that the clock was always ticking in my head, and the major competition was lurking just around the next bend. I needed to commit fully to selling, and Kaplan allowed me to do that.

Now, to get someone as good as Kaplan, who brings so much to the table, you have to give up a sizable piece of the action. We could have gone ahead without him, but I doubt that we would have been either as successful or as profitable.

Q: *Once the product got wide placement and you were shipping good numbers of units, what issues were you concerned about?*

A: Aside from maximizing reorders and coordinating production, my major concern was figuring out when to *cut back* on production. In a fad business like this, you definitely don't want to carry over too much inventory. When an item dies, you're lucky to get back ten cents on the retail dollar for it. I'd rather be clean of inventory at the end and lose some sales than give back my hard-earned profits.

We took a number of steps to address this issue. In the toy industry, there is a service that you can subscribe to that gives you weekly reports on your sales (and those of your competitors) with the major retailers. As a result, we were able to track our sales against Trivial Pursuit and new incoming games by the week. The report also gave the inventory on hand of each game for each retailer. We could therefore tell when Trivial Pursuit started to catch up in deliveries.

This service was used mainly by the large toy companies, because the smaller ones considered it too expensive. It cost us about $2,000 per month, and it was the best investment we could have made. Using that data, we could see clearly when we should stop making more goods. We cut back just as our over-the-counter sales started their dramatic decrease, as competitors' games hit the stores, and as Trivial Pursuit finally became available in sufficient quantities.

Aside from this service, we talked regularly to reps and buyers regarding sell-through and future projections. Many stores gave us actual sales figures, by week. We could see clearly the point when decline began. Today, most major retailers are on EDI, and you can get sales results by day by individual store.

Q: *Was your personal reputation at great risk if the game didn't sell at retail?*

A: No. As long as you keep your word, your reputation stays intact. Buyers understand that you can't guarantee that a product will sell. (That's why stores have markdown books.) But if I promised a store ad and didn't deliver, if we had seriously missed delivery dates, if quality had been compromised—these are things that would have hurt my reputation, and deservedly so.

You can also take steps to minimize this problem. For example, you can prevent an inexperienced buyer from purchasing too much on his/her opening order. This is good for you, as well: better to have a buyer buy 300 units and sell out, than to have him/her buy 600 units and only sell 400.

Q: *What convinced you that there was an opportunity to develop a new trivia game?*

A: There were many factors. We knew, for example, of the tremendous success of Trivial Pursuit in Canada, and we knew that Canada sometimes leads the market in game trends. We also knew that Selchow & Righter [who marketed Scrabble] were having trouble meeting demand, and that for the time being, this problem wouldn't get solved.

What else? Trivial Pursuit was a very expensive game, and we thought that created an opportunity if we could come in below them. Consumers were then tiring of computer games, and were looking for a more socially interactive type of game. Trivia games were gender-neutral and had appeal both to kids and adults. We felt that if we could beat the schedule, we could go ahead with minimal risk.

Q: *Explain the "two-tier" distribution strategy.*

A: Smaller companies generally lack the funds to promote a new product and thereby create consumer demand. One way to solve this problem is to introduce your product in the first year to upscale retailers like department stores. By giving these stores a cooperative ad allowance (a percentage of purchases, which eliminates risk), they will advertise your product under their banner for you. This also appeals to their strategic impulse to be first to market with a new item.

What's the difference between a department store and a mass merchandise buyer? The department asks, "What's new?" The mass merchandiser asks, "What's selling?" Given this fact (which has diminished in importance slightly in recent years), you can follow a sequence: Go first to the department stores, and build up a track record. Then approach the mass merchandisers. Sometimes it may be wise to alter the product or package for mass.

In the case of the *TV Guide* game, our anticipated product life span was so short that we felt we couldn't wait a year to go to the mass merchandisers. Everything had to be compressed into one season. We accomplished this by listing department stores in the first ad (Sept. 15). By using the eight regional splits of *TV Guide,* we were able to list more than 60 retailers. This first ad stated a $25 retail price. Three of the intervening ads had no retail price stated. The last ad, which ran on December 8, was exclusive to Kmart, and had a six-day sale price of $16.96.

This two-tier strategy doesn't work for all products. But it can be very effective for certain kinds of products. It entails very little risk, and minimal advertising investment.

Q: *Your second letter to* TV Guide *gave them two options. Why would you give two options when one of the two was clearly better for you?*
A: It's true that one was much better for me. But it's always a good idea to give people choices—it shows that you are fair and candid.

In this case, *TV Guide* was new to licensing. What I was saying through my two options was, in effect, that if they felt that my preferred option was too one-sided, then *they* should exercise that option and serve as their own manufacturer. The fact is, however, that we never believed that this was a serious option for them. How could a company doing close to $1 billion worth of publishing business create and market a brand-new game in a timely manner? Who, exactly, would do it? There wasn't time to go hire someone; and even if there were, what would you do with the person when this job was finished? It seemed a no-brainer to us that *TV Guide* would choose *not* to be a manufacturer.

Remember, too, that *TV Guide* was the only partner we wanted. Our success depended on getting them. To further complicate matters, as noted, we needed an agreement *in a hurry.* To accomplish this, we felt our initial proposal had to be transparent, fair, and appealing. The two options helped us accomplish that.

A break-even analysis

I'm always amazed when business students attempt to pass judgment on the *TV Guide* game without understanding the economics of the deal. As is true for most Harvard Business School cases, the important details are there; you just have to find them, and work with them in the right ways. In this case, you have to compare the up-front investments that the venture required with the number of games that would have to be sold in order to recoup that investment. After that, as they say, it's all gravy.

Here's how my breakeven looked.

Costs:

Product (including assembly)	$3.10
Factor (1%)	0.125
Inventor (5%)	0.63
TV Guide (10%)	1.25
Advertising (5%)	0.625
Sales commission (20%)	2.50
Total:	$8.23

Selling price	$12.50
Cost	8.23
Per unit profit	4.27
Initial investment:	$50,000
Breakeven:	11,709 units ($50,000 ÷ $4.27)

Key success factors

All told, I can point to 12 key factors in the success of the *TV Guide* game. They were:

1. *A growing market category.* Obviously, Trivial Pursuit was hot, and it created a new category of trivia games. All other factors would have been irrelevant if R&R had not been entering a hot and growing category.
2. *A major pricing umbrella created by the market leader.* Trivial Pursuit wholesaled their game at $19.00. This meant that full-margin retailers like department stores and gift stores sold the game at $39.95. Established games like Monopoly, by contrast, retailed for less than $10.00. This wide disparity, and the success of Trivial Pursuit at a record-breaking retail price, was an invitation to competitors with new products to enter the market, and to sell at a price lower than Trivial Pursuit and still enjoy a healthy margin.

It should be noted that the big discount store chains tend to continuously decrease their selling price on a hot product, even if it's in short supply. Many chains sold Trivial Pursuit at the peak of its popularity at their cost. Why? The theory is that this strategy builds traffic. The further opportunity for the *TV Guide* game in this scenario was that retailers could sell it at the same price as a heavily discounted Trivial Pursuit—and make a good profit on the *TV Guide* game.

3. *The Reiss experience factor.* My knowledge of our industry, and how to get things done quickly within it, was key. In my opinion, a newcomer to the industry could not have succeeded; there simply wasn't enough time in the schedule to accommodate a learning curve.

4. *Relationships and mutual trust.* This is linked to the previous point. A network of relationships and mutual trust was in place. This network had been in the making for a quarter century. It allowed top reps to be hired overnight, Sam Kaplan to be recruited, the inventor to start at once, buyers to place orders based on prototypes, and—most important—*TV Guide* to enter into a contractual relationship with me. The fact that $3 million worth of orders were taken before the first game was manufactured is testimony to the strong relationships that were already in place.

5. *The* TV Guide *connection.* The agreement with *TV Guide* gave R&R instant credibility. A small player competing against established game giants like Parker and Bradley normally has a difficult time of it, and this is particularly true in a hostile retail environment. Retailers were then consolidating. They did not want one-item companies on their books, demanded heavy advertising support for the product, looked for brand identification, and demanded extended dating terms. On top of all of that, of course, their buyers were hard to get in to see.

TV Guide cut through most of these problems. It gave us instant brand identification. It had a circulation of 18 million, was known to virtually everyone, was the authority on the game's subject (TV), and was already on the shelves of most mass merchandisers—many of whom also advertised in *TV Guide*. The agreement with *TV Guide,* with the specified five free ads worth $425,000, quieted the retailers' concerns about advertising. These ads were crucial in securing advance orders quickly. By promising retailers that their name would be in the ads, the critical sell-in was achieved. This was essential, because the big game companies were in the process of developing their own trivia games (more than 80 were available by the end of the year).

The *TV Guide* connection was also critical in creating the 6,000 questions that served as the guts of the game. R&R was relieved of the responsibility of hiring people to perform this huge task (and of worrying about the accuracy of the product). In fact, *TV Guide* insisted on this—to protect the integrity of their name by ensuring that all answers would be accurate.

6. *Timing.* The time element was critical to our success. Many new ventures overlook or downplay the importance of this critical component. In our case, it was paramount. The game prototype and the distribution network had to be in place by the time of the all-important annual Toy Fair in New York. If we didn't make *that fair, in that year,* we were dead.

The chart below shows all the time pressures that had to be overcome.

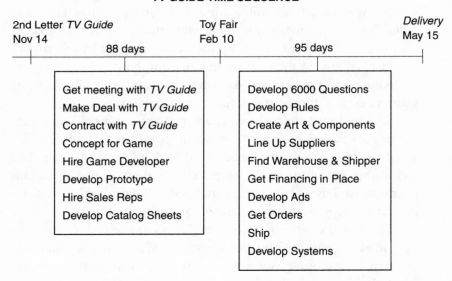

TV GUIDE TIME SEQUENCE

2nd Letter *TV Guide* Nov 14		Toy Fair Feb 10		Delivery May 15
	88 days		95 days	

Get meeting with *TV Guide*	Develop 6000 Questions
Make Deal with *TV Guide*	Develop Rules
Contract with *TV Guide*	Create Art & Components
Concept for Game	Line Up Suppliers
Hire Game Developer	Find Warehouse & Shipper
Develop Prototype	Get Financing in Place
Hire Sales Reps	Develop Ads
Develop Catalog Sheets	Get Orders
	Ship
	Develop Systems

7. *The deal structure.* The deal structure contained several key pieces. One was **incentives:** many people got financial incentives to motivate them to quick action and total commitment. Alan Charles, the inventor, was given a percentage of sales to persuade him to

put other projects on hold and create a prototype and rules of play at once. It worked out well for him. Instead of receiving a typical one-shot fee of perhaps $15,000, he took home something like $230,000. My sense is that if I call him up in the future with a great project, Alan will be responsive.

Sam Kaplan, too, did well, in part because the incentives were there. He devoted large amounts of time, energy, money, and expertise, in return for which he received 50% of the profits of Trivia, Inc. He took home about $1 million within the year. And—if his version of the story is to be believed—he was motivated by the prospect of having some fun, and working with me.

The reps, too, were experienced and considered the best in their area. They received an above-average commission rate, and the prospect of getting a hot game. (Most major companies don't use reps, so reps are normally cut out of this type of deal.) It should also be noted that based on their past relationships with me, these reps knew they would get paid, their rates wouldn't get cut, and they would be treated fairly.

A second key feature was the use of **variable expenses.** Swiss Colony was hired to assemble, store, and ship the games. They also billed our customers for us. There were no up-front fees (except for the $2,500 required to set up their computers to handle us). All of our payments to them were on a per unit basis.

Reps were paid on a commission basis, with no up-fronts or guarantees; this, too, kept our fixed expenses low.

We employed a factor (see chapter 5), who was paid on a percentage basis. Again, there were no up-fronts or guarantees. This saved us the costs of checking credit and collecting money. The factor also ensured that we got paid: once they okayed shipment, payment to Trivia, Inc. was guaranteed. Obviously, they had far greater leverage in getting invoices paid than we did.

The 6,000 questions created by *TV Guide* were paid for on a per question basis ($3.00 per question). We therefore knew up front that developing the questions was going to cost us exactly $18,000. This might have been a considerable liability if we had contracted with the *TV Guide* people on an hourly basis.

The third critical feature was **the free ads.** Besides getting our license, our major objective was to get as many free ads as possible. *TV Guide* offered us two options: a low royalty (8%) with no ads; or an escalating royalty for five free ads. (This escalation was not explained in the case at the time it was written, because *TV Guide* was then a private company and didn't want details of their business made public. Since then, they've been sold to News Corp.) What did this mean? Basically, they started out with an 8% royalty that escalated 2% at various volume levels, peaking at 20% for games sold in excess of 300,000. There were no guarantees or advanced royalties.

We were thrilled to accept this option. First, we could afford it. Second, it solved our problem of how to get quick and assured placement of goods in major retailers. Most royalty agreements seem to run opposite to this structure, decreasing in rate with volume. This was the first product royalty arrangement that *TV Guide* had ever entered into, and they asked us to draw up the contract. I submit that *TV Guide*'s approach is smarter, because when volume gets to a certain level, your initial costs are recouped, increasing volume means lower costs, and you can afford to pay higher royalties.

In drawing up the contract, we asked to pay royalties quarterly on monies received, rather than on shipments made. This was counter to industry standards, and obviously was very favorable to us. I made a point of drawing *TV Guide*'s attention to this, and they (naturally enough) asked why I was red-flagging a potential sticking point. "Because," I told them, "you are rich and we are poor." They laughed and signed on. From their point of view, this was trivial; to us, it was very valuable indeed.

8. *Unsatisfied demand.* It was clear to many in the business that the makers of Trivial Pursuit couldn't keep up with the astounding demand for their game. This allowed us to get a lot of spring orders. In fact, we were constantly receiving calls from major retailers like Toys "R" Us and Kay Bee to ship *at once*—they were out of Trivial Pursuit! This was not a major factor in our decision to pursue the opportunity; we would have proceeded even if they had been shipping on time. It did help us, however, in getting to a higher volume than we otherwise would have.

9. *Flexibility.* As I've said many times in this book, flexibility is an important characteristic in almost any entrepreneurial venture. Our second letter to *TV Guide* underscored our intention to produce a game without a board. This would allow the consumer to play on the board of any other game, or, to play without a board entirely.

From our perspective, it would have allowed us to get the retail selling price under $10.00 and still protect our high margin.

But *TV Guide* then made one of their very few demands. They wanted their game played on their board. We quickly saw that we wouldn't win this one, and agreed. They were our customer, and the customer is always right. I suspect they were also right in an objective sense. The increase in the *perceived value* of a game with a board was much higher than the incremental cost of the board.

10. *Creativity.* The best example came in the use of books, rather than cards, for the questions. This was Sam Kaplan's idea, and it was a good one. The problem that Trivial Pursuit's manufacturers were experiencing lay in collating all those individual cards. We put our 6,000 questions and answers in four books that had vintage *TV Guide* covers on them. These booklets could be produced quickly, and had a tremendous cost advantage over cards. So we solved the production bottleneck, created a significantly more profitable product, and created a game that you could play—e.g., in a car—without having to worry about losing the cards. The books also enabled us to leverage the very familiar *TV Guide* cover and format.

11. *Sales mentality.* Everyone involved with Trivia, Inc. knew that sales were the key to success. My deal with Sam Kaplan was most important in this regard, because he took over the business end of the business and let me sell, sell, sell.

12. *Luck.* Let me say it again: Luck almost always plays a part in success. Make sure your ego allows you to recognize this fact.

We were incredibly lucky that the publisher of *TV Guide* answered my cold-call letter. (How many CEOs of $700 million-plus corporations would have done so?) We were lucky that they met with us so quickly, and were able to cut a deal so quickly. We were lucky that they were entrepreneurial, and understood our needs. We were lucky!

The decision on "WHOOZIT?"

Something like 90% of the students who discuss the R&R case vote not to go ahead with WHOOZIT?, the proposed new product introduced at the end of the case.

Those opposed to the new venture tend to cite a changing market (true), a market now flooded with trivia games (true), the lack of an advertising relationship (true), and the lack of brand identification (true). Perhaps the strongest argument made against going ahead with WHOOZIT? is the argument that the *TV Guide* game rode a rising tide, while WHOOZIT? would be born in a declining market.

Those brave souls who advocate going ahead with WHOOZIT? tend to point to our recently assembled network: reps, Swiss Colony, the factor, the buyers, the suppliers, and Sam Kaplan. Why not drop another product into this pipeline—especially if that game was a better playing game, and might generate good word of mouth and a resultant longer life?

We went ahead. Why?

- Our breakeven was even lower than that of *TV Guide,* which was extraordinarily low. WHOOZIT? had a breakeven of about 6,000 pieces. This was the primary reason to proceed.
- We were excited about the "play value" of the game. (As noted in chapter 7, "falling in like" with your product is a good thing; falling in love with it is usually a bad thing. We were "in like," or maybe a little bit in love.)
- We thought we could position WHOOZIT? as a "picture strategy" game instead of a trivia game. As it turned out, this distinction was lost on everybody but us.
- We figured that the game wouldn't take much effort to develop. If we could sell only 10% of what the *TV Guide* game sold, we could make more than $200,000 per year with very little effort.

What happened? Most retailers, including those who had done very well with the *TV Guide* game, wouldn't even give us a chance to test the new game. Trivia games were then in heavy closeout mode; management wouldn't sign an order for a new questions-and-answer game, *no matter what it was called.*

We sold enough units to recoup our costs. This illustrates a key lesson of low-risk, high-reward entrepreneurship: Going against the odds is not a bad strategy as long as your risks are minimal and controlled. The break-even calculation is a crucial piece of this strategy.

When the market for trivia games was exploding, we focused on the upside opportunity. When the market for trivia games was declining, we focused on managing our downside risk—by keeping our breakeven as low as possible, and by leveraging resources that were already in place.

Appendix 4

INTERVIEWEES

Following are the individuals interviewed in the course of research-ing and writing this book, along with their institutional affiliations. I am indebted to them all for being generous with their time and their ideas.

John W. Altman   Founder of six start-up companies and currently the Robert E. Weissman Professor of Entrepreneurial Practice at Babson College.

Jonathan Axelrod   Founding partner of Axelrod/Widdoes, a Los An-geles, California–based television production company.

Don Bakehorn   Founder and CEO of American Stationery Co. of Peru, Indiana, a mail order catalog specializing in personalized paper products.

Peter Benassi   Founder/CEO of MRI (Media Resources Interna-tional) Ltd., a barter company.

Dan Blau   Co-founder and president of Kidsbooks Inc., publishing company of Chicago, Illinois.

Dennis Boyer Founder and former CEO of Brothers Gourmet Coffee and now founding director of the Center for Entrepreneurship at Florida American University.

Chuck Burkett Founder and CEO of Monogram International of Largo, Florida, a manufacturer of impulse gifts, toys, and souvenirs, founded in 1971 and sold in 1999.

Peter Danis Former president of Boise Cascade Office Products, a New York Stock Exchange company that has purchased many entrepreneurial companies.

Bill Doyle Vice president of licensing and acquisitions for Johnson & Johnson.

Stephen Gordon Founder and CEO of Restoration Hardware, a national specialty retail chain trading on the NASDAQ exchange and headquartered in Corte Madera, California.

Edmund A. Hajim Chairman and CEO of Ing Furman Selz Asset Managment LLC, and previously chairman/CEO of Wall Street's Furman Selz LLC.

Mike Hsieh President of LF International of San Francisco, the venture capital arm of Li & Fung of Hong Kong.

Jim Hunter Founder/CEO of James Hunter Associates, an industrial distributorship based in Elm Grove, Wisconsin, and teacher of entrepreneurship at the University of Wisconsin-Milwaukee.

John Korff Founder/CEO of Korff Enterprises, Inc., a sports marketing and event management company.

Len Levey Former president of Sibley's Department Store in Rochester, New York, former president of furniture manufacturer Levey Barrett, and now chairman of America's Cost Reduction Corporation of Chicago.

Raymond Lo   Hong Kong-based entrepreneur who participates in numerous consumer product start-ups.

Amy Love   Founder and publisher of *Real Sports* magazine, a national consumer magazine focused on the drama of competition involving female athletes.

Jim McCann   CEO and builder of 1–800 Flowers.com.

Keith Mirchandani   Founder/CEO of Tri-Star Products, a direct response marketer of consumer products.

Hamid R. Moghadam   Co-founder and CEO of AMB Property Corp., a real estate investment company.

Earl Peek   Founder/CEO of Intellectual Technologies, Inc., a game company.

David Permut   Founder of Permut Presentations, Inc., of Beverly Hills, California, a motion picture production house.

Bud Pironti   Founder/CEO of National Syndications, Inc. (NSI), a direct response marketing company based in New York.

Don Seta   Founder and chairman of the Seta Corp. in Boca Raton, Florida, one of the largest jewelry mail order catalog houses in the world.

Jerry Shafir   Co-founder and CEO of Kettle Cuisine, Inc., a manufacturer of refrigerated fully prepared soups from natural food ingredients, based in Boston, Massachusetts.

Barbara Todd   Co-founder and president of Good Catalog Co, a national mail order company based in Portland, Oregon, and sold to Reader's Digest in 1998.

Sid Young   Founder/CEO of Young's Maintenance Ltd., painting contractors in Los Angeles, California.

ACKNOWLEDGMENTS

In my most egotistical moments, I never imagined myself writing a book. And now, somehow having done it, I want to recognize the contributions of all those people who have been so generous with their time and made the book possible.

The project started when Jim Robeson—former chairman of the marketing department at Ohio State and Miami University, dean of the School of Business at Miami, and a member of six corporate boards—sat in on a talk I gave to John Altman's entrepreneurship class at Miami of Ohio. Although I didn't know it at the time, Jim subsequently got in touch with Bob Wallace, vice president and senior editor at The Free Press, and suggested that I might have a book in me. Bob contacted, me and the ball started rolling. So both Jim and Bob share in the paternity of *Low Risk, High Reward*. Many thanks to them both!

After floundering for a few months, I knew I needed help. Bob Wallace put me in touch with Jeff Cruikshank, and things began to move forward. Jeff's experience, talent, and low-key demeanor were exactly what the project needed. Without his guidance, wordsmithing, and encouragement, I doubt that I would have wound up with a satisfying product—to me, or to any potential readers out there.

I need to thank the 27 entrepreneurs whom I interviewed for this project, in an effort to develop a broader perspective on the sometimes elusive subject of entrepreneurship. Their names and affiliations are listed in Appendix 4. I learned a lot from them.

Many people also read all or part of the manuscript, or made other valuable contributions. These include: Teresa Amabile, Jeff Armstrong, Duane Barnes, Carl and Damon DeSantis, Jay Dial, Dan Ebenstein, Alex Giampetro, Howard Greene, Jeff Hahn, Mike Hsieh, Amy Love, Murray Low, Joe Mancuso, Melissa Previdi, Jim Robeson, Harvey Roth, Joe Rubin, Jerry Shafir, and Jeffrey Tannenbaum.

Thanks, too, to a second group who helped with specific questions or opened doors for me to get those answers. These include: Judith Anderson, Ellen Blahut, Carl Boyer, Bill Deitch, Ron Goldstein, Terry Hill, Nina Hwang, Larry Klatt, Tom Madden, Michael Marasco, Ray Negron, Sara Pilafas, Bob Savage, Cliff Schorer, Stu Seltzer, Larry Sherman, Ken Solomon, Alan Stein, and Peter Van Raalte.

Special thanks go out to those people—the salespeople and reps—who are closest to my roots and who gave me new insights into this wonderful profession: Bill Ericsson, Alan Grubow, Bill Kelley, Ralph Liberatore, Bob Martinson, Ed Miller, Jock Miller, Tom Powers, Lee Root, Stu Spizer, Dick Waldinger, Bob Wolf, and Sherwing Zimring.

I should single out and acknowledge the contributions of Howard Stevenson, Harvard Business School professor, successful entrepreneur, and one of the best teachers I have ever met. I greatly appreciate his kindness and encouragement as I wrote this book. Even more important, of course, is the friendship that he and his wife Fredi have always shown to me and my family.

Saving one of the greats for last: Thanks to my loving wife, Grace, who has always encouraged me in my work (including this recent effort). She never gives up, and she always aspires to the best—and is a great source of pride to our family.

INDEX